A HUNDRED YEARS
OF MODERNITY 1889–1989
A PARADIGM STORY

A paradigm, like an ocean on its way to extinction, shrinks around its edge; its ebbs never matched by its flows, leaving behind lagoons here and there.

A HUNDRED YEARS
OF MODERNITY 1889–1989
A PARADIGM STORY

A Treatise in Sociology

F. Birtek & P. G. Laszlo

VP Vilnius
2020

A Hundred Years of Modernity 1889–1989: A Paradigm Story
Faruk Birtek & Paul G. Laszlo

Editor: Aytaç Demirci
Designer: Taci Miraç Dey
Cover design: Birtek & Dovydėnaitė

VP Vilniaus Akademinė leidyba | VP Vilnius Academic Publishing
Ž. Liauksmino g. 3, LT-01101, Vilnius, Republic of Lithuania
www.VP-books.com | info@VP-books.com

Printed and bound in Istanbul by Talat Matbaacılık

ISBN 978-609-96020-2-8

This work of fifteen years is dedicated to my teacher,
Neil Smelser, who taught me how to enjoy and
"think in theory", he remains to be my life-time teacher;
and to our students, who made me rethink what I taught.

Contents

Preface

I would like to forewarn prospective readers before they embark on this reading journey with me. This is not an ordinary book. It might not even be a book in the proper sense of the word but an experiment in writing. It does not prioritize facticity and clarity. It often puts theory before fact. It is most speculative and without any fear of flying, non-metaphorically speaking.

It raises a big question. With the conviction that the recent rise of ethnic politics, public religiosity, evangelical and fundamentalist politics arose due to *the decline of the paradigm of modernity*, it asks the question of why that has been the case. To the big question it gives a rather "soft" answer: the hubris of the modernist paradigm led to its overextension to areas of its irrelevance. Away from the base it was easy to mimic in the name of progress, and without its core it succumbed to a kidnap by nationalism. Eventually it was overrun by the Hyksos in their neighbourhood in 1940. It was made to procrastinate by artificial respiration until its apparent utility expired with the end of the Cold War in 1989.

I believe the stronger parts of the collection are in the building blocks of the argument and not the argument itself. I believe the chapters on Weber's "ideal-types", "paradigm theory", "dialectical narration", "dialectical essentialism", and some parts of "Durkheim's Sociology" are original, and the superficial rendition of some aspects of the nineteenth century in Chapter Seven is, hopefully, entertaining.

I beg my readers at this moment who do not have the patience to read these rather "thick" pages for a "thin" argument to stop reading and not to forsake their *amitiés* for me.

For my acknowledgements to the wonderful people who contributed to this writing, I have mentioned them in the Post Preface. Instead of enumerating many names, my gratitude is contextualized for a true appreciation, and that requires more than the space that a preface allows.

In this work we have made a division of labour. Paul Laszlo did the historical research and Faruk Birtek undertook the writing.

Chapter One

Statement of Purpose and Discussion[*]

Synopsis and Overview

This is a hundred-year analytical history of the Paradigm of the Modern. Leaving momentarily the definitional questions of what is a paradigm, what is modern, which and why a hundred years, an analytical history. This is, thus, in part a treatise on sociological theory. The following chapters will try to tell the story of the demise of the modern as a dominant paradigm, a demise arising I argue from its inner tensions. For that understanding a journey into the inner depths of the paradigm is called for, akin to what Parsons does in the first

---

[*] Before this lengthy exegesis, however, I must make one thing clear, and that is my bias. This is not written with any sympathy for the so-called "post-modern", a perspective I find too hard to understand and, when I do, find rather too obvious. I am a firm adherent of the paradigm of the modern as it is the culmination of a long historical struggle that finds its first and clearest expression in Kant and continues with great passion in the works of Marx and in the curative language of the sociology of Émile Durkheim. The principal reason for writing this long essay is to commiserate with my reader, the demise of the paradigm of the modern as the global locus of collective aspirations. That I find is the real reason for the rise of religiosity and more strikingly the rise of Islamism and the emergence of fundamentalism as a brutal force in the Middle East—both being only recent resurgences. The question is not whether religion is an indissoluble social category but rather what place it has in public life. When Mark Lilla rightly claims that Islam would trump secular politics, it is not that it is inevitable but rather, I believe, that it becomes the case when morality is re-transported from the individual back to the community as the paradigm of the modern wanes away. The recent rise of ethnic identity is the other aspect of the same phenomenon.[1]

chapter of *The Structure of Social Action*. Here the logic of my argument is very close to Parsons's, but with one big difference. He looked into methodologies in terms of how they get "unstable" in their logical extensions; I am trying to track down the instabilities as they arise, in the successful practice of social paradigms. My search for the inner tensions of the paradigm is to track down *faiblesses* for its amenability to *hijack* and *kidnap* (see Chapter Four). My search is to find a way to overcome these *faiblesses* by unearthing them for their better understanding and for their possible purge. What I will argue is that what often has been chosen as the target of attack by its enemies, e.g. Bauman, is not part of the modern's essence but only its transfigured version arising from a series of betrayals. Post-modern critique comes in that niche.

I postulate that the paradigm of the modern and the paradigm of Durkheimian sociology are two different names for the same paradigm. Thus the rise of the one is the rise of the other, and the demise of the one fully inheres in the demise of the other for the same reasons. The following study is an analytical history of that paradigm, an analytical history embedded in its particular essence. Only through an understanding of its essence, I suggest, can we understand the strengths and weaknesses of a paradigm over time—the strengths and weaknesses that are revealed in the consequences of its "paradigm practice" (see Chapter Five).

I take it as axiomatic that every paradigm is amenable to only certain hijacks and kidnaps specific to its own nature, specific to its own innate logic, and so is the case with the modern.

Taking the Parsonian track, I will see what happens when a paradigm overextends itself. The greatest hubris of all paradigms for their nemesis is their innate tendency to always "overextend" themselves. For us each paradigm overextends differently, hence each has a different history of nemesis, and each has its characteristic hubris (see Chapter Three). In their essence we discover the origins of the peculiarity of their own hubris. For the modern I am going to *fin-de-siècle* Paris to discover the roots of that essence (see Chapter Seven).

In trying to trace the betrayals of the modern, I will define a hijack as what happens when the paradigm is extended beyond itself by its practitioners, which leads to the undermining of its essential logic. By definition, hubris is the culprit of this type of deviation (see Chapter Four).

For example, in this vein I will try to show below how the rational public order required for the enhancement of the individual—a core value of the modern as a true child of the Enlightenment—is extended to embrace the rationalization of individuality, only to undermine the paradigm in the long term. Here vanity is often the reason for this susceptibility. A highjack, in these terms, occurs when the paradigm is taken over by a contrary logic due to its overextension by its own practitioners. One example would be the seduction of the modern by the elegance of instrumental logic, and by its extreme technicism, which in their practice would destroy the ethical anchor of the paradigm of the modern, that is the enhancement of freedom and liberty for the exercise of responsible moral choice. These two axes, individualism and freedom constitute the logically necessary context of Durkheim's "moral individualism" which I take as the core value of the paradigm of the modern. The question then is how this individualist moral core historically gets betrayed in the history of its successful collective practice.

The modern is the Will to organize the public domain, anchored in its "four humours": universalism, legal-rational political authority, scientific outlook, and *laïcisme,** putting Kant's idea of practical reason at

---

* I have to use the French expression, as secularism is not its substitute. See Appendix I.

the core of Durkheim's sociology. Hence, the paradigm of the modern not only has the four public-defining elements at its core, but, because it necessarily includes a Will to realize them, it is also a political project.

Once a political dimension is thus implied, at that juncture, another threat of a betrayal comes in through the backdoor: another story that configures either as a kidnap or a hijack, at the other extreme, nationalism, often seeps in as an instrument for setting a new order yet only pregnant with new forces which might threaten the initial project.

Let me briefly anticipate some of my arguments below. I mentioned one type of kidnap above. Another story that configures at the other extreme, and that will play a central role in my discussion below, is nationalism. Nationalism has been an "efficient" combination of hijack and kidnap. The main contradiction implicit in the practice of nationalism is that it often arises to enhance individual freedom—the instances in which this has not been the case will be discussed later—yet its collectivist method never goes away (see Chapter Five).

Appearing historically as an instrument of the vanity of the modern, nationalism took over only to radically betray the modern. As a social ideology, the modernist paradigm sought collective action to enhance its individualist credo but either got entrapped in its collectivist means, never to return to its moral individualist core (as was the case in Soviet socialism), or fell prey to nationalist Romanticism, smothering the individual in a communitarianism of a new kind, at times surfacing as the question of community and identity.

The worst scenario occurred when the two extremes met in a backward loop. When nationalism met technicism and love of "rational order", mimicking the empirical results of the modern yet with a deep resentment of its fundamental credos, a most archaic result ensued: the unique horror of the Nazi regime, the Holocaust, and Stalinism.[2]

Bauman takes these cases as the defining moments of the modern; I take them as its antitheses, as cases of its radical kidnap. Bauman's confusion might also underlie the rise of so-called post-modernism.

Discussion

In looking at Durkheim and in constructing the Paradigm of the Modern I want to see how much it is in its essence and how much in its kidnap that we can discover the betrayal of the individual, the individual who is the raison d'être *of the Paradigm of the Modern and Durkheim's principal concern, the moral individualism. My position is, in its kidnap, the individual is betrayed.*

Marx saw Capitalism as the reason for its aborted birth. Capitalism, for Marx, both relied on individualism and undermined its future history. For Marx that was why the revolutionary overthrow was necessary. I do not think that Marx at this point is disputable. Here all we can do is to wait for the revolution. Yet this is too grand a stage, proletarianisation is not universal, there is enough space available for other modes of instrumentalisation of the other. If this space is available, there really is nothing to write about other than technical tracts. But then how are we to account for the extensive transfiguration of the individual, even in the absence of proletarianisation evinced in the so-called post-industrial society?

I will argue that this transfiguration was not in the logic of the Modern with its Enlightenment ancestry—in exact opposition to Bauman—but that its kidnap was due to its innate (of its particular nature) vulnerability. I believe for Durkheim his sociology was to counteract that vulnerability. As long as Kant's practical reason was forti-

fied with Durkheim's sociology and the Paradigm of the Modern with the individual as its kernel, that kidnap could be offset. Yet Durkheim tried to do two things in one. One to parry that danger of kidnap, and the other, to repress an innate weakness (faiblesse) once individuality becomes the cult.* This is the component which I will designate as Dada.

I must explain at the outset what I mean by my rather free use of the term Dada. At the core of Durkheim's individualism, as moral as it is and not mechanistic like that of the Utilitarians (Bentham) and Dewey,[3] lies the vide, that is, the question of meaning, precarious, always ready to leap into an abyss even larger than life. The remedy to that doubt, very Pascalian and not Montaignesque, lay, I thought, in the make-believe world of surrealism. Surrealism was the antidote to a waning meaning, not because it tried to nullify it, but, on the contrary, because it fully embraced the vide to make it joyful, playful. This combination of the meaninglessness and playfulness of the surreal, as the two faces of the Modern would, I thought, be best expressed by referencing Dada for its history, for the vain life of Tristan Tzara, and for its Swiss habitus. Hence my liberal use of the word Dada in the text. I beg my readers' forbearance for this shorthand expression for the combined tragedy and comedy of modern man once God, community, family and the rest is turned to nothingness on the road to the freedom of the individual. For me, Pascal and Dada waltz to freedom in the same manner as Polanski's vampires once did. Once more back to the "void" and the "word", but the "word" now most ephemeral and make-believe, leaving a most heroic, a most Promethean, task. Pascal perhaps was the first modern, and Goethe, for his individualism, its late harbinger.

Moral individualism is moral because it necessarily presupposes

---

*   Durkheim's word; cult is not a pejorative word in French.

choice. Yet choosing necessarily implies not choosing. That is where the vide, what Durkheim called (in English translation) "meaninglessness", the void seeps in; one could claim that the whole of Durkheim's scientific edifice, institutional functionalism,[4] is about finding ways to dispel the intrusion of the vide into everyday life. It is in that "vide-space" that the surreal arises and embodies the vide in its core. The surreal and the vide are two sides of the same coin. I use Dada as a term to encompass both.

If Durkheim had had a dialectical method he would have considered Dada not an alien corn to fight but part of the true logic of his paradigm, the Modern. Durkheim's Moral Individualism is moral because it contains Dada. It is its Yang for its Yin.[5]

For Durkheim for Dada to be offset, the nation-state was to be embraced. Yet the nation-state was open to a kidnap by collectivism in the name of safeguarding individualism; that was Durkheim's first problem, and furthermore that collectivist stream could get much worse in its near future.

For Durkheim a robust Modern with its four humours (i.e. universalism, legal-rational public space, scientific outlook, and laicism) in sway would not allow any chance for primordialism to arise. That is convincing. But when the robust modern is in sway, how are we to account for individual identity to emerge? The Modern's universalism is not attentive to differences but tends to absorb all elements of identity into a public persona necessarily and legitimately construed as universalistic. The unfulfilled burden here is to account for the individual self apart from the public persona. Public persona, citizenship, after all, is a vehicle for the self to participate, hence to grow freely in the public sphere. Thus moral individualism can only be sustained in the distance between public persona and the individual self, a distance which is also

the measure of democratic regimes. This is also the core political princi-
ple of the Paradigm of the Modern.[6]

It is, of course, true that nothing in the logic and the theory of the
modern is there to appropriate that space, but what of its safeguards?
When nationalism of any kind is embraced that distance is most vul-
nerable; its only defender is Dada as it would be the last to replicate the
normative public's rationalist discourse; otherwise rationalist discourse
at the private level is too indistinguishable from its public counter-
part to set itself apart in everyday practice, to resist its absorption into
the latter. Pirandello's six characters sing their gibberish song "Cho chi
chin..." for the effort of this demarcation.

We once more return to the same issue. It is a robust Dada which
safeguards the normative practice of a rational public to curb it from
its self-corrupting expansion into the private, thus to keep the private
from being annihilated by an over-zealous public.[7] *That, I find, is per-*
haps the most important function of Dada in curbing the normative
public from corrupting itself by trespassing its natural borders. Dada
is the true guardian of the normative public and thereby the guardian
of robust citizenship, which necessarily, as its prerequisite, inheres in
a fortified private. Hence, I argue that Dada is Durkheim's necessary
mirror image: it is the source of its real existence. His survival, his
paradigm's health, depends on the health of its Dada; Dada as the par-
adigm's Dragon is where the paradigm of the modern is saved from
its own corruption, from its own destruction and ultimately from its
kidnap by the Devil (Chapter Four).

In other words, only by vigilant recognition of the Dada embedded
in the essence can the collectivist means be kept in abeyance, and na-
tionalism, however innocuous in kind, not obfuscate the moral indi-
vidualist ends of the modernist project.

Durkheim's endeavour, rightly, was how to keep Dada for the private while safeguarding the viability of a rational public order, which only underscores the significance of keeping the private and the public spheres strictly separate but adjacent. Yet, in my view, this excessively "linear" concern with rational public order also requires appreciating the curbs it needs in order not to obfuscate itself with its heightened social ambition.

My contention is that for a robust Dada there is a desperate need for a rationally constituted public order and that, conversely, for a robust rational public order a strong Dada is imperative, so neither will trespass its boundaries to undermine or obfuscate itself. Essentialism in that regard is the guide for generating the proper boundaries of the public sphere. That also, I believe, was Durkheim's position, though not in such clear words. That will be one of my tasks in my rendition of Durkheim's paradigm (see Chapter Six).

For Durkheim, the nation-state—a civic nation-state founded on the four humours—was to be embraced to offset Dada. Yet the nation-state, of whatever kind, was open to kidnap by collectivism in the name of safeguarding individualism. That was Durkheim's first problem, and, furthermore, that collectivist stream was to get much worse in the history of the paradigm (see Chapter Five). Rousseau's *volonté générale** was to open that gate. The nation-state was the friend of the modern, and nationalism its foe. The danger arises when the nation-state so readily avails itself of nationalism, even if only of the civic kind. It is for this reason that a politics of vigilance based on the essential premises of the modern, the four humours as we have called them, is the ultimate bedrock of moral individualism.

---

* İlkay Sunar suggested (in personal communication) that *volonté générale* often becomes "the will of the generals".

My thesis would be that Durkheim in his cerebral preference would align with nationalism, albeit with the civic kind, in order to assuage the Dada, at even a greater potential cost.[8] *The question is whether Durkheim built sufficient substitutes for the forsaken primordialism he had purged, other than some catechisms of his modern republic, and the "professional organizations",*[9] *to prevent the possible gravitation of his civic nationalism to its anti-thesis, the ethnic, the primordial kind! As would happen, when one day the ethnic would kidnap Dada for the Holocaust to descend, as the Devil that by its nature kidnaps paradigms, once turns around to kidnap an unattended Dada. That was the case of Hitler.*

The Devil that devours Dada is now Satan, almost intergalactic, a force out of this world unfitting to all its past and history, a force as never before, descending in its horror from another universe for which madness is too innocent a word!

For Durkheim in his geometric logic a robust Modern with its four humours in sway would not allow any chance for primordialism to arise.

The cure for primordialism would be found in the solidarity embedded in universal citizenship, sustained by secondary organisations.

For some adversaries of the Modern, the intellectual lacuna is their inability to account for the individual self apart from the public persona. The question is whether the context of Durkheim's institutions of Civic Morality and the professional ethics they engender, and the republican education they impart, could provide sufficient ingredients for the survival of robust moral individualism. For Durkheim (and for myself as well) the answer would be in the affirmative, as long as the modernist paradigm is ascendant and has the wind of its Will behind it.[10]

As a parenthetical issue, my other contention is that the grey that at times permeates the modern is not part of its essence but rather the consequence of its practice. It is sociological but not essential, once more attesting to the need to unearth the Dada lying at the core of the modern. It is the strife for the austere in which the modern indulges in its struggle against the *belle époque* that makes the modern so easy for Protestantism to mimic. Without Pascal, Descartes is no beginning of the modern, and Camus without Ionesco is incomplete. If the *belle-époque* circus had the ludic as its mask, the modern has the austere. The danger ensues when the mask, from too frequent use, begins to replace the hidden self. The only safeguard against it lies in reflection and an essentialist self-understanding, and their incessant daily practice, with the ludic to vouch for the ever-present doubt and the vide that creep in through the backdoor.

So far all of this methodological discussion is in full accordance with both Marx and Weber. It is, in fact, more a replication of Marx, as Weber never develops such an extensive scheme for the study of a social formation. Yet Weber is much more in tune with the hazards of the modern's practice even though, I feel, without developing a "deep theory". He has only a tragic vision and thus no remedy.

This study, however, radically parts company with Marx when the paradigm of the modern is described normatively. Marx would have described it in terms of its inner processes with regard to "labour extraction and the formation of surplus value". I am focusing on the normative mindset. A lengthy discussion of this choice will be presented in the Method section (Chapter Three). I take the modern as a more general case than capitalism as the modern avails itself to different modes of labour extraction, as has been historically evident.

In formulating the Modern as a unique historical case and finding its culmination in the Paris of the fin de siècle, I am parting company both with Marx and with Weber. It is not part of an evolutionary process as it would be in Marx's historical stages, nor is it a necessary consequence of long history of Western rationalization as Weber almost metaphysically would have us believe. Mine is non-evolutionary and historically unique. Hence it has no claims to being a general state that all societies would have to go through. The task is more akin to archaeology—not in the Foucault sense since he also has a subterranean evolutionary scheme—in unearthing a particular historical episode. My reason for the birth of the modern is no reason at all. It is chance, it is historical conjuncture, and that attitude itself is as un-Modern as it could be. It is weak causality compared to the Modern's constant search for hard causality akin to the natural sciences, which later would confuse so many of Durkheim's followers!

The paradigm here is the "normative modern", which is found, I argue, bona fide in Durkheim's work. That will be the subject matter of the following pages. It must be clear that however much of a Durkheimian I am, at this juncture it is Weber's hermeneutical methodology that best suits the task at hand and not Durkheim's. Here, in discussing the paradigm in brief and in depth, it is Weber's inner understanding (the true meaning of the word Verstehen), his essentialism, that is operative, and Durkheim's structuralism has to remain mute. But when essentialism is put through a historical process in a forthcoming volume,[11] it will be the structuralist methodology that will have the primacy for the comparative analysis of the history of the "demise" of the modern in the world's changing context.

This is then also a treatise in sociological theory. It intends to investigate the hundred-year life of the sociological paradigm and *inter alia* the paradigm of modernity. It is, in one sense, sociology studying itself, but only after a proper methodology is developed for that purpose (Chapter Two).

Its theme is the question of the "historical stability" of Durkheimian theory as a theory of modern society in "essentialist terms". While for Parsons the "stability" of theoretical paradigms was a question of whether or not the internal coherence and consistency of a paradigm can be maintained when the model is logically extended,[12] what I have in mind here by "historical stability" is how well a theory as a social paradigm endures its successful historical practice.[13]

Contextualisation of the Question

For that historical question, my focus here is the story of the paradigm of the "modern", which in its different ways structured the globe roughly for a century and a half. Most of its ideas had originated in the Enlightenment with Voltaire as its harbinger. It was rooted in the French Revolution and, in its paradigmatic form, came to life in the "science" of sociology. Its theoretical master was Émile Durkheim. Its locus of practice was *fin-de-siècle* Paris. Its defining core was what Durkheim called "moral individualism", as opposed to a utilitarian, Benthamite use of the term individualism, which Durkheim radically debunked as he debunked its allied concept, the pragmatism of Dewey.[14]

It was in Durkheim's scientific work that a most ingenious epistemological innovation was formulated to make sociology as a scientific discipline possible. The innovation was to formulate society as an autonomous realm of theory and scientific discourse. Durkheim's society was to render coherent what the elements of the paradigm of the modern had already evolved in an unclear and disparate manner.

For the reasons below, I will take the hundred years from 1889 to 1989 as the lifetime of the paradigm of the modern (Chapter Seven). This essay, then, is an analytical history of the paradigm of the modern in the hundred years from the building of the Eiffel Tower to the razing of the Berlin Wall in 1989. Its practice emanated from the Paris of the *fin de siècle*. Its politics was best reflected in the Radical Socialist Party.

The central piece of the paradigm of the modern was what Durkheim called **moral individualism**, and the modern is the way to organize the public order for the realization of that moral individualism. The following chapters will try to tell the story of the demise of the modern as a dominant paradigm, a demise that arises, I argue, from its inner tensions, issuing from its successful historical practice.

In other words, I want to pose the question of what might be the structural instabilities that are hidden in the logic of the paradigm and come to the surface in its **successful** historical practice. What I will argue is that what has often been the target of attack by the enemies of the modern is not part of the essence of the modern but only a distorted version of it arising from a series of mutations at the hands of its betrayers and antithetical imitators.

Two axes, **individualism** and **freedom**, constitute the logically necessary pillars of Durkheim's "moral individualism", which I take as the core value of the paradigm of the modern. The question then is, how does this individualist moral core get betrayed in the history of its successful collective practice?

Hence, Durkheim's sociology is the *grammar* of the French modern. I claim that there is no other modern than the French modern of the *fin de siècle*. Its political practice was embodied in the Third Republic after the 1880s and represented by the Radical Socialist Party.

Before we proceed I must emphasize that the definition of the modern is no less contentious than in the case of the elephant and the seven blind men. From defining it in terms of the revolutionary advance of technology to the enhanced rationalism of the human project, hundreds of authors have marshalled hundreds of definitions, at times at odds with each other. Here I insist on one definition: the social organization of **public** life for the ascendance of **moral individualism**—a definition I take as most loyal to Durkheim. They refer to two strictly separate and yet most interdependent realms.

What Durkheim called "moral individualism" is a very special project of individualism. It is rooted in the Enlightenment project of individualism. There already exists a very strong idea of individualism in the Renaissance. In the Enlightenment, it is an organic idea of individualism; a project of development, of the constant pursuit of enhancing capacities, of self-growth and learning, whereas in Renaissance individualism these capacities are givens and the concern is how to use them. Renaissance individualism borders on unscrupulousness, on cynicism,[15] whereas the moral act that Durkheim's sociology requires radical self-abnegation of the physical self. Uplift (*Aufheben*) arises from the denial of self; i.e. the self is enhanced by its own denial of its egoistic pleasures. Self is to transcend its selfishness, a self which is "*Bildung*-ful" and autonomous—to pursue the ends of its species being as Marx after Hegel would have called but ends that are processes and not fixed goals. This is the basis of the paradigm of the modern: a private self at the core and the public domain for its realization. For that moral individualism to be realized, the public domain has to be defined by four essential elements. They are the logical prerequisites for this endeavour, in the manner of Kant's categorical imperatives.

To repeat, the Modern is exclusively about the public sphere— how to organize it so that moral individualism can best arise, expand, and strive to realize itself. Consequently, in contrast with post-modern discourse, the lynchpin of the paradigm of the modern is the strict separation of the private and the public—in the same vein as Durkheim's methodological separation of sociology and psychology—and its exclusively public nature in the Weberian sense. The great challenge is to derive, find, and establish the normative premises of that fundamental divide at the micro level. As long as where and how that line is to be normatively drawn remain theoretically enigmatic, the empiricisation of this enigma becomes the fodder of post-modernist discourse.

Politics in the real sense is very much about that issue of demarcation, about how to safeguard the private (and lately, in particular, the individual's privacy) without, on the other hand, allowing the public to be ransacked by the encouraged expansionism of the private; i.e. how to find a solution to the Hobbesian question without a Leviathan!

The Political Underpinnings

The following endeavour is to recapture, to resurrect modernity from its kidnapped essence: the conceptual nexus for that exercise is a conjoined discussion of the Enlightenment, the idea of the nation-state, the practice of modernity, and the power of instrumental reason. In other words, how can we contravene the dismal rules of sociology; how do we keep the ends from escaping their dismal sociological destiny, how do we in practice *defeat* sociology.*

With similar political aspirations in recent history, socialism with a human face failed to become a stable solution. It lacked the necessary theoretical foundation. It was merely pragmatic. Social market capital-

---

* I am grateful to Philip Selznick as a teacher.

ism was a strictly economic solution. It did not alter the hegemony of private greed, other than taming its activities with over-regulation and corporatism; and, by its logic it remained mute to individuals' capacities for making moral choices—the very Kantian premise of modernity—other than by the occasional ballot.

What is necessary is to fortify the Enlightenment against its possible kidnap, distortion, and the like. It is how to fortify the ends such that the means do not bend them to make them constantly near but principally inaccessible; a road that constantly goes astray, a "circulinear" trajectory for a straight path.

The nation-state is one such locus of distortion; it was created as a vessel of the Enlightenment: how to make individual liberty possible so that "capacity" can in principle be expanded, and reason can rule without any impediment? The nation-state was seen as the terrain for realizing that goal. This was, for example, the Durkheimian nation-state, but it was kidnapped by mobilisational ideology. In that case three logical alternatives follow: disband the state, or build into it structural safeguards that prohibit the "power to corrupt", or fortify the Enlightenment so that the state remains only an occasional tool well bounded and unable to kidnap the initial moral individualistic goals of the Enlightenment. Here I shall take the third road. The same analogy remains for the idea of modernity; it is nothing but an instrument of the Enlightenment. In many ways, its history well coincides with the nation-state, and is often coterminous with it. The debate on modernity thus arises frequently from the same quarters. It is inspired by the same disillusionment with the nation-state. The danger on both occasions has been to absorb an anti-intellectual irrationalist position; in other words, in response to kidnapped reason, in rebellion against the self-defeat of the Enlightenment by its own instruments, a hyper-romanticism is unreflectively taken as refuge. It is true that part of it is due to the hubris of the late militants of the Enlightenment who abandoned self-reflectivity for the sake of efficiency or efficaciousness. This was most true when instrumental reason defeated reason, positivism took over critical methodology, technology kidnapped purposeful labour—the labour of homo faber as the storehouse of "freedom in a larger sense" à la Hegel.

I will thus start by purging this hubris that overshadows the critical anchor of the Enlightenment and annuls the self-reflectivity of reason as its distinguishing quality, the core of its essence. But this need for a purge also attests to the vulnerability of reason's critical essence. The first task then is, in the same self-reflective vein, to discover the sociology of this vulnerability, rather than faulting the kidnappers. That will be what I shall pursue next.

Essentialism is necessary for this purge. Hermeneutics, contrary to what Habermas has suggested,[16] is the source here of a radical safeguard and not always a conservative knee-jerk. That is to say, whether conservatism in the Habermasian sense is laden with freedom or not, depends exclusively on the content of the paradigm to be conserved. It is not the attitude towards change but the content that ultimately matters for the expansion of individual freedom and liberty. The big problem for some critics has been that the Enlightenment and the Modern might have failed to satisfactorily account for the reproduction of the autonomous self: how can we sustain a will for *Bildung* without rooting it in some type of primordialism? Is the power of practical reason in itself sufficient to sustain moral individualistic Will, as opposed to the greed-based economistic individualism of the Utilitarians and their felicific calculus? Durkheim's critique of the Utilitarians in this regard remains unmatched.[17]

Conclusion

This monographic study is issued in the conviction that the Sociological paradigm is one of the best ways of unearthing history's dialectical motions whenever and wherever they occur, but only with a correct methodology. Here the sociological paradigm is the subject matter of that very dialectical investigation. That will be one of the issues below.

Sociology in its "totalizing instinct" has the potential to best capture history's dialectic as "irony", the "surprise",[18] the "unintended consequences" of social action as the real stuff of sociology within its "totalizing" framework. Merton with his "middle-range" theories is far better sociology than Parsons's grander analysis. In economics the same function is served by the concept of externalities. Although it is often the negative externalities which are studied by the economists, understandably as they relate to the questions of "proper" pricing and the cost of public goods, it is the positive externalities which are crucial, I propose, for the study of change and conflict at the paradigmatic level. Marx's greatest contribution to sociology was to argue that it is in the interstices of the positive externalities that the new interests arise and where the Will for conflict thrives. Whether it is the externalities or the "unintended consequences", they either arise in total randomness and thereby remain irrelevant for sociology, or they are systematic and patterned to form the bases of sociological investigation. It is the latter which best describes the real substance of change and is the subject matter of sociology. Systematic externalities, on the one hand open new avenues of interest and the potential for change, and, on the other, often also reinforce the existing institutions and relations. It is in that niche that social conflict becomes the substance of sociological analyses. Here I am taking this track, where Merton and Marx meet, and where Weber and Parsons are often silent.

This monograph will thus try to do several things at once in the belief that the virtue of its practice is in the telling of these various stories concurrently and jointly. It will try to concurrently construct a stylized narrative of a semi-abstract* historical nature of the hundred-year history of modernity and connect that with the later crisis of the sociological paradigm. Concurrent with that "theoretical" history, it will, as its second task, develop a new theoretical methodology which will run as the subtext of the historical narrative. I will develop that methodology which I will call "dialectical essentialism", in Chapter Four. It will incorporate into a coherent unified holistic methodology which had been assumed to be indifferent, or at worse, hostile to it. In other words, it is to have Marx and Weber join hands in the appreciation and critique of the Durkheimian paradigm. This unifying framework—i.e. not eclectic but synthetic—purports to explain the history of the rise and the decline of the paradigm of the modern in a manner not offered before.[19]

The two building blocks of our theoretical narrative are Weber's "ideal-types" (Chapter Three) and a theory of social paradigms (Chapter Four). They will follow a discussion of the methodological framework (Chapter Two). These will constitute Part One of this study.

Part Two is empirical/descriptive. Here, we will construct the paradigm of the modern—first analytically investigate it in its historical practice (Chapter Five), then reconstruct it in its normativity as found in Durkheim's sociology (Chapter Six), and finally we will describe the paradigm in its historical context (Chapter Seven). Each requires an essentialist reconstruction à la Weber's conceptual and historical ideal-types.

---

* Semi-abstract since it will only make scanty reference to historical "facts" but will rely more on intuitive interpretation of a handful of "essential" facts, à la Weber.

Appendix I

The Four Humours

The four humours, which lie at the core of the paradigm, as a totality define it as a "historical ideal-type" à la Weber (see Chapter Two). They are not empirical deductions but they are the four corners of the paradigm's logic. They are *musts* for the paradigm; they are the neccessary prerequisites of the Enlightenment idea of "organic individualism", whose subject and object is the self-improving rational individual. They are thus deductively construed tenets. Each one of the underpinnings which define this paradigm is, of course, historically extraordinary.

Let me give some examples to underscore the uniqueness of the four humours. When I identified one of them with the French term *laïcisme* and not secularism, it is because, in its logic, *laïcisme* is modern and secularism is not. Because the paradigm of the modern has not been sufficiently studied in rigour, secularism and laicism are often confused and at times are put on a virtual continuum without being clear which is the extreme of the other. They are, theoretically and normatively speaking, antithetical. Secularism is to find a medium for lessening the influence of religion in everyday life. Laicism is militantly against religion because it tries to restrict its social sphere and in its theory hems it into the individual's own inner self. In doing so, it absorbs it into a fundamental tenet of individualism, which is the fundamental principle of the modern, which in turn necessitates the four humours that define its life space. And that is individual freedom of thought. In other words, laicism absorbs religion into a principle of individualism, and its politics negotiate with religion in terms of its territoriality and argue about the boundaries. Laicism restricts territorial space to the inner self and in its practice it lets it reaffirm the principle or, as Durkheim said, in the cult of individualism. This contrast between laicism and secularism impinges on the separation of the public and private, and arises from "Render unto Caesar what is Caesar's and unto God what is God's". Secularism cannot maintain such a division.

Let me turn to the universalism of the paradigm of the modern. I deliberately did not use the word egalitarianism, because the question is how to allow differences without violating the principles of universalism—i.e. all rules apply equally to all individuals, again a historically most unusual and extraordinary laicism, to which Christianity at its origins made a great contribution, and gradually the Church adapting to its historical context, most radically modified this precept as otherwise it had been a most unusual claim in human history, until perhaps almost yesterday, that all persons are to be equal. Imagine what an Arab, a Frank, a German would have thought of that strange proposition. The Church created God-given hierarchies as they appear in everyday practice. Now this idea of anti-hierarchicalism when taken in the form of equality, in the French *égalité*, as in *"liberté, égalité, fraternité"*, *égalité* here is what we would translate as universalism, and the idea of equality in English is better represented by the idea of fraternity.

Appendix II

Embedding the Discussion

The first serious book on the mentality of the modern was Edmund Wilson's *Axel's Castle*.[20] It was a brilliant analytical paradigm study, perhaps the first of its kind. It was a timeless classic, a radical systematic critique—in contrast and far superior to Nietzsche's aphorisms however well celebrated they have been—of the Enlightenment and the modern as a shallow and mechanistic world-view, but it remained at the threshold of the 19th century. What he took as two rivalrous perspectives, the Enlightenment and the rebellion against it, Stuart Hughes put into one as he narrowed the span of his period and restricted it to the *fin de siècle*. I will hence argue against Edmund Wilson's dichotomy. I will instead argue for its totality expressed anew in that particular modern of the *fin de siècle* as the individual comes to occupy the central stage. I will argue that Dada and Reason constitute a whole, an inseparable totality of a yin and yang. That was Durkheim's momentous realization.

Stuart Hughes's *Consciousness and Society*, a landmark tough it was, it was also superficial for not going beyond appearances.[21] It lacked a particular sociology! It neither paid sufficient attention to the historical milieu nor was it analytically rigorous. It is especially the second aspect which I find more relevant to any type of a paradigm study. Yet, I think, notwithstanding its superficiality, it was a breakthrough. His frame is what I follow here: his is the guideline, his is the map. Yet, here I want to fill in its broad contours, and add the cartographic third dimension to Hughes's two-dimensional mapping. In unearthing the inner essence of that paradigm, I want to trace the inner instabilities that ensued in its successful practice. That, I think, is the novelty of what I propose below. Here I am sure the use of the Marxian methodology is obvious.

A few counter-examples might help to underscore the particularity of my view in looking at the history of the practice of the modern. Tourraine looked at it, but it is hard to distinguish the innate ideas of the modern in a systematic and analytical manner, as I claim to do, from mere a hegemonic paradigm: what is modern and what is hegemonic is not clear. In other words, how much Foucault is about the modern and how much about anything is not clear. At the other extreme, for Rabinow, the modern is French but not sociological. He is too narrow while Tourraine is too broad in covering the modern. As we shall see, the modern is sociological and hence Rabinow's French misses the analytical problems—Tourraine too broad, hence unspecific, Rabinow too narrow and misses the point (errors type I and II). I am going to take the Parsonian track. I will see what happens when it extends itself. The greatest hubris of all paradigms in their nemesis is their innate tendency to always "overextend" themselves. For us each paradigm overextends itself differently, hence each has a different history of nemesis, and its hubris is specific to it. In their essence we discover the origins of the peculiarity of their own hubris. For the modern I am going to *fin-de-siècle* Paris to discover the roots of that essence. I shall discover its nemesis in its political practice abroad, which saves it from the distortions of the local interests, the cover-ups available with ease, which prevent us from seeing its distortions and self-effacement. Abroad, I shall later discover how its political practice would reveal its innate weaknesses, as Parsons' paradigms showed their instability in their logical extensions. The Modern as a paradigm with political practice at the forefront is to be seen best in its political practice.

The last book which made any impact as far as I know on the discussion of the Modern has been Bauman's.[22] His is antithetical to what follows here, and to rebut him has been one of the motivations for publishing the following essay. Žižek, fun that he is, meanders so much as to lose sight of the real stream.[23] Bauman, I will argue, is not about the Modern but is about its kidnap and as such gives us no understanding of the Modern, though as he has regrettably been most influential.

Notes

1.   "Charb's is the voice of a classic French republicanism, willing to ground everything in individuals and nothing in groups as groups. [...] The only effective and honest way for the left to help French Muslims is to focus exclusively on racial and economic justice and the rights of individuals," which truly summarizes the point of view taken in the current work. See Mark Lilla, "How the French Face Terror", *The New York Review of Books*, Volume LXIII Number 5 (2016).

2.   Albrecht Wellmer, *Critical Theory of Society* (Herder & Herder, 1971).

3.   Robert N. Bellah, ed., *Emile Durkheim: on Morality and Society* (Chicago: The University of Chicago Press Books, 1973).

4.   Mark Lilla, "How the French Face Terror", *The New York Review of Books*, March 24, 2016.

5.   Dialectic is so alien to the French mind that even Kojève could not alter it. See George Lichtheim, *Marxism in Modern France* (New York: Columbia University Press, 1966).

6.   Faruk Birtek, *From Kant to Tristan Tzara: Unwitting the Negative Dialectic of the Enlightenment* (forthcoming).

7.   Faruk Birtek, "From affiliation to affinity: citizenship in the transition from empire to the nation-state", *Identities, Affiliations, and Allegiances*, ed. Seyla Benhabib, Ian Shapiro and Danilo Petranovich (Cambridge: Cambridge University Press, 2007).

8.   Karl Löwith, *From Hegel to Nietzsche* (London: Constable and Co. Ltd., 1965); Franz Leopold Neumann, *The Democratic and the Authoritarian State: Essays in Political and Legal Theory* (New York: Free Press, 1964).

9.   Émile Durkheim, *Professional Ethics and Civic Morals* (London: Routledge, 2013).

10.   It has become common parlance to suggest that republican modernism could not satisfy a presumed innate need—almost akin to human nature—for individual identity; hence the recent prevalence of a search for it. In

principle, I oppose any societal arguments grounded in human biology. My suggestion would be that the recent rise of a search for primordial identity has been rather due to the waning of the paradigm of the modern owing to internal and external reasons, the subject matter of this essay. It is my observation that contemporary society is on the threshold of two fundamental fault lines: universalism versus particularism, and urbanity versus tribalism.

11.   Faruk Birtek, *The Durkheimian Paradigm on its Foreign Travel* (forthcoming).

12.   Talcott Parsons, "The Positivistic Theory of Action", *The Structure of Social Action* (Illinois: Free Press, 1949).

13.   It is the successful practice of those models, I claim, that made their inner contradictions possible, in the very manner in which Marx described the success and the demise of capitalism. If they had not been relevant, powerful, and seductive models for historical implementation, they would not have developed in such a way as to give rise to the inner vicissitudes of their political practice. The big question is: are contradictions endemic to every paradigm as part of its nature; or are they due to sociologically inevitable processes; or are they true for only some paradigms and not for all? If the second or third, they are curable, for example, by avoiding optimization. To repeat, to prevent any misunderstanding, I am a firm adherent of Marx and Durkheim as theorists, who, hopefully, have shaped my work.

14.   Émile Durkheim, *Pragmatism and Sociology*, ed. John B. Allcock (Cambridge: Cambridge University Press, 1983).

15.   Gide's Lafcadio is its newer version. In the Enlightenment, individualism is the *Bildung* of the individual. The individual is no more fixed but is constantly striving for his own improvement, perfection, betterment. The individual is the possessor of "a priori synthetic judgment". This is a tremendous attribution. This is the revolution of Individualism, an individualism whose format was shaped in the Renaissance but without its substance. It is not Castiglione's Courtier or Machiavelli's Prince, but Hamlet who is the *bona fide* modern! It is the possibility of a constant positive-sum game. That is what makes the question of practical reason so all-important: how to keep this

organic, self-generating substance within the bounds of moral rationalism, a Kantian question solved ontologically by Kant, sociologically for Durkheim.

16. Jürgen Habermas, *Knowledge and Human Interests* (Cambridge: Polity Press, 2015).

17. Émile Durkheim, *Pragmatism and Sociology*, ed. Allcock (1983).

18. I am grateful to Madeline Landau, who always insisted on the "surprise element" as the core of any sociological investigation.

19. I would claim that the modern continues willy-nilly as parts but with no will of its own, i.e. continues only as cultural sediment. The European Union, in the name of reviving the gains of the paradigm of the modern, is only a betrayal of it, an example of over-regulation in the name of defending what was sacrosanct, i.e. moral individualism and the expansion of choice. It takes a corporate road à la Scandinavian, modern here being construed as well-being but not the expansion of individual freedom: eliminating the individual in the name of defending individualism at the altar of so-called "low risk society", which only crowns accountants as the adjudicators of "the good society". Once more the means take over to submerge the ends. Our challenge is how to safeguard the welfare state with a public order that maximizes— NB not optimizes—moral individualism: the heroic struggle of the responsible, choosing subject (this was written before 2008). For the more recent EU context, see Claus Offe, *Europe Entrapped* (Cambridge: Polity, 2014).

20. Edmund Wilson, *Axel's Castle: A Study in the Imaginative Literature of 1870–1930* (London: Collins, 1961).

21. Stuart Hughes, *Consciousness and Society: The Reorientation of European Social Thought* (Brighton: Harvester Press, 1988). He relies partly on Parson's *Structure of Social Action: A Study in Social Theory* (New York: Free Press, 1968).

22. Zygmunt Bauman, *Modernity and Ambivalence* (Ithaca: Cornell University, 1991).

23. Slavoj Žižek, *Living in the End Times* (New York: Verso, 2011).

Post Preface

A Life in the Modern:
Berkeley in the 1960s
Faruk Birtek

Acknowledgments

One problem with the hubris of the modern is that like the primitive men it has a low recognition of chance and luck as Lévy-Bruhl once commented. I begin my story of Modern as the dominant paradigm with the inauguration of *Tour d'Eiffel* in 1889 for the Paris fair, an edifice of greatest design, and end my story with the fall of Berlin Wall which collapsed in 1989 by a moment of misunderstanding, pure chance and luck—obvious to everyone to observe in visiting the relevant exhibit in Berlin. It was a mis-event, most apropos: providence playing a game of hide and seek with the modern, or as I shall argue, a providence which was of modern's own making!!!

Here I am going to commit one big fallacy of the modern man and connect the biography and the subject matter of this book. There is a latent hubris in that. It attributes its author full agency. I find that aspirations of causality as a best representation of the modern's metaphysical superficiality. I will yet indulge as I think the narrative in itself, without any claims of causality, will help my reader connect with my narrative. Biography is where the micro and the macro meet.

I am no Mr Travis of Lindsay Anderson yet I have been a very very lucky man.

Biography and the Subject Matter of the Book

I will begin by a biographical sketch to introduce my reader to my text. I hope to set my reader for the narrational context, to help my reader to eventually become part of the narrative, find it obvious and natural. Indeed, one major tenet of the Modern is to connect, to imply a causal relationship between the author's biography and the text. This extraordinary stipulation is almost a necessity after God's death. In Greek tragedy, the author was only a reflection of the text. In Medieval thought the author could only be God. In the Modern, biography and the narrative are bundled into one. They are bonded by a causal relationship. This indeed is so new and so extraordinary that we today take it with non-chalance and naturalness. This indeed is the power of any paradigm, to make otherwise the most extraordinary into the most natural.

The Modern Self's essence is revealed in the narrative when we construct a causal link between the two. In fact, this causality is built logically and any chance element only weakens the narrative. When argued well if chance is the final definer of things, this again only remains as a demonstration of the causal relationship but now in the obverse. Chance overtakes momentarily only to demonstrate that there is the ultimate substratum of logical construction which necessarily connects the attributes of the actor with the narrative. For chance element to be meaningful causality must be ordinary and natural and expected.

Thus, reading the self helps us to read the text. Self is the context of the narrative. Freud only turned this upside down, the clue to the self is in the narrative. In either case there is the stipulation of a causality. Gérard de Nerval broke that chain: the narrative was to stand alone and without a causal link; it would drift like a dream but without any connection to its author. Dream is the context, and self is fractured, it faces its void in the dream, the non-causality that permeates the context is the cause of self's denial of its own totality. This was very modern as it was very anti-modern; its silent nemesis. André Gide also broke the causal bond between the author and the narrative by randomizing the acts that coalesced as the narrative, but Gide's randomization was not to create senselessness, not the vide, it became meaningless meaninglessness. In this manner Gide contributes nothing to the Modern. On the other hand, Michelangelo Antonioni broke that causality between the author and the narrative, to replace it with another context, now subterranean and all-embracing boredom. This was very much the modern, now causality is one aspect of the self, the void, the meaninglessness the self confronts. This is the Dragon of the Modern which I shall extensively discuss.

Another author, to contrast with the modern, is Laclos who had become so modern in his reception after three hundred years, has a narrative but no author. The author of the act is two-dimensional, we know nothing about him or why he is acting the way he is. Hence with no possible attributions of causality, the actor actively induces changes in his context and the context eventually changes on its own to render a tragic death of the actor. Laclos was so appealing to the modern reader as a breather to his otherwise causally knit narrations. Laclos's extreme individualism was pre-modern. Laclos with his contemporaries remained amoral as Durkheim observed for the seventeenth-century philosophers. For Durkheim the driving force of the modern actor was moral individualism, that was the causal connection between the social actor and the narrative; the breakdown of that causality under lay society's malaise, weakness, breakdown, and the modern society's need for the institutions to sustain and replenish that causal connection.

I shall accordingly start with a biographical excursion to assist my reader with the narrative that will follow.

Acknowledgments of a Very, Very, Very Lucky Man

What will follow is an analytical account of the Paradigm of the Modern, and a search for the source of its demise in its own inner workings. For such a grand story one might think one has to be either of the intellectual maturity of a Cassirer, an Eliade or a Goldmann, the geniuses of paradigm archaeology, or a fool (which, of course, the fool himself cannot detect), or an analytical genius like West Churchman. I am none of those except perhaps the fool, but I have also been a very lucky man to have met all the people—my students, my teachers, my friends—who taught me so much of my paradigm, to have lived in the cities that bespoke the language of my paradigm, and to have been, by pure chance, in the midst of events that were mostly the lived tensions of that paradigm of the modern.

What will follow is a theoretical study, often of a very abstract nature. Its research roots are introspective, intuitive, and experimental—no different from the way the Greeks developed their science. In that respect, without my wonderful luck in meeting the wonderful people I have met in my lifetime, this work could not have been written. All the credit truly goes to them. My acknowledgments in this regard then are necessarily autobiographical and a bit *inevitably* tongue-in-cheek! To paraphrase Freud, every biography is a gateway to its century's sociology. **In auto-biography, the macro and the micro meet.**

This therefore cannot be simply a set of acknowledgments of the customary kind. It cannot be for a work that has arrived where it has over more than four decades of reading, teaching—a most formative experience—and most importantly, discussing with a lot of very intelligent people. I find it a little too vain when authors, when they are not heavenly like Kant and Mozart, ignore the people, the milieu, and the places where they have formed and absorbed their ideas, and acknowledge only a few works and a few people and places.

When Eugene Wigner received his Nobel Prize, his first thanks were for Dr László Ratz, his high school mathematics teacher in Budapest. Ratz and Wigner were extraordinary people. I am an ordinary man who has had extraordinary luck. I met some exceptional people in my life. They prefigure all that might be of interest in the following study, and sometimes they must share some of my burden of error.

This is the story of a very lucky man. That luck was mostly possible because it reflected its age, the modern at its height, and unbeknownst to itself, in its dying decades. At the time my story begins, there was a unified intellectual language and an abundance of student grants, and no visa was required to cross borders other than for the US and the Communists. A phone call was a dime. There was no Internet and no ban on smoking. The written word was carried from place to place by humble postmen and women. People around me spent all their time either discussing with each other in bars, restaurants and coffee shops in clouds of heavy cigarette smoke, or in the library reading their nights out. I was twice locked up on the ninth floor of the UC Berkeley Library, where the bound volumes of *Past & Present* were housed, only to be saved by the night watchman. Most of my contemporaries at Berkeley worked part-time in the library for their subsistence. It was a wonderful time to be a foreign student in America.

All acknowledgments are written retrospectively. My ideas did not come from heaven. I was a late bloomer. My ideas come from having been whirled in the blender of a very lucky life; my ideas come from the brilliant people I have met, from students, friends and teachers, and from all the wonderful places I have lived. Among those places, one stands out as the most crucial for my story. For places, I owe the most to Berkeley, where I came off age intellectually. Before that I was at best an infant.

A Life in the Modern

My acknowledgments can thus only begin with my contemporaries, the wonderful people, the last of the moderns, the Berkeleyites of the sixties, and the place where I met them. I suppose the story of that Mohican-land must be written from afar and through the gaze of a young foreigner. The other wonderful people I have met since have had an impact on me because I had my autobiography set in Berkeley in 1964.

I doubt my luck would have helped me as such if I had not chosen to go to Amherst instead of Harvard at the time, which I did for very silly, rationalist reasons. Amherst had a better admission's record for Harvard graduate school and that was why I chose it. I think if I had chosen Harvard, I would have most likely stayed on at Harvard, and, given my then insecure and pompous Turkish self, become a very different person—a person too dumb and pompous to *hear* the wonderful people I would later meet. For all my encounters to be lucky breaks, my life had to have begun in Berkeley in the sixties and seventies, and I had to have had Berkeley to shape my mind and spirit to hear them. To Berkeley I owe myself and whatever I have had of curiosity, passion, a little disorganization, and a great love not for, but of, learning.

There are many ways of writing one's own biography. Here, I will take my biographical track for acknowledging a profound debt of gratitude to the people—men and women—who enabled me to write this book. Had I not had the good luck to know them, I would have been a different man. "The moving finger writes; and having writ, moves on."

On the other hand, any man would be a fool to ignore his father in his autobiography. Yet this is not the place for that account. I take that as given, a firmament to be shaped by experiences, by the people one meets, by the places one has been, by the events that one, by pure coincidence, witnesses and the times one lives in.

In acknowledging the people and the places, the events and the particular times I have lived through but of which I was no author, this autobiographical sketch might, indirectly, also serve an unintended end. It might, in very different categories, in very different language, convey a representation, a reflection, an incoherent summary, of the abstract and "grand theory" of the modern this book purports to tell at a personal, microcosmic level. My personal experiences took place in the last decades of the Paradigm of the Modern, with which I have fully self-identified. In their final decades, paradigms often come to their full realization in Hegel's sense, as well as experiencing the beginnings of their inner fracturing.

Biography and Dedication

This is the story of a very, very lucky man (referencing Lindsay Anderson's extraordinary film of the same name). He was born to a rather affluent family to an elderly father with considerable prestige and social power in a cosmopolitan and international ancient city with a great history but then in its years of relative decay living through the worst agonies of the conflict between the cosmopolitanism of the early part of the century and of the chauvinism of the middle. A man who has been to the best educational institutions of his times.

A man acquainted with, or better, befriended by the best minds of his times, and by pure coincidence became a direct witness to, or participant in, the most tumultuous events of his times, in Berkeley and Paris, and who now waiting to die in modest security as an emeritus professor. His must be—to say nothing of the inner self—one of the luckiest of stories, socially speaking. Having had not only the best teachers, I also had the best students of the century. This book is above all dedicated to them.

Let me for a moment go to the beginnings. My journey had started in 1962 from a port in the Levant. When I came to Marseille, the French–Algerian war had just ended. Marseille was full of *piednoirs*. Support for Salan was widespread. "De Gaulle assassin!" was inscribed in capital letters on many of the city's walls. Men in trench coats and black Citroëns chased each other through the streets. They would first walk at a fast pace, then start running before being arrested. Sometimes shooting followed. From Marseille I took a long-haul train to Antwerp, traversing Europe from south to north. After a few days in a small seamen's hotel near the docks I boarded a small freighter. Since then I have loved Antwerp, just as I love Hamburg now. It had great novelty for me. It had all the characteristics of a northern European port, different from the ports I knew of the Levant. Whenever I read about Dutch Marxists, I always visualize them in Flemish Antwerp.

My freighter was carrying frozen chicken from America to a still war-weary Germany. I caught the freighter on its empty haul to Florida. I was going to the United States to go to university. I was from a land that took the practice of the Modern most seriously and militantly but with little cognizance of its essential roots in individualism, liberty and choice. I did not know then that I was going to the other edge of the Modern, where its roots were so sanctified yet its practice and its institutions so lacking. In the end, I think I am fortunate to have experienced two one-sided Moderns for the better part of a lifetime.

Our captain was a gentleman in his early fifties. He had seen the war as a junior officer. Burnt out now and running the chicken haul from America to Germany. He hated the Nazis. He was from Hamburg and a seaman, who lived in Blankenese. I never saw the Captain again, but Blankenese later became one of my favourite places. During the voyage we ate at his table and had wonderful long conversations every night after dinner, burning the midnight oil. I learned so much from him, of the navy, of Conradian-like intellectualism. Since then I have always been most fond of the German custom of the after-dinner cigar and the serious conversation that goes with it.

We landed in Florida on Labor Day weekend and officially could not get off the boat. Customs was closed for the holiday. There was no air-conditioning on the boat. That September was no exception in Florida, most humid and hot. That day stuck on the water in the sweltering heat felt longer than the fourteen-day Atlantic crossing. Eventually, we were let off the boat to visit Cypress Gardens for a few hours. Cypress Gardens was another story. It was my first culture shock. I still cannot fathom it, perhaps because I have never been to Disneyland! The next day I took the train from Tampa to Grand Central to go to Amherst College. Only in the previous year more people had begun crossing the Atlantic by air than by sea.

And that is how my road to Berkeley began, and there my paradigm of the Modern would take shape.

The Place and the People

After a year at Amherst I transferred to Berkeley but not before wandering half a year in Europe, as was then the custom and the chique. My going to Berkeley was out of no foreknowledge but due entirely to chance. My luck was due to two disconnected events. First, my deep discontent with New England "churchiness", which made me drop out of Amherst at the end of my freshman year; and second, when, by pure chance, I came across a Berkeley Course Catalogue among the new arrivals in the tiny library in the basement of Cambridge (UK) City's town hall. The catalogue impressed me. It had all the things I wanted to read, from existentialism to Dostoevsky, from Jung to Nietzsche, nineteenth-century intellectual history and Sociological Theory. I sent my transcript by Western Union to beat the deadline.

In those days you could get an air ticket from London to Berkeley that included a helicopter ride from San Francisco Airport to Berkeley Marina. The flight at night over the Bay was like flying over a jewel garden. In retrospect I think my adult life started that evening when I flew to Berkeley. Me as I know it began then, in January 1964.

Berkeley in the 1960s stood on the western precipice of the modern. The hills behind set Berkeley apart, as if it were an island. The Pacific in front looked endless, as if Berkeley would melt away into the ocean were it not for the Golden Gate Bridge forming a barrier. In that little patch of land between San Francisco Bay and the hills that separate Berkeley from Nevada and Arizona, a culture had been developing for some time that encapsulated all that the Modern meant, with its promises and its agonies, the certitudes and the void, the individualism and the collectivist politics, with its analytical rigour and poetry, Nagel and Rilke all in one, just as Paris had been in its *fin de siècle*, in 1900.

For all that, Berkeley was a pressure cooker. If Parisians had escaped to *fin-de-siècle* Normandy or Biarritz, where did Berkeley people go in the sixties? One way was to go south as far as the Big Sur. At the time, Highway One was a one-lane country road, Monterey had not yet been hit by tourism and Clint Eastwood, and the canneries were still in operation. In Cannery Row one could smell the ocean in the sardines being canned. One could sleep on the beach if one did not mind the cold, the seaweed and the back pain. On the way, one could stop over in Santa Cruz. Where the University campus is today there was the woods. It must have been a state park. There one could spend the night under the pine trees if one did not mind the curious raccoons chewing on one's sleeping bag. This was the long haul. One did not always have the time between course work and a charter flight to Europe to venture south often. For a short trip, Palo Alto was near, but it was a different continent. Stanford had a wonderful faculty but sat at the end of a very long, interminable bridge. From Berkeley we thought the Hoover Institution ruled the place. Its politics offended us as much as its coincidental name at the time. Just on the other side of the Berkeley hills, almost as if in Arizona, stood the sleepy towns of Walnut Creek and the like. Yet they were to us as far away as the moon with their landscape and the way their people talked. Whenever I had to go there, two songs from the fifties would ring in my ears, "purple people eater, take us to your pre-si-dent."

A much more customary route was to Marin County, Sausalito and Mill Valley. The part-wooden bridge to Tiburon was beautiful on the drive. As one crossed one was met with a huge, deserted wooden building on the left that might have been a silo of sorts. It had a four-digit San Francisco telephone number from the twenties inscribed on its side in big letters. Each time I went by the building a Bacall–Bogart dialogue in black-and-white would play in my head. In Sausalito they made wonderful avocado-and-shrimp salads at the Trident, owned by the Kingston Trio of "Tom Dooley" fame. However posh and endowed with a marvelous terrace on the water it was, there, in those days, even a student could afford a light lunch of an avocado sandwich. A dime was a dime, and a dollar was a dollar.

In 1964 the department of sociology was still at South Hall. Barrows was under construction.* Blauner and Matza were the younger of the professors, Blauner brilliant and radical, perhaps a little more junior, Matza forever youthful and endlessly inspiring. They were kind enough to let me take their graduate seminars in my senior year, and I wrote a paper for each that I still find extremely insightful in my less modest moments! Smelser was ageless in his forever-mature way: always the mainstay of the department, helpful, attentive, diligent, superb. I owe Neil Smelser the rest of my career, but more on that later. His having been a Rhodes scholar reinforced my thoughts of going to Cambridge after Berkeley.

Returning to the department, Kenneth Bock gave extremely lucid lectures. I learned a good deal of my Marx from him. His favourites were Toynbee and Sorokin and Margaret Hodgson, who has a wonderfully lucid book, unfortunately forgotten now, on the historical geographical sociology of England before the Industrial Revolution, in which she argues that all innovation occurred where there had been immigration that broke the back of conventionalism. Bock looked the Berkeley grandee even in his Marx lectures. He looked as if he had been at Berkeley since before the university had even come to the hills. He was there already when the department was called the Department of Social Institutions. Bock was always very courteous if a bit distant.

---

* A part of this appears in my Berkeley Sociology Alumni's blog.

We all read Marx very carefully. Our favourite contemporary radical sociology writing then was that of Ralf Dahrendorf! We took him as one of our heroes. We considered so-called conflict sociology a true alternative! A bit of a mistake in retrospect. Randall Collins fell for it. That was before we discovered the Frankfurt School.

In the mid-sixties Berkeley had an excellent undergraduate program before it got axed after the Free Speech Movement. We felt in no way inferior to the graduate students. Sproul Plaza was the core of the campus. It was largely dominated by the sociology, philosophy, political science and English majors. The engineers would not come down too much, but would hang out north, where the fraternities were. The law students stayed in the north in isolation. The psychologists had already run to the other side of the campus to become professional. Next to them were the Department of Social Welfare and one or two state institutions of social service. The agricultural experimental farm with its open space provided the light for that corner of the campus, forever saving Oxford Street with its airiness. The historians were not yet in the picture; in those days in America the history departments were where the football players were parked for their semi-academic sojourn.

We all gathered on Sproul Plaza, by the fountain or in the adjoining cafeteria, for heated post-lecture discussions. Zellerbach Hall had not been built. From Sproul you could, on a clear day, have a magical view of the Bay, San Francisco and the Golden Gate Bridge, sitting like a crown in their midst.

Berkeley was an open university. Evening seminars never ended in the classroom as scheduled. They would continue many hours into the evening in one of the beer joints on Telegraph. One favourite was Robbie's, a Chinese-run hofbrau! It had the cheapest pitcher if not the best beer.

During the day in the lecture halls around Sproul on the other side of Sather Gate, we would go to any lecture of our choosing. Everyone had his favourites. Mine were Carl Schorske's history lectures in Dwinelle. I never took his course but hardly ever missed his lecture around noon three days a week. He remains the best lecturer I have ever heard. Listening to him with his free associations, recounting the ironies in Western history, was pure joy, a delight unmatched by anything else. I am sorry that his written work has been no match for this volcano of a lecturer. People cannot get to appreciate him as much as he certainly deserves! If it was not a Schorske day, my early afternoon excursion could be either to Hubert Dreyfus's lectures on Existential Philosophy, a subject we thought broke through conventional thinking, or Alfred Frankenstein's lectures up the hill on Renaissance art, where he made the symbols come to life.

One day, opposite Dwinelle, in Wheeler Auditorium, John (more on him later) and I went to listen to Koestler. We both admired him very much. His *Darkness at Noon* is, I believe, still a classic. He was then preoccupied with "the thirteenth tribe". We were a bit disappointed with the lecture, but it felt great to shake the hand of a great man—on that we didn't change our minds. Berkeley education was not only in the classroom; it was everywhere!

Years later, in the late sixties, it was at Sproul that I would meet Marcuse, who would bring that holy place to its pinnacle. But let me continue with the Sproul days before Marcuse and return to the years 1964–65. These were still the years of the beginning, before Marcuse, before Vietnam, before Kent State, and the dream of the general strike and the sit-ins.

On Sproul Plaza, on a beautiful sunny day in late 1964—it must have been around noon—we surrounded a police car that had come to disperse us. A very fine man, Mario Savio, whom I, as a habitué of Sproul, had seen and exchanged many greetings with, climbed onto the, by then immobilized, police car carrying the bullhorn he had for the occasion. Mario in his light brown leather jacket climbed onto the police car in his white socks but only after he had instinctively removed his shoes! This is the image I have of the day after more than forty years. Not the details of what he said, but that innate elegance, that civility, is to me the unforgettable thing about that moment that has remained with me forever. It remains as one of the softest spots in my heart. That was the beginning of the student movement. It was Berkeley, 1964. His elegance in no way detracted from his passionate and radical speech, punctuated with a wonderfully witty and acerbic portrayal of the university administration. He expressed for all of us the fears of what might become of the university in the future. Clark Kerr's idea of the multiversity was already in the air. Kerr wanted to integrate the university with the giant corporations on the outside; we believed in the ivory tower. This was the start of the Free Speech Movement. Nineteen sixty-eight had started in Berkeley, four years ahead of the world.

That evening the students held a sit-in in Sproul Hall, which was the University's administration building. I wanted very much to go but couldn't. Something came up... I went to Ernie's, which was then perhaps one of the best restaurants in San Francisco, and had my first Duck à l'Orange. I still think it was the best I've ever had.

In 1964 a conflict had been brewing for some time between the students and the administration with regard to whether leafleting tables might be put at the entrance of the University for the upcoming California elections, which Ronald Reagan would eventually win. I remember how dark we felt when several months later we listened to his inaugural speech as the new governor one late California afternoon on the lawn where the University's undergraduate library now stands. The University had put up loudspeakers, as if to forewarn us of the coming events. In the Free Speech Movement struggle the students wanted no restrictions on political speech. The University claimed they wanted politics not to be allowed on campus. I could see the University's point. I knew if we wanted an ivory tower it had to cut itself off from society. On the other hand, the University had a bad record of denying tenure to Marxist faculty. It had a history of demanding the oath of allegiance from its faculty members. Only a few years earlier the same issue had led to a violent skirmish when the House Committee on Un-American Activities, a legacy of the McCarthy days, had met in San Francisco, and Berkeley students had a big role to play on that occasion only to be hosed down the stairs of City Hall by city firemen. Perhaps those were the first seeds of the coming student movement!

Berkeley had become the vanguard of the student movement. Already by the early sixties many bright students from the best colleges in New York and other parts of the East who had seen the rough side of the Civil Rights Movement in the South had transferred to Berkeley. Berkeley had become the place where the bright and committed middle and upper middle-class children of professional parents chose to complete their university education. They had no patience with aloof, academic *savoir faire*.

The police car and the Mario Savio episode say so much in retrospect. Not only did Mario take his shoes off to climb onto the car, in the later hours we would bring coffee and sandwiches to the two cops who had been trapped so long inside it. What strikes me is the innocence, the purity—the naiveté in the positive sense of the word—that characterized the early days of the student movement. I find that completely commensurate with the assumptions in which the whole paradigm of the Modern was anchored—alas, at times at its fragile expense! I find that civility, innocence and optimism about human nature much more germane to the Modern as an Enlightenment project than the atrocities, the violence, the Holocaust (Bauman) perpetrated in its name. I will try to argue that point in the later chapters.

The Free Speech Movement wreaked havoc among the faculty. Some saw in it the Hitler Youth; some saw it as another version of the juvenile "rebel without a cause". They were wrong. The students were also wrong to imagine they could get involved in the world but only on their own terms. The administration handled the situation very badly in the beginning. They had no experience with any of this. Every movement at some point has a need for dialogue and recognition. The administration instead totally shunned the students. They could have built a bridge between the students and the faculty. By the time they tried to do that, it was already too late.

A very intelligent solution was eventually found. The small strip of land at the South entrance of the campus where students had the leafleting tables was turned over to the municipality. Thereby, the students could continue having their political tables but now they were not on campus but on a land which belonged to the municipality. I do not know whose ingenious idea that was.

Incidentally, for my two protagonists at Berkeley, it is no irony that Neil Smelser and Mario Savio were at loggerheads during the FSM demonstrations. Savio and Smelser I believe met several times. When they met, Savio was apparently rather rude in his rebellious posture and Smelser taciturn in his Budha-like manners.

Four years later, in late 1969, I returned to Berkeley as a graduate student after Cambridge (UK), Paris and the New School, and a little working time in East Africa. The department had moved to the fourth floor of Barrows Hall, where all the social sciences departments had also moved. Herbert Blumer had built the best department in the country—at least that is what we thought, and what the country thought, as the top students from the top colleges congregated there. These were the years of sociology. Herbert Blumer represented George Herbert Mead in the department. He had been Mead's student. Blumer was a wonderfully warm person. Huge as he was, he would put his arms around your shoulder with the greatest friendliness. Rumor had it that he had been a professional football player in Chicago to put himself through college and was once married to a beautiful fashion model. Blumer filled the corridors of Barrows's fourth floor with the magnanimity of a department chair who had created the best department in the country by recruiting sociologists whose methodologies were most unlike his—an exceptional quality indeed in academia! When he and Smelser gave the graduate theory course it was a feast. It was said that to make his methodological point he once asked Smelser, "Neil, have you ever seen a norm walking down the corridor?" Leo Lowenthal was the highbrow German intellectual, very sophisticated and acerbic, quite in the centre even before we had all discovered the Frankfurt School. Marcuse's fame had not yet fully moved north from San Diego—or was he still at Brandeis then, I cannot remember. At the time, Habermas was only a mimeo we circulated among ourselves as the bright young new German sociologist. The text was his "Science and Technology as Ideology", translated by a fellow graduate student, Hans Muller. It very much enchanted us. Foucault's *Madness and Civilization*, his best work, might have just been translated! David Matza was to review it for *American Sociological Review*. Bendix was remarkably erudite. Lipset, I never met; he was always on leave. Kingsley Davis had already established his turf at Demography. Goffman had gone to the East Coast the year before

I came to Berkeley, but his fame still lingered vividly in the corridors of the department. Kornhauser, still young, was resting on the laurels of his *Politics of Mass Society*—I think he took an early intellectual retirement after the book. It was de Tocqueville made contemporary. I realize now, when I reflect retrospectively, that this Tocqueville "secondary organizations and democracy" advanced a formula that messed us all up. France had almost no secondary organizations until the 1890s, but Germany had a lot of them. They both went Fascist in the mid-thirties, yet France resisted better with its deeply entrenched state, whereas Germany could not! Hannah Arendt certainly has been much more perceptive on this issue and the rise of Fascism.

Berkeley had become much more of a graduate institution, perhaps a little in response to the Free Speech Movement. Sproul had lost its earlier focus as the principal forum. Intellectual activity had shifted more to the departments. For us, the social scientists, it was Barrows Hall. Sproul had become more the promenade with lots of Hare Krishna song and dance. The cafeteria had become more amorphous, and the new Zellerbach Hall now obstructed the magical vision of the Bay and the Golden Gate Bridge. One good thing was that the student movement had totally turned the law students around; they had now become mature, political and active. With the more graduate character of the university, the research institutes had come to play a more dominant role, often at the expense of the departments. One institute that had become a highbrow intellectual centre was the Center for the Study of Law and Society. There, Selznick was the duke, subtle in mind, elegant in manners. From him I learned so much. He was magnanimous and most generous with his time and his ideas. I spent many seminar hours at the Center. Philippe Nonet was the other member of the Centre's faculty who I saw a lot. He was most generous with his time and most rigorous in his intellectual demands. He was most kind to be in my oral's and dissertation committees. I am most grateful.

The following year I had the great fortune of being asked by the department to give Selznick's theory course while he was on sabbatical. A great experience! It was my first true teaching job. I believe I was very successful. I gave a tough course and a tough final exam and was rated very highly by the students. Habermas was then on my reading list and his "science and technology as ideology" was the dominant theme of my essay final! It was the beginning of my academic career. I had already been a Teaching Assistant for several years. I had enjoyed that very much. It was a great learning experience. As a Teaching Assistant I might have been a bit too serious for the job and a bit too pompous. On reflection I sometimes feel embarrassed. Teaching my own course might have taken those silly edges off my demeanor. No better cure for pomposity than a little self-confidence!

The other most gratifying and educational experience was being on the editorial board of eight of the *Berkeley Journal of Sociology*, a graduate student journal whose board was selected by fellow students. We spent hours arguing over manuscripts. It was a wonderful way of getting an education. Manuscripts were reasons to argue over methodologies, politics and theory. It was a great education and tremendous fun. I will return to it below.

The *Journal* gave me one of my most memorable experiences, which I still recall with great pride. For the *Journal*, Karl Kreplin and I taped Herbert Marcuse in a fully packed ASUC auditorium. He was brilliant, beautiful and moving. Marcuse had become my hero and he still remains so.

Berkeley's mindset in those days was shaped by Marcuse, Kuhn and the Beatles—the first of whom I still adhere to academically, and the second of whom I now abhor for his lowbrow academism. Since then, Marcuse for me has remained a perennial talisman. Listening to the

Beatles now is even more moving an experience. Today they bring tears to my eyes, tears of nostalgia for the Modern. Yet Pink Floyd have become the most potent in my consciousness since they sound the death-knell of the Modern from its own involution: "teacher, teacher you're just a brick in the wall..."

I had returned to Berkeley in 1969 on the heels of the flare-up over the "people's park", a strip of land used by political groups that the University wanted to take to build new dorms. I was told about the great episodes of that conflict when I arrived. A year later was the time of the greatest eruption: the Kent State killings, the escalation of the war in Vietnam, and the invasion of Cambodia. It was a total event. A good many of us in Sociology got involved with writing leaflets to mobilize workers in the flatlands for a general strike. What phenomenal excitement, what fabulous education, what fantastic solidarity.

The anti-war movement was in full swing. As teaching assistants, we were holding teach-ins on capitalism, imperialism, and the war. Baran & Sweezy's *Monopoly Capital* was our handbook. Retrospectively now I feel a little ashamed of how we put the engineering students through such an ordeal when they lacked all interest. They were intelligent enough to bite the bullet, go through the episode most obligingly, and not jeopardize their grades in their social science electives. I think the University handled that occasion better. Yet I do not know how much they were in on the helicopters that sprayed our Sproul Plaza meetings with tear gas. That was brutal and silly. The helicopters only agitated us and made our will all the stronger. It was Paris all over again as I knew from the year before, but now on the Berkeley campus. We thought Berkeley was Paris! The issue was one of war and killing, of empire and the draft!

But it was not all politics and campaigning: Berkeley was a city of cinemas, from the most regular kind to the walk-ins, like the two at

Northside. The crown however belonged to the Pacific Film Archives. Tom Luddy had made it one of the richest sources of the "oldies", from *Nosferatu* to *Pandora's Box*, two rare films to be viewed every night. I would run into Luddy in Paris on the Boulevard St Germain, and we would nod and pass by as if we were on Telegraph Avenue. I must have been at the Pacific Film Archives almost every other evening. It was a tremendous source of education in black-and-white which I am sure, has contributed immensely to my chapters on the life of the Modern. The Pacific Archives has now moved from Durant to Shattuck in a typical modernist betrayal. Many grand works the modern built in its hubris only to lead to lose their true functions. The Archives were a step from hub of the campus to where one would drift in and out momentarily if not stopped at the Swallow next to the Archives, for a lemon tart or a quiche. Now at Shattuck on the edge of campus the Archives is a movie theatre miles away. By then we could just pop in, watch a black-and-white film and return to the library. Modern edifices often defeat their *raison d'être*. If that was not enough, one went to the Surf Theatre in "Frisco" by the ocean at the other end of the city. I believe the Surf no longer exists today. People there wore black turtlenecks and smoked like Juliette Gréco. Walking the paved streets—as they were then—around the Surf Theatre on a sunny day and then topping it off with a brief visit to the Musée Mécanique at Pigeon Point remains for me something to yearn for forever.

The Marcuse of those days on has remained my beacon. He has always been there somewhere, hidden or apparent, in every course I have taught for the last thirty plus years. Some people are both place and persona in one. It was also at that time in Berkeley that I met three friends from whom I still keep learning, İlkay Sunar, Claus Offe and Steve Cohen. To them my gratitude remains immeasurable.

How could I not consider myself a very, very lucky man! Berkeley was a fantastic place. No place has yet come even a distant second for my learning experience and for the depth of its lived days.

My social geographical account ends here. Let me turn now to the people I met in a chronology of personal acknowledgments, to thank them for enabling me to write this book.

For the people who shaped my lucky life, let me once more go back to my undergraduate years at Berkeley for a moment. At Berkeley, still before 1965 and before the student movement, every day I would read T. S. Eliot in the mornings and afternoons, and every day I would gravitate to Berkeley's Morrison Library—a beautiful wood-paneled reading room—to read whatever appeared that day on the "new arrivals" table. Next to it stood the table with current journals. There, I started reading one of the first issues of *The New York Review of Books*, to which I have since subscribed for so many million years. Next to it were *The New York Times*, for which you had to sit close to the table to catch one of the few copies before somebody else got it; there was no California edition back then. From the same table I avidly read the journals, *Encounter* and *Commentary*, which the CIA had been supporting, unbeknownst, of course, to us. We did not know much about the CIA then. One day on the new arrivals table I discovered the first English translation of Apollinaire's *Alcools*. It has since radically configured my understanding of the Modern, as I write below in a way quite different from all the ways the Modern has been understood and rendered by many others. It was thanks to what I learned from John Steele that I would so much enjoy the Morrison Library and Apollinaire. Without him I might have become just a bookworm sociologist in the Reserve Book Room next door!

But my Berkeley early education (1964–65) was not only the theatre of the absurd and German expressionist drama. In fact, Martin Esslin's introduction to *The Theatre of the Absurd* only reinforced my choice of sociology as a major. It was not the contextualization of those theatrical texts, which he intelligently does none of, but his discussion of their—to use another neologism—subtext that struck me as so Durkheimian. I had read Marx and Durkheim on many occasions. My search in sociology was not for public conscience or a Fabianist type of "do-goodery" [sic]. However much I commend them both when done privately, I abhor them when done academically. My search was for a conceptual understanding of how societies exhibit particular cultural forms in particular times in their history. There, I wanted geometry and rational discourse. I never had patience with descriptions that pretend to be theories the way Giddens would practice later. In my first term in Berkeley sociology, Neil Smelser's course on theory was required. I found in its systematic rigour, analytical depth and comparative skill what I had been dreaming of at Amherst. That is when I decided to study sociology as the real thing. It is the best course I ever had in the many thousand years of my education; it set me the model of teaching for which I have received so much praise, adulation and reward, and I have traveled with it on demand to many different parts of the world. Smelser made me into a medieval craftsman who carries his means of production with him, never to depend on anyone else. He gave me my métier, an incomparable gift! I took Smelser's word to many places around the globe, and it has given me a purpose and prestige. I consider I had three principal teachers, in the Yaqui sense (Carlos Castaneda, *Teachings of Don Juan: A Yaqui Way of Knowledge*): my friends, Scott Lindbergh and John Steele, and Neil Smelser. Neil Smelser is my third teacher, yet so different from the other two—of them I will say more later. Thanks to Smelser's geometry, their contributions complete the circle and become meaningful. It was so essential for me to see where geometry ends and where poetry begins, where reason must prevail and where unreason is to be admitted. That was also Durkheim's problem; in a deep reading of Durkheim it becomes obvious that unreason is ubiquitous, always there, robust and hard to keep at bay. Courage, as Esslin mentions in his introduction to his book on the theatre of the absurd, was to survive rationally in the face of its fragility, by facing the deep truth of unreason that lurks behind reason. Nietzsche in his struggle is as modern as Kant. Weber never was.

I have since taught a theory course on Smelser's heels with a different emphasis. Marx and Durkheim got more comprehensive and longer. For Durkheim I included his Kantian essays and for Marx Hegel, and I dropped Smelser's Michels and Parsons to include a little Weber as a conclusion. I have never failed to mention Smelser as the originator of the course each time I taught it for over thirty years in many places, and, to Neil Smelser's credit, I was often elected best teacher by the students. Neil Smelser has had more impact on my life than anyone else; he made me into an academic. My loyalty to him would never waver.

When I went from Berkeley to Cambridge to read Economics in 1965, Frank Hahn and Nicholas Kaldor taught theory in the same elegant, rigorous manner. There is no better training in logical analysis than good economic theory. Again it was my luck that I ended up as an economist at Cambridge. I had wanted to read European history. But Cambridge would not let me do European history without Latin—very sensible indeed. Reading my second choice, Economics, at Cambridge proved most valuable in the long run, much more than history, which I read the most now. Frank Hahn must have been the most intelligent person I have ever met. I had never seen wit and logic combine so well. His article, co-authored with Matthews, on economic theory is, to my mind, still the best model for any analytical theory thinking and still my guide to the way I organize my theory lectures.

After Cambridge I found myself in Paris in 1968. I do not have to recount the story of Paris in 1968. Obviously, the French students might have been politically much more mature than the American students, but they were naïve about university education when compared to my Berkeley cohort. The crisis was as much of the state and the universities, as it was of the unions, which had been mothballed politically in part because of their relationship with the atrophying Communist Party. The youth rebellion was against both. In the grand auditorium of the Sorbonne I was tired of warning them over and over again of the pitfalls of the "relevant education" they were clamoring for. The French university had been moribund for a long time, but I thought the answer was not more relevance, as I knew from my Berkeley days, but more university. I had Clark Kerr in mind! I could never convince them of the errors of their vision. Eventually Edgar Faure would give them a model of relevant higher education and prove me right. French students must be far unhappier now than before. Only many years later did I meet Daniel Cohn-Bendit in person. Then and now a wonderfully intelligent and admirable fellow who heroically never tires of politically defending the tenets of the political modern, he gets lonely now in the maze of the European Union's Leviathan.

After a year in the turbulent Paris of 1968 and a brief stint in East Africa, I went to the New School in New York. I wanted to go to the New School because it still had remnants of the "university in exile". I had a tremendous admiration for German Jewish scholars and felt a particular affinity with them, especially after my year at Amherst, which was, of course, in my mind the opposite. The urban context of New York suited me well. My *fin de siècle* and the Modern were still lurking in the East Village, where most resident shopkeepers spoke Polish almost exclusively. I lived on a shoestring on St Mark's Place near

Tompkins Park. I loved the intellectual atmosphere at the New School and that part of New York. I had no money to go beyond 14th Street except on foot. In the tiny, cozy library in the 12th Street basement of the New School I discovered *L'homme et la société*, which had articles by Lévi-Strauss, Georges Gurvitch and Lucien Goldmann, who, I believe, were also the editors of the journal. Its content and orientation—what they called Philosophical Anthropology—I still consider the most sophisticated intellectual example of the human sciences, a model that has unfortunately become archaic.

The next year I came to Berkeley as a graduate student. I was TA-ing and I loved it. It was most educational. One learns best by teaching, I have always found. The Berkeley department had become a haven for the best students in America. Barrows Hall graduate lounge was the meeting place where I learned an infinite amount from my fellow students. We organized to meet one evening a week at Karl Kreplin's house on College Avenue. Art Stinchcombe would come to these meetings. That was where some of the best theory discussions took place. Outstanding times! This was education at its very best. Sometimes we also met at Art's house on Henry Street. Stinchcombe was one of the best minds one could meet, clear and rigorous, challenging and superb. He was always most cordial to me. I learned so much from him on those occasions. Berkeley was a total learning experience.

Yes, Berkeley was a total learning experience. From sociology people would also go to other departments for seminars, lectures, discussions. One of my favourites was Steve Cohen's at Urban Planning.

I have not seen anyone who could elucidate the instrumental grammar of the modern with total cynicism the way Steve did. Kolakowski, very famous then, came once to teach for a term in Political Science. It was very exciting at the beginning, yet the lectures turned banal after a while. Visitors often did not have a knack for lectures the way Berkeley faculty did. One exception was Amartya Sen. I learned my Harrod–Domar from him—a tough job to teach—in my junior year when he was visiting faculty: a very bright, conscientious, and fine man. Lectures were central to Berkeley teaching, and that suited me far better than the tutorials of Cambridge.

Two other people at Berkeley would also contribute significantly to my thinking with their systemic approach. One was West Churchman, whose *Design of Inquiring Systems* I read like a medieval monk with his holy book every day for several months at the Graduate Social Science Library, where the only copy of the book could be found. The other person who influenced me in that regard was Benjamin Ward. By then I had had a relatively good training in Economic Theory at Cambridge. Ward gave informal seminars at his home with great generosity and cordiality. Along with West Churchman's book, I also read Ward's *What's Wrong with Economics?* more than a few times when it was still in manuscript format. I do not know whether it ever got published in that original, thoughtful, rigorous, radical language. It was an almost Kantian critique of the science of economics. Nothing beats the rigorous reading of economic theory for developing an analytical logic, checking one's assumptions, delineating one's lines of causality, and recognizing the logical boundaries of one's theory. For my thinking, for an analytical perusal of mental paradigms Edmund Wilson set the model, then the works of Élie Halévy and Ronald Meek. Parsons showed me the practice of talking in terms of cultural paradigms as bundles of Will, and Churchman how to look at their underside. But nothing is as indelible an experience of a live lecture as Schorske, always a giant in that regard. How sad that his written works, though so germane to the concerns of this study, remain in my eye somehow not on a par with his giant intellect—yet certainly better than Peter Gay's superficial dabbling in the same subject. Again in the vicinity of the issues into which this study wants to delve, it was Gay's failure that prompted me to first unearth the mood to capture the sensibilities of a period, and to do that best tongue-in-cheek and with humour, which Gay, so lowbrow, darkly lacks.

To begin with, from Berkeley, in retrospect, two people stand out in my memory of the Berkeley faculty: David Matza, totally enchanting, outstanding, brilliant, a loner, most lovable for his exceptional mind; and, above everyone else, Neil Smelser, our Buddha figure forever. Finally, for my academic superiors, two others after Berkeley have to be mentioned once more for their immediate impact on this work: Donald Black at Yale, political and logical positivist, most invaluable for his double challenge, without which this work of mine could have degenerated into metaphysics or astrology; and Offe, who, with his passion for abstraction and critique, with his search for rigour and geometry, I still feel sits on my shoulder the minute I turn to my text.

As far as friendships beyond intellectual camaraderie are concerned, Jeff Prager and Karl Kreplin were the two people from the department that I saw most often: brilliant people, brilliant minds with kind, generous, warm hearts. Knowing them was pure pleasure. Jeff later went to UCLA to teach. I got to see Karl for a longer period. Karl stayed in Berkeley to eventually teach millions of hours a week at the local community colleges. A very, very sharp mind that connected the micro with the macro so well but that hit the political glass ceiling when it came to employment. I learned so much from Karl—a brilliant sociologist in the best tradition.

It was also then that I had many wonderful evening discussions on the theory of the state with İlkay Sunar. I would venture to say we were the first to deal with the question when the state was still only "an agency of resource mobilization", to use Parsons's words, in American social science. My dissertation came out of those discussions, as did my later connection with Pierre Birnbaum. After I returned to Europe, Pierre and I developed a wonderful friendship that was not only fun but also of great learning. To me Pierre stands as the true edifice of the Republic and the French Modern, which this book is about; hence, my gratitude to him is most immediate and real. With great amazement I note the later rise from that wilderness of the industry of the "sociology of the state"! After Sunar's in political science, my dissertation was the first in sociology to put the state at the centre of a comparative historical discussion, in my case with the extensive benefit of Schumpeter and Selznick's sociology of organizations. Theda Skocpol, whose work I much admire, and others writing on the state came only after a decade. With Sunar then, a mind sharper than mine, and since then each time we converse—now for almost half a century—I have to rethink what I thought I knew, and each time a new understanding emerges. What great joy and elation.

Claus Offe, the master of systematic abstraction and of state theory, was Berkeley's other gift to me at the same time. That concern—rare for the day—with the theory of the state was again the basis of our almost immediate intellectual solidarity in Berkeley in the early years of our camaraderie. There is no single person I owe as much as I owe Claus Offe for his stoic patience and generosity with me; and for making academic opportunities available to me that I otherwise could not have obtained on my own. Thanks to him, I discovered Budapest, which would later play such a central role in my life. Thanks to him I spent so much intellectual time in Germany, which in itself is a full education when in the company of Claus. He is one person whose goodness I can never fully reciprocate. Intellectually, our discussions, which often went on until dawn over Hennessey or Armagnac, and often with the contribution of Sabine, his then wife, have left a strong imprint on the text below, especially in Chapters Two and Four. Time with Claus is still a tremendous intellectual joy. Based on our Berkeley friendship, founded in 1969, we have been getting together in different parts of the world for an evening or two of intense discussion every year for the last forty years. Claus is my true guide to the modern, my master for the story I will soon be telling. I also benefited from being witness to the subtle disagreements between Claus and Pierre on the state and modernity. On that my position was closer to Pierre's.

I first met Steve at the Max Planck Institute in Starnberg in a seminar Claus organized in the early 1970s. Since then Steve has become one of my best friends. He was my savior when I got writer's block with my endless dissertation. Yet he is much more than that to me. Steve is the most cynical radical brilliant insightful person, and great fun. Great to see him run circles around anything and still maintain a great sense of humour, and to hear him, with his tremendous intuition and theoretical insight, debunk all existing conventions tongue-in-cheek and with the subtlest humour. One of the most intelligent persons I have met in my life.

So much fun! So much to admire! So much to learn from! Yet, before I conclude recounting my days in my Berkeley intellectual rose garden, I must relate one experience that I have never stopped retelling for its irony. It was at Berkeley, on one of those days Marcuse had come to town and was staying at Leo Lowenthal's house in San Francisco. As a favour to me, Leo asked me if I would take Marcuse on his afternoon stroll in the city. It was the best gift anyone had ever given me. I duly went, of course, and we set out on the walk. I discovered I had nothing to tell him! I was totally dumbstruck. I never felt so stupid. In total awe, whatever I mumbled was rubbish. The old man, very generous in his way, very handsome and very elegant, bent over backwards to engage me. It was to no avail. It must have been the lowest point in my life of over six decades. Today, I tell the story every year to my students as a warning to curb one's hubris. Life is full of irony and contradictions! My angel of luck must have been busy somewhere else that day!

One micro-cosmos where I grew intellectually might also interest sociologists of later generations: Berkeley Graduate Student Lounge.

The rectangular room on the fourth floor of the east side of Barrows Hall was the sociology graduate students' lounge, a room lively as no other department's in Barrows.

The intellectual centre of the room was the seating arrangement: a lounge and two armchairs at the left side of the room by the left wall. It was the centre of gravity as Ann Leffler, always a little quiet; Margaret Polatnick, jovial yet extremely reserved; Carole Joffe, whom I always found the most brilliant of our cohort; Sue Halpern, most insightful but always quiet; and the very sedate and serene Ann Swidler sat and carried on intense conversation. The late Carol Hatch, when she could escape from department work, would join them, and also Fred Block when he came to the lounge. At the table by the window in the north-east corner—usually the boys' corner—Harry Levine would sit, he a brilliant conversationalist with a great voice, a charismatic and brilliant guy who had been a part-time cab driver in Manhattan, and told lots of wonderful stories with the greatest sense of humour; I talked to him a lot. Again, on the east side, one table south, again by the window Sue Greenwald would sit and at times carry on a distant conversation with the women's side of the seating arrangement. I liked Sue a lot. A woman, like so many of the women in the department, whose parents were from the DC area, Sue was, I believe, from Alexandria, Virginia, and her father was in the foreign service. At the time it was very prestigious to have parents in public service, as it is today to have a "business background"; these were still the Kennedy years. Richard Apostle would quietly drift in and out of the lounge as if watching it all but saying not a word; David Hummon would come in, always with a friendly smile on his face, a good voice, and a lovely personality; Jeff Alexander would burst in like "the force" with an overwhelming presence and a booming, deep baritone voice; Jeff Johnson and wife were slightly standoffish and looked conceited with a little unwarranted snobbery; Jeff Johnson was unable, I think, to survive the sociology lounge; he later transferred to the Law School—a very intelligent choice, I think—and I'm sure has since become a very famous lawyer in Texas, where he was from. Karl Kreplin, my mentor, from whom I learned so much in conversation, would come in the afternoons in his preferred colors, beige and brown. Jeff Prager, whom I liked very much and spent good times with, was always most amiable and intelligent and personable; I was awed by his father's having been in the Lincoln Brigade, which to me was the highest accolade one could get—I would always ask him about his father and his stories. David Minkus was intelligent and always a shock value in terms of what he had up his sleeve. On some days Jeff Weintraub would come in with his slick blue Italian bicycle—which he would take along even when he went to the men's room—but chose to remain a little aloof to the lounge's intense sociability. Jerry Himmelstein was a very nice fellow, earnest in his theory interests and intelligent, a person with whom I had long discussions on Marx and theory; I enjoyed him a lot. He was one of the mainstays of the lounge.

Around the coffee machine on the right Tom Taylor, whose father had been the architect of the US policy in Vietnam, and another friend, whose name now escapes me, who had already as a graduate student published in the ASR, remained on the high right-wing of the department at a distance, holding the south end of the room against the prevalent left. I always admired Taylor for his reticence and his courage to come and go with no loss of poise in such an anti-war atmosphere. To be at Berkeley at the height of the Vietnam conflict must have required a lot of courage. I admired him for not losing his composure, keeping his chin up, and courteously going about his own business, never engaging in any political discussion—very hard in that common room—but never apologetic either. There were also two people who would occasionally hold court in the lounge. They were from an earlier cohort, senior to us, but with a little too much sound and fury. They were Irwin Sperber and Hal Jacobs. I never found them as intellectually powerful as the members of my cohort.

At Berkeley, lectures ruled. That was where the education most entertainingly occurred. They were great. Berkeley as a whole exuded education, from the Film Archives to the museums. The Graduate Lounge was yet another site where our education in sociology took place. There, getting annoyed with Eric Olin Wright—Erik, a year or two my junior, was the "sociological engineer" who alienated everybody with his opinionated aloofness and highhanded manner—and, on the positive side, adoring Ann Swidler, being envious of Jeff Alexander—Jeff was an exceptional figure, Foreman's Mozart: radical, rascal, rebellious, very sharp; trying to figure out Fred Block and enjoying Carole Joffe's conversation were all part of my education. Stuart Buckley, an Englishman, I found even more difficult than Fred Block to decipher, my English sympathies notwithstanding. Another Brit, Rosemary Taylor was the model personality, solid, helpful, polite, gracious and intelligent; David Hummon, a good fellow, intelligent and always helpful; Margaret Polatnick had the most disarming smile, but I rarely managed to talk to her. In the meantime, in one of the offices next door, Jeff Paige, with whom I later developed a strong camaraderie, was trying to do something very unique, putting Marxian theory to a Durkheimian statistical test. His book, *Coffee and Power*, would one day crown this very special intellectual endeavour.

Once in a while some faculty also drifted in; among them, Troy Duster was the most amiable and most-liked. He had the great talent of holding the department together—a great feat for all that tension and radicalism. What I would give today to be back in that lounge for just half an hour to be with all those intelligent, earnest, gregarious and brilliant young people, especially the brilliant young women, like a scene out of a Tom Stoppard play.

But in my mind, nobody compares with Carole Joffe. Carole, who was without a doubt by far the sharpest mind among us all was at her best in one David Matza evening seminar—the most brilliant seminar I ever had. Carole Joffe's intellect was exceptional. The best course, undergraduate or graduate, I had was no doubt Neil Smelser's theory course. Neil Smelser was the theory's master. Nobody could do it like him. There was also Art Stinchcombe, from whom you learned the heavens by talking to him, but never in his lectures. Selznick was the intellectual aristocrat who best practiced the sociological dialectic: the negative surprise of good projects, the irony of good intentions. Leo Lowenthal, the Frankfurt School itinerant, brilliant and intolerant, was Marxist and elitist, radical but archconservative, very sociable but hating people at the same time. Leo, a bon vivant with refined taste, was the prototype of the German bourgeoisie before all was destroyed by the Holocaust. Robert Bellah was different. Whenever I saw him I could not but visualize him as a lanky old man with a staff in his hand, wearing sandals, a wooden cross slung over his neck, sweet-talking infidels into Christianity. In retrospect, it might be too harsh to see him as the first post-modern in the department, the beginning of the end. This was in radical contrast to his brilliant earlier book on the Japanese samurai—a book that, unbeknownst to him, was, I think, in the best Schumpeterian tradition, which later much formed my historical sociology. Schumpeter, once the president of the American Economic Association, had then been all but forgotten. When I borrowed his books from the library, they had not been checked out for twenty years. My dissertation was much lodged in Schumpeterian institutional economics, which was then practiced only in one or two places south of the Mason–Dixon line.

Around the campus, lively conversations educated me in the coffee shops and backyards, and for that I am most grateful in particular to Bob Dunn and Elliot Currie for the brilliant discussions in their backyards. There must be a hundred other fellow students whose names I do not recall now. I am grateful to them. They make up the Berkeley that I feel so loyal to.

From Berkeley to Yale

From Berkeley I went in 1974 to teach at Yale, where I met a very exceptional person, Donald Black. Donald combined rigour, logic, geometry and sociological theory so well that I felt reassured in my Kantianism in that period of unnecessary confusion. His cottage in Hamden was almost the Vienna Circle abroad for its theoretical rigour. Going there for an evening of pure intellectual feast was the high point of my days at Yale. He was Wittgensteinian not only in his elegant manners but also in his mind: morally most upright, most civil in his ways, and most impatient with any lapse of logic. That was the type of theory construction I cherished. I have since made it the locus of my sociological efforts. I was building on what I learned from Neil Smelser, Philip Selznick and Frank Hahn. For more than three and a half decades I taught theory on several continents and it was always voted the best course wherever I went. From Donald I learned to insist that poetry and geometry should not mix, and that the poetic aesthetics of a good theory's logic might recall the aesthetics of Eliot's *Wasteland*.

I am grateful for the respect my colleagues showed me at Yale despite my being only a junior member of the department. I am grateful to Donald for being instrumental in creating that atmosphere for me by upholding the ultimate rule of collegiality, the presumed equality of member intellects. As a Wittgensteinian, Black could have become my other Yaqui teacher had time permitted. But I left Yale after two years.

I must acknowledge here one more debt of gratitude. Regardless of the fact that I was only a junior fellow, the Yale faculty always treated me with great civility, equality and respect. Donald might have had a hand in that. I was an academically active junior faculty member, vocal and intrusive for my rank. I have always been over-committed to my profession, perhaps making myself overbearing at times.

At Yale I also spent many rewarding times discussing theory with Seyla Benhabib, who has since remained a brilliant mind with admirable intellectual seriousness. I am very glad that our intellectual camaraderie has continued so well now over four decades. I cannot also fail to mention Mark Cooper. He was a very bright young graduate student, perhaps the best I have ever seen. We used to spend hours in my kitchen on Mansfield Street discussing, exploring totally new ideas, and opening new avenues of research in historical sociology. I owe a great deal to those moments with Mark for my later work and thinking.

One other very memorable person I met at Yale was Feza Gürsey. A great physicist, he was an academic sage, a model scientist, and an admirable human being, a role-model for many of us.

My luck had not deserted me at Yale!

My Text Ran Ahead of Its Grammar: The Lucky Circle

Looking back, let me rerun the cycle, return, go back to the beginning, and recount, to punctuate my luck for the places, friends and teachers, to connect that personal narrative more directly with the story below, for my reader to make more sense of my text, and have my Berkeley cohort pitch in briefly to set the stage in the many ways I cannot figure out.

For discovering the *fin de siècle*, I am most grateful to icicle-like, self-righteous, alien and alienating New England's stiff upper lip that made the search for the *fin de siècle* the means of my survival, its sensibility the most radical antidote to New England self-righteousness. That context helped me to see the *fin de siècle* as Will and un-Will, its *vide* as a perennial fixture at its core. I will later call that *vide* the Dragon, the ever-presence of meaninglessness, the Beckettian absurd as the principal aspect of the *fin de siècle*'s coherence, which became so intelligible to me in the midst of New England certainty, self-assuredness and hubristic arrogance. This, I think, is crucial to the peculiar way I tell the story of the modern below. It was my neighbour Scott at Stern Hall reading *The Ancient Mariner* aloud every other night is what, I think, brought it about. Scott broke my rationalist mindset cast in Turkish Republicanism and the positivism so handy for a young man so insecure. Without his tutelage in Blake and Coleridge I would have been a very stiff man, and this book could have never been written. My intellectual debt to him is nothing but enormous. My luck was to have Scott for my neighbour at the dorm. He was my first teacher in the Castenada sense.

In contrast, my other intellectual kin and some of my teachers at Amherst, who pushed me in the direction I went, and later my neighbours at my bed-sit in Cambridge for the cheap wine and silly nights, have to remain anonymous since I cannot remember their names after four decades; but, remembered, undoubtedly, has to be Stuart Hughes's *Consciousness and Society* at Amherst. It shaped my initial mind as it did the minds of many of my generation, swaying me directly into the *fin de siècle* so impatiently that I dropped out to search for it in Europe at the end of my first year.

Thanks at a more personal level are due first to Scott at Amherst, and then to John Steele, my second life-time teacher, whom I met in my very first semester at Berkeley during an irrelevant public lecture at Dwinelle, for sharing part of that destiny, though always from his abyss—a duality between the sharpest mind and the most elusive metaphysics—to make Berkeley the fount of my youth and the source of all of my later intellectual impatience and aspiration; and for jointly reading Jung and T. S. Eliot in a course of his choice, for the beginnings of my orientation, for unknowingly getting me on my path to Berkeley and Cambridge; and to Scott for setting me off from Amherst and on to the marvels of the *fin de siècle*, and for introducing me to Blake, Shelley and Coleridge. They both remain my teachers to the ultimate degree. I am grateful to Scott also for quitting Amherst, which we did together. Amherst was too bland for his wonderfully erudite metaphysical mind.

I am grateful to Steele for helping me to discover Dada in a very special way, so I could here read Dada and Modernity as inseparable, the Yin and Yang of reason and unreason, which I find, very immodestly, the most fundamental message of the text below. I am thus grateful to him for seeing sociology in its fear of the Surrealists, of German Expressionism, of the Pascalian fears of Durkheim.

Finally, all my generation owe everything to the Beatles' music and to Marcuse's intellectual passion. I am so fortunate for having been a "lucky man", to have traversed the sixties so well situated and so naively; to have seen The King's Road and Mary Quant, to have been at the Sorbonne in 1968, to have been on Sproul Plaza with Mario Savio in 1965, to have been in love when the world turned upside down, to have walked Telegraph Avenue when helicopters were spraying Berkeley with tear gas, to have had the teach-ins for the Law School and the Engineering kids, reading them Paul Sweezy during the Cambodia crisis, and to have spent endless nights composing leaflets for the working class below San Pablo, debating Stalinism against Régis Debray in the editorial meetings of the *Berkeley Journal of Sociology*, disagreeing with Jane Tatum and admiring Karl Kreplin.

At Berkeley at the time—I don't know how it is now—each department had a different doctoral qualifying procedure. In Sociology it was the oral exam. It was pivotal. That, I think, was one reason why the sociology degree at Berkeley was so strong. We took it very seriously. I did, too—read almost everything under the sun for my areas and beyond. That preparation was the bedrock of my sociology for many years to come. I loved that period of most serious, extensive reading and discussion. I did very well in my exam. I enjoyed it tremendously. It was fun and serious at the same time. It was thorough and exhausting. I am most grateful to my committee. I wanted to pass with distinction.

I did not. That year Hardy Frye did. He must have been very, very good. I knew him well. He was a very bright fellow. Oh, what a wonderful department! Oh, what wonderful times!

Finally Most Personal

But all was not of course all pink and rosy, as it was not for Lindsay Anderson's Mr Travis either. There were many dark moments of brown and melancholy. They connected me to Apollinaire's "Le pont Mirabeau".

Thanks to my soul brother Osama Doumani, I survived, literally, the "butt ends" of those moments, and thanks to him I am still here writing. He saved me from a stretcher lying in the corridor of the El Cerrito Community Hospital! Without his intercession, I would certainly have died. For those most formative days exceptional thanks goes to Brenda Cummings. Her personal brilliance, her stamina and above all her British sense of humour at its best, which made me see the orange and the sunshine even in the days of the "darkest side of the moon". She will forever remain my soul sister.

As this book is about the rosy and the pink and my exceptional luck, I do not have to further acknowledge here the dark days of my past. Apollinaire, from the first day I read him at Morrison Library, bridged for me the brown and the pink, the melancholy and the joy. Let that remain as my acknowledgment of those brown days.

In retrospect one more reminder is also in order! The downside of all that luck, of all those lucky trips and encounters, those coffee shops, cinemas and lecture halls was that "a rolling stone gathers no moss". One day soon people will say "oh, how his hair has grown thin, how he wears his trousers rolled", on Amazon he has nothing to his name.

The End of One Diaspora and the Start of Another!

A day came at Yale when, despite myself, I could no longer be the foreigner and a local at the same time. It was not fair to my departmental colleagues, who had embraced me as a fellow faculty member. My commitment to the department, which ran deep, would contradict my wayward conscience. Would I be a passerby pretending to be permanent? I had to either mentally naturalize—an awful expression—or go back home. I chose the latter.

It was a Weberian dilemma. I wanted to be more publicly involved than I could have possibly hoped to be as an academic in America at the time. I packed and went home, or actually went back to what I imagined to be home. I could not have known what I was getting into. Only with time did I discover that everything looked the same but had changed drastically in the almost two decades I had been away. Someone must have wished on me the Toyota ad, "You asked for it. You got it!" Since that return, my engagement in public service has never ceased to be intense!

Thus, I ended one Diaspora for another. It was the beginning of my Diaspora from the Berkeley of the 1960s. But then again, wasn't that only an Atlantis? John Steele is in LA now doing his aromatherapy, and sociology has now been toppled from its pedestal, where the best and the brightest once had sought self-expression.

But what of the other choice? Public activism in my land, as I discovered in the end, was no different from being on a treadmill, where one tries hard, runs and sweats buckets with the illusion one is moving forward while in fact one remains in the same spot; the good days and the bad days differ only in how steep the treadmill is set for that moment. The agency the modern paradigm presumes for its actors might be no more than an extension of their hubris, as Kierkegaard so painfully realized!

In this *longue durée*, I was the beneficiary of the generosity of several institutions. Ford Foundation's MEAwards gave me a grant with which I spent a term studying the documents pertaining to the post-war period at the then Public Records Office, which is now called, by a very un-British name, the National Archives. They form the bases of my writing the end of the last chapter. I am very grateful to that institution.

I must thank two other generous institutions for giving me space and for providing me with most exciting company, in parts of writing this book. The first institution to which I owe a great debt is the C. V. Starr Center for the Study of the American Experience, Washington College, and its director, Ted Widmer. This book, in the actual, physical sense of writing, began there in Chestertown, where the College is located. For me, the evenings of the dreamlike winters of Chestertown, spent in the only pub in town, The White Swan, chatting the world away with Ted and the occasional visitors from New York, remain very memorable. In Chestertown I also had the great fortune to meet Townsend Hoopes. His *The Devil and John Foster Dulles* is a truly great work, surpassing Weber in many ways. I learned so much about America and its "inside" politics. I am most grateful to Ted for making all that possible for me. Needless to repeat, I am a lucky man—the down side: so impossible to repeat those wonderful moments, and life too short to find anew.

The third institution that very much shaped this book is the late Collegium Budapest, which the Hungarian Government has since closed for very un-academic reasons. The Collegium was a true intellectual beacon in central Europe. I am most grateful to Fred Girod at the institute for our lengthy conversations on world matters. They were not only intellectually most exciting but also most educational. The city of Budapest made me rethink and rewrite my chapters describing the modern. I had not earlier thought of how different Habsburgs were from Durkheim's modern which is central to the book. But without the Habsburgs contrast the understanding of both Paris and Durkheim would have only remained most shallow.

Roquefort les Pins, 2015

In the final stage of preparing this book for print I have enormous debt to several people. To begin with, Serdar Metin, my student, later my assistant and my colleague who helped me much to shape this work. He helped me to clarify many of the concepts and consequently with his degree of involvement shares some of the blame in their rendition. I am deeply grateful to him for assisting me so invaluably in so many years: a young man with great promise and erudition. Ms Ginger Saçlıoğlu edited some of the chapters which today are more intelligible than the others. I am most thankful. I had the similar benefit of Binnaz Toprak's editorial review of Chapter Seven. This is not the first time I am grateful to Binnaz for her great talent for writing clearly and be so generous with her time. Reşid Canbeyli, my colleague and academic neighbour to whom I owe so much for being himself the wise scientist to admonish me often when I might have gone astray. Sarhan Keyder who I often consulted as my guide to contemporary French *mentalité*. His insights have always been most astute and perceptive. Dobrinka Cidrof came in the final stage to make the work to take-off with her extraordinary dynamism, goodwill and optimism, and enabled its completion. In the final stage Mr A. Demirci was indeed indispensable in preparing this manuscript for print, for which I am most greatful.

İstanbul, 2017

Personae

Chapter Two

The Question of Method: Introducing Dialectical Essentialism

The Theoretical Ambition: Remembering Kant

Facing these questions raised in Chapter One, here will be the venue to introduce the elements of a "new sociology". A sociology which I shall call *analytical sociology*. It is signified by its methodology, which I will call dialectical essentialism.[1] Its methodology, I hope, sets it apart from the field's recent confusion of description and theory,[2] or the rise of subjectivism and relativism in the name of subalternism. "Analytical" here is not to recall Freud, but refers to Euclid and rigour; it is a choice for geometry over poetry. The discussion of analytical sociology and its method, dialectical essentialism, will constitute the subject matter of this chapter.[*]

Unless one agrees with Hegel's idealism, the "dialectical method" in the hands of the post-Marxists had become "mush". In opening all doors, it was left devoid of any particular door. Stalin had amputated it to a universal engineering technique.[3] Wallerstein, at the other extreme, in stretching it to a disproportionate historical size, turned it into an incontestable, almost extra-terrestrial myth akin to the medieval Black

---

[*]   Neil Smelser taught many fortunate of us the great joy of engaging in rigorous logical analysis of sociological theories. I believe he was the first, and I think he still remains the best, in doing that. The edifice of his *savoir faire* is which after fifty years still remains as the model work. Here I am referring to Smelser-type analysis by naming my method, analytical sociology. Dialectical essentialism is my twist.

Death—both ahistoricizing it to offend Weber and mystifying it to blaspheme in the name of Marx. In other words, in contemporary endeavours, the questions of both timing and determinacy of the dialectic remain in abeyance.

Here the purpose is then to turn Marx upside down, not to find Hegel but to catch the same Marx in a different format, a format more akin to his earlier writings.[4]

This is not to deny the power of linearity in history, but good sociology, I believe, is about unintended consequences, about ironies and surprises. I take them as the principal stuff of dialectical essentialism. In history the two logics, linearity and dialectics, compete, often intertwined at any particular time. Here, I am looking at the cases when dialectical logic would prevail. On the other hand, this is not a renaming of the conventional dichotomy of "change and stability", which, I find, is more a definitional issue than a question of substance.

Dialectical essentialism will be built on the methodologies of **both** Marx, for his dialectics, and Weber, for his essentialism, viewing their work most complimentary and not rivalrous. In this construction, we would always have Nagel's idea of analytical rigour in the background. By making the analytical precepts of "theoretical rigour", and "empirical reference" (the latter, I will call, "narrating the dialectic") into pre-requisites—and thus to parry Popper's criticisms—"dialectical method" would thereby be immunized against its metaphysical renditions which in fact were full betrayals of Marx (e.g. Wallerstein), and "essentialism" would be immunized against its ahistoricization, so antithetical to Weber.

The principal dimension of my method, "narrating the dialectic", is to radically counter these abductions. My method identifies the contradictions through an essentialist reading of a particular historical formation (e.g. Marx's "Capitalism" but not his "Socialism" and "Communism", which escape the dialectical methodology to leave their discussions very un-Marxian), and then sifts through its particular larger empirical/historical context to seek an explanation for its outcomes, i.e. in Hegelian terms, the way it would unfold, or, for us, also not unfold at any particular juncture. In this scheme, not all contradictions in history get resolved, and if they do it is the historical context that determines the timing.

Hence, my key conceptual apparatus, **narrating the dialectic**, has two complementary aspects: (i) contextualizing the contradictions, and (ii) historicizing the context. In our study, for example, the contradictions are specific to the context of the paradigm of the modern, and the context for its demise will be historicized in terms of the Paris peace negotiations of 1920.[5]

Pivotal for our history is the Great War. Coming only twenty years on the heels of the First, the Second World War concluded what had started in 1914.

Narrating the Dialectic: Contextualizing the Contradictions and Historicizing the Context

The content, the focus, the subject matter of this methodological expedition is to tell the analytical history of a paradigm. This is not ordinary history, but an analytical history, the type of history that Marx and Weber did. It might offend the historians, in which case we can always call it the "analytical story" of an historical subject. Its precedents are perhaps rooted in the epics of the ancients, i.e. the myths of Mesopotamia or the tragedies of antiquity. In these ancient narratives, the story is told to convey its essentialist content—the pinnacles, the "anxieties" (apologies: there is no better word for the anxiety of collectivities than this rather personal, individualized term)—of their societies, of where they saw the dangers of their "hijack" and the pitfalls and the glory of their sacrosanct values. All these are the stories of their paradigms told with an essentialist logic. Here, with some distance now from sociological texturing, I am attempting the same for modernity, with one other difference: here, it is a story told in its empirical validity, a true story of a past paradigm. The ancients were about paradigms told in terms of their moral message, not a true story but a story told in the imaginary.

I will first construct my paradigm in terms of its inner grammar, and then follow its story in terms of the logic of this inner grammar as it unfolds through its own motion driven by its own success. Once we establish our paradigm's inner logic by an essentialist construction, both in terms of its empirical-historical contexts and by comparing it with other social paradigms, or, better, "half-paradigms", again in essentialist terms, we can "catch the conscience" of the paradigm and test its validity in its travel for reasons of historical conjuncture.

Hence our story has the aspect first of constructing a paradigm's inner logic. This logic is then put into an historical test in its travel to understand the analytical boundaries of our historical paradigm—where it is strong, where it is ridden by internal contradictions, and where it is too weak to face a conceptual challenge. These analytical faces of the paradigm come to the fore as it moves forward in its historical success to let its inner logic unfold. Hence, the second part of our story is a travelogue, the travelogue of a paradigm.

Recovering the Dialectic

This is a theoretical travelogue, written in terms of analytical sociology, to capture the unfolding of the inner logic of the paradigm, with real events and empirical evidence. The strength of analytical sociology is that it connects the very abstract, often metaphysical, language of a dialectical observation—if one can at all call that "observation"—with a real historical narrative. This is the tremendous salvation of the "dialectical methodology" that was dismissed by Anglo-Saxon scholars for its very abstract nature—the French could not divorce themselves from their Aristotelian Cartesianism to even have a glimpse of the dialectic, with the exception of Kojève's influence in the 1930s.[6] As for the works of Althusser and Balibar, to mention a few Marxists in France, even their logic of analysis is geometric but not in the calculus-like manner of the dialectic, i.e. variables do not change their character over time, and they do not interact. In other words, neither Althusser nor Balibar sees the interactive contextualization and the transformation of the variables as the contradictions unfold, e.g. in their work both the working class and the ruling class remain the same, to use their vocabulary, all through the unfolding and crisis stages of capitalism, and for that matter, of feudalism.

Hence, one purpose of our analytical sociology here is to save dialectical methodology for its own use. And the second stage in my methodological exercise is to save essentialism.

Saving Essentialism

The purpose is to save essentialism, but only in an analytical language with real practices and real episodes, with real Will and real challenges, and most importantly, in temporal motion. Essentialism took essences as constant—without their historical motion—and wanted to study culture by crystallizing it. (The exceptions are few, and one such example is Huizinga.) It is crucial to observe essences in their real historical motion. This is what I am bringing to essentialism. What we are hoping for then is "dialectical essentialism", conducted by analytical sociology, i.e. the sociology of causal relations of the third order. Not a description but causal statements; yet because of its texture a causality that starts with geometry and hence is tautological but rigorous, and then moves toward calculus.

For this dialectical essentialism, Weber had the pieces of its methodology in what I shall identify below as "historical ideal-types", but other than the grand exception of *The Protestant Ethic* he shied away from constructing more complete pictures of a paradigmatic nature. When his focus moves abroad to the East, to Buddhism and other religions, he was laying down the crude elements of a paradigm, but he restricted them too much to their abstract nature without recognizing the real practices of real people. It was, I believe, not necessarily that Weber shied away from what Marx called the real practices of real people (I don't want to get into the dead-end epistemological debate about materialism/realism vs. idealism) but rather that he was too far afield to benefit from that type of investigation of real things. Here, Weber was in the world of abstraction. Here, he admittedly much abbreviated and short-changed Eastern religions.

One final thing about dialectical essentialism: we have seen the elements of analytical sociology; now for the essentialist dialectic. At this juncture, I part company with Marx for the first dialectic.[7] Marx begins his dialectic with man's confrontation with nature (just as Durkheim would do as well, yet Durkheim's nature is primarily nature within the individual) and with the satisfaction of basic "physical needs". That road later leads him to an impasse when, by the extension of his logic, he finds himself in a world in which the question of basic needs is resolved by the giant step of capitalism. There Marx has to have recourse to the cyclical nature of capital accumulation—a brilliant anticipation of contemporary economic theory—or the discontinuities capitalism engenders in creating inequalities while resolving the need problem. This is clearly getting away from the level of analysis Marx had been conducting. In other words, do the contradictions disappear if income inequalities are relatively flattened out, as in the example of the welfare state? Equally, what happens after the revolution when the capitalists are disappropriated as presaged in the *Manifesto*? At this moment, after fully embracing Marx's dialectical methodology of "real people with real things", i.e. ridiculing Hegel yet using his instrument, Marx in the end gets caught in the same problem in his last stage of development, i.e. in communism. Here, I submit to the primacy of Weber's dialectic—the relationship of societies with their own values, whether constructed when they face the ultimate question, the question of the afterlife,[8] or, relatedly, when they face the question of the heavens, or as they face themselves within their cultural totality. Weber and Durkheim come closest here, once in a very rare and unlikely rapprochement. Hence, I take the symbolic world, and the cultural essence that lies behind it with its inner logic, as primary for the study of recent societies. This is not to forsake political economy but to put it into its secondary place, to drop it as the first cause of Aristotle and make it the second cause. My proposition is that essences face the political economy they create, and reveal their weaknesses and strengths in this real context they create for themselves where culture and power are interwoven. Here, we shall capture in terms of analytical sociology the inner guts of a paradigm, its anatomy and morphology, its structure and its moving parts and how they complement and/or contradict each other. I want to understand a human being when he is up in a tree and trying to challenge the birds; only then I can best understand his structure and his morphology.

We shall first lay the groundwork of our theory, to get the matrix within which we shall construct our paradigm of Durkheim and modernity. Then, for its inner unfolding, for historical conjunctural reasons, we shall take it abroad, abroad as a consequence of its victorious deed, as an extension of its historical success, and in that travel we shall narrate the *dialecticality* of our paradigm. It is crucial to sustain the narration of the dialectic, a dimension I claim to be unique, never seen before, and to salvage the dialectical methodology.

The dialectical methodology here has to be defined and defended. The weak, evidentiary nature of the dialectical method has been its greatest weakness. Its indemonstrable nature made it viewed as akin only to astrology or metaphysics, depending on the viewer. To save the dialectic from its catch-all nature, the fundamental antidote is to find a way of solving the timing issue. In other words, *when the dialectical movement is to take place.* This also solves the Popperian objection with regard to determinacy. If the dialectical movement is predetermined with regard to its undefined consequences, then it gravitates toward metaphysics, and if the empirical evidence does not have the medium of its causal connection with the motions of the dialectic, then it is akin to astrology. We then have two problems, one, timing and determinacy, a single issue, and the other evidentiary, i.e. empirical evidence and its causal relation with the theory. I am going to solve the first question by way of a simple "value-added" model à la Smelser.[9] I will posit that the motions of the dialectic come to the fore when it coincides with the motions/values of its context. The dialectic has consequences when the conditions "add" to its motions, or, conversely, when it simmers and does not fully reveal itself when conditions offset its consequences. In this way, I am circumventing the determinacy question but making the dialectic into an operational variable by analytically connecting the motions and the conjunctures. The conjuncture is the intervening variable here, a condition that makes the dialectic acquire its full process. About evidentiarity: dialectical discourse has always remained abstract and unconnected to its relevant sphere of facts which it tries to explain causally. Here, I am introducing the device of "narrating the dialectic", whereby motion and consequence are intimately related and become empirical referents for each other. These two are crucial and, I believe, important steps forward in bringing the dialectic back as a sociological method. It has to be noted that only within the bounds of rigour that analytical sociology (the other contribution of this monograph) offers can we use the dialectic with its necessary rigour and predictability and not gravitate to its somnambulistic nature, where its actions are impossible to predict and where it becomes disconnected from real events other than, at best, in retrospect, and even then, only most circumspectly.

One last point that has to be asserted here is to discard the supposedly conflictual rivalry between Weber and Marx. For the Cold War Marx was to be challenged by Weber. This is all very trivial although it occupied many hours of lecture time, millions of lecture rooms, and trillions of young minds. What a pity, if not downright brutality. Marx and Weber are no different in terms of their epistemology. Weber is no Bishop Berkeley, and no Hegel for that matter. Empires, Rome, Buddhism do not exist before societies, as Plato would have stipulated, or as Berkeley believed, or Hegel, who had his history oriented to the full fruition of a single idea with a single definition. Weber's historical ideal-type, for example, amply shows that the Roman Empire, in that example, is an historical entity created by humans and comes out of full *Existenz*, as Marx would demand from Feuerbach. So, no Idealism here. As for Idealism, if it means that Weber thought ideas and ideals, cultures and symbolic things mattered, yes, certainly, but that is no philosophical idealism. This silly confusion has prevailed for a long time: the confusion of the epistemological issue with the somewhat ontological issue of relevance. It is simply that for Weber "ideas are as real as physical needs" and "facing the heavens is as fundamental a question as facing nature". It is here that Marx and Weber differ, but this is no epistemological question; it is a question of prioritizing the "real" in writing history. Marx wanted to use one dimension that would cover human history from the cave to the future. Weber, looking at a shorter duration, considered societies that have developed enough organization around symbolic things and heavenly questions to take these issues as more fundamental. The difference here is in the nature of the "real" world they are looking at. If one could take "religion" as the "material" of everyday life, the way the French might use the same word, for example, both are materialists. The bigger difference is the extent of the use of the dialectical method, which I shall discuss below. But all the idealism/materialism of the Cold War debate was just that, a means to divide East and West, a Berlin Wall of sorts, built this time by the West. Both the wall and the Marx–Weber contrast caused tremendous loss of time and energy, and, most importantly, of people. One killed, the other wasted in much larger numbers. Who was more brutal? I presume the East. And who more wasteful? I guess the West. But the West created resources much faster so it could afford, and perhaps, even needed to be so wasteful, whereas the East could not afford as time has shown. Its brutality created a demographic deficit. Not only the great loss of human life it engendered, the disenchantment the Wall caused, led many to die trying to cross it.

Here below, we merge Marx and Weber into one to study Durkheim's paradigm, the paradigm of modernity in terms of comparative essentialism.

The Theory: In Defence of Essentialism

It is Marx no doubt who most successfully stood Hegel on his head. It is time now to turn Marx upside-down. It is ideas that fill the sinews of the economy to fix them in a particular direction, to push them at times into most "uneconomical" conduct. The economic instinct is much more malleable than Marx thought, and the Will more rigid and unyielding than the prospects of economic gain.[10] No doubt resources matter for Will to move history in the long run, but until the long run there are many ways to mobilize resources, to extract human sacrifice, to blind people to their own material well-being, or to reconcile them to mere subsistence—all emanating from a cultural, moral compulsion. This was Weber's point. What Hegel was for Marx, Nietzsche was for Weber. Behind the veil of human action was not political economy but essences, cohering as cultural systems, as systems of Will and Unwill—all emanating from a cultural, moral compulsion arising from a bundle of sensibilities embedded in a cultural paradigm expressing their historical essence. Political economy determined their historical course, their destiny, in the very long run, but certainly not their origins or their shape.[11]

Marx solved the problem of the Will by making use of capitalism's competitive logic. He short-circuited the issue of the Will by making "success" the pivotal variable. In terms of the logic of his theory, this was a valid solution. In the contradictions of capitalism's mode of collective accumulation, Marx solved the problem of the Will by looking only at the successful accumulators. It was enough; it was a good logical boundary. He did not have to explain why they would have the drive for accumulation, nor did he have to think about what Joan Robinson calls "the animal spirits". (Rumour has it that it was Joan Robinson who coined this term for Keynes.) In that regard, the threat of falling into the ranks of the proletariat in case of unsuccessful accumulation was sufficient.

Marx studied the consequences of the successful! But if we were to pursue the construction of the "will" itself, then Marx's solution is of course no solution at all. Marx had also run into a similar problem with the revolution and the proletariat. Short-circuiting through the study of the successful would not work here as we were studying the "unsuccessful". The stumbling block of Marx's explanation of revolution appears in the form of a most enigmatic transition from "consciousness-in-itself" to "consciousness-for-itself". Marx here did bad psychology. For Marx, immiseration was a process that would secure the transition. In this bad psychology, Marx at worst had to admit a shadow of Hegel's idealism, or at best, submit to a teleology that brought him closer to Kant. The second position is certainly stronger and more germane to Marx and is what guides us here. Here, the emancipation of the species is the consequence of the resolution of the endogenous contradictions in the logic of capital. That is to say, either Marx would claim, in the Hegelian idealist chart of things, that the proletariat would move from consciousness-in-itself to consciousness-for-itself, à la Hegel, to break the historical deadlock of the accumulation crisis, or he has a teleological argument with an ultimate assumption of the "necessary freedom of the human species", which brings him closer to Kant. The latter argument is certainly stronger where the crisis is endogenously created from the internal contradictions within the logic of capitalist accumulation. In that sense, one had to go to the more philosophical Marx of the earlier years to solve the problem of the Will necessary for *Das Kapital* and the *Manifesto*, to resolve the problem of the capitalist contradiction in its last but most necessary stage—here, obviously, Lenin later found the lacuna to intervene and put the party in its stead.

This is not to advocate a methodology of voluntarism based on the Will. It is to recognize the power of thematic substructures.[12] Here, Will embodies the sensibilities and carries the cultural paradigm forward in history. It represents a collective "knee-jerk" for which societies often battle for little reason. Here below in Chapter Seven, for example, I will take Durkheim's as one example and the belle époque as another, and with some minor analogies in the form of "Berlin" and "Budapest" as cultural loci. The way they will be discussed and compared will be to treat them as representing and embodying different sensibilities, different cultural systems, each identified by its own particular essence.

The Dialectical Methodology

In all this, of course, there is a description of change and a recognition of uncertainty, but never the source of change itself. The only change Weber had in mind was an even longer *durée* than Marx's, a metaphysical notion of "rationalization", the destiny of all cultural systems—or maybe only of the West, not very clear—after their subsequent rise and fall and conflict and rivalry, a subterranean, almost sub-continental drift to rationalization, a trend that often in the secondary literature gets confused with the organizational exigencies that cultural systems respond to and the interests that develop in routinization. These are short-term processes, a process of, so to speak, "despiritualization", but they are endemic to the particular histories of each cultural system.

In the West they only coincide with, and hence amplify, the super-process of rationalization.

For change we need Marx's Hegel, i.e. contradictions of success but with two caveats: firstly, not all systems suffer from it, i.e. rationalization, hence Marx rightly chooses the study of the ones that in their particular logic are inherently burdened as such, e.g. Durkheim's paradigm (Chapter Six) below as another example, and secondly, how they unfold and how the nature of their crises would mutate depend on the larger global context—once more Marx can dismiss that since his example was about the most global of any system ever.

Structures and Change

The destiny of essences and the structures that carry them forward make them historical. For change we have to then go to Marx and beyond. Marx was too busy with changing the world and forgot in his theory to go beyond the change itself. Here, we will adhere to Marx's methodology more than what Marx himself did in his theory. We shall take the dialectic to its purported generality rather than abandoning his theory as Marx himself did, once it had served its purpose. We shall recover the Hegel in Marx as the best student of Marx, i.e. as the early Lukács did later. For the change of the essences, we shall step outside of Weber's world. In Weber the dialectic appears only as irony; in Marx it is the source of new motion. Both forget the dialectic's external process; they forget that the dialectic is also an enlarging process, where the "beyond" will be sought. In Marx, the dialectic creates its own vibrant alternative; in Weber it creates only atrophy. The dialectic in Weber is an ossification problem: essences are taken over by bureaucracy, or by organizations of a similar type, to solve the resources problem, which is part of the general problem of stabilization and routinization. The essences overwhelm the "spirit", and the interests of routinization ossify the essences, but each in its own manner, i.e. each system of essences ossifies in its particular way in terms of the interest it creates internally in the process of routinization, in the manner perhaps of Hobbes's assumption of perpetual motion, i.e. ossification is essence-specific.

While paying homage to Marx, we also want to take him to his logical extreme, the dialectic and beyond. In an earlier study, I used the same dialectical method in my discussion of the demise of the British imperial economy in the nineteenth century. In both cases, success transforms the environment, but also internally reinforces the embedded organizational forms. In its boundedness (in, for example, Durkheim's paradigm) by its endemic assumptions (of, for example, culture); endemic because they are pivotal—the paradigm cannot change because of its totality. In the British case, the economic rationality of the imperial economy, as enmeshed in the success of the public schools and the corollary economic organizational form of collegiality, creates a stalemate that can only be broken by another dialectic. Here then is the double dialectic, internal as well as exteriorized, changing the environment while internally self-perpetuating as the dialectical beginning requires. Marx leaves us in only the first stage. (Note the great confusion of Socialism in one country, or Trotsky.)

Now to clarify our methodology: conjunctures, actors, essences and structures combine to weave both an historical account and the rethinking of political agendas, for both Weber and Marx.[13] Rethinking past conjunctures and resuscitating their actors possibly creates apertures for conjuring new potential essences, and accordingly, working politically for new structures. *History is nothing but a history of conflicting, com-*

peting essences, and of the structures that succeed or fail to transport those essences over time. Actors in opportune conjunctures can work as "switchmen" for essences to rise, to fall, to defeat their alternatives or be defeated by them. Not all alternatives are always realized, nor can all actors' projects as projected essences materialize unless the proper structures are historically possible and classes, or other structured interests, are forthcoming to structure them.

Essences create their own particular political economies. Furthermore, each system, when understood in terms of its internal logic—the essence—is vulnerable to some kidnaps and more resistant to others; that is the comparison of the pre-modern empires, the national empires, and the nation-states.

Double-Contextuality

Ascendance, contradiction and conflict, and perhaps, subsequent demise have so far been dealt with here as a part of a totality, as one complete episode of the rise and demise of the Durkheimian paradigm of modernity. Success as ascendance, and contradiction and conflict as multiple crises, will however unfold in our model according to their global context. They all come to a crescendo if the global environment "feeds"—elective affinity—or numbs the internal processes to simmer. In the former case we will have the success or the contradictions and conflict coming to the fore, in the latter a simmering crisis moving sideways, corroding its context but not transforming it. We will, in our "story", see the examples of both motions.

Without the two paradoxes of the Marxian dialectical model operating historically at the same time, whether a paradigm dissolves or

simmers at increasingly lower levels of equilibrium depends, I argue, on its historical contextual factors. That is what I call double-contextuality, that is, the coincidence of the paradigm's own context (contextualizing the contradictions) and the historical context (historicizing the context) of that context globally defined. For example, I believe the Soviet revolution occurred in the context of the War where Lenin and the party could intervene. It was due not to the coincidence of the two Marxian paradoxes but to the global context, which secured it. If the Russian war in 1914–17 had taken a different course, Russian history too might have taken a different turn.[14] Historical illustrations of the above theoretical argument in broad brushes, can be found in Chapters Five and Seven.

The external international environment will thus in our story determine the timing of change, that is, whether the crisis unfolds or whether it simmers, with the society thereby constantly drifting to "lower-levels of equilibrium". For this second layer of analysis—an analysis not of the structural sources of crisis but of the way and the time that it is revealed—I shall use Smelser's model of the "value-added" in a simplified, two-stage format not dissimilar to Dahrendorf's "superimposition", yet Smelser's and my model are hierarchical and Dahrendorf's is not.[15]

Historical Grounding of Double-Contextuality

Let me first repeat: narrating the dialectic has two complementary aspects, contextualizing the contradiction and historicizing the context.

Let me discuss some historical examples in broad brushes of double-contextuality to elucidate my points: the proposition is that the surrounding conditions, the very historical circumstances, whether created by the activities of the paradigm itself, as in the example of the British imperial economy, or externally given, as in the examples of a global war or even a severe winter, ultimately matter for unfolding or not unfolding of the Marxian dialectic.

I will briefly begin with a less customary example, the Turkish experience of modernity.[16] The Turkish case is the story of the ascendance of the Durkheimian paradigm through its struggles with, and ultimate victory over, the British in 1923. The historical global context facilitated the Turkish success internally and externally. These are the years when *fin-de-siècle* modernism sways the global context. The British, on the whole most alien, mostly unsympathetic and at best indifferent to the French model of modernity that fuels the Turkish project, feel strong hostility to it when they see it in Turkish hands. Yet, exhausted by an unexpectedly long war, they decide instead to retire to their imperial somnambulism in Paris and will muster up only scant will to fight the Turks, choosing instead a proxy to fight the war for them. Historically this time, being most war-weary, they will go only so far. They only drop their proxies when the battle goes too much against them, whether that be the Whites and the Murmansk project against the Bolsheviks or the Greeks and the Chanak affair against the advancing Turks. I claim that it was the Durkheimian convictions of modernity which gave the Turkish fighting elite the mettle to successfully battle the end pieces of the British victory and occupation. It gave them the conviction and self-assurance which the British by then had lost (the Greeks were no Americans that face the Germans in 1918, and Trikopis no Pershing!). It was the same self-assurance that they were with the "times" that gave the Turkish modernizing elite the radicalness in building their Durkheimian Republic in the 1920s.

In the Turkish case, after several decades of ascendance, the Durkheimian contradictions arising from its own success—mainly a conflict between the political centre and the economic periphery—will eventually unfold in their own time and manner with the world economic expansion of the 1950s on the heels of the Korean War. Finally, the "new town society" created by the narrowly bounded success of Durkheimian modernity when contextualized by the post 1970s global environment, and both encouraged and energized by the American mode of modernity, creates inner conflicts that force the Durkheimian Turkish state into constant isolation, forcing it to hover above society with the international support it procures for its "unnatural condition" thanks to its geographical position. The failure to resolve this crisis, the simmering of an unresolved conflict, on the one hand requires the Durkheimian paradigm to engage in constant double talk about "undoing" democracy in order to found the institutions of democracy and to abolish civil society intermittently in order to create it. In this gravitation toward lower levels of societal equilibrium, more the external support becomes constantly necessary. Here, my argument necessitates *a double dialectic*: firstly, had the Durkheimian paradigm been prevalent globally, the Turkish internal crisis would have been less severe. Secondly, in spite of an internal crisis arising from the mismatch between the Durkheimian state and the new global economic context, this conflict is repressed by another global concern, the geopolitics of the Cold War—the Cold War saves the Republic but perhaps retards its capacity for its dialectics to unfold.[17]

Finally, Durkheim's crisis and the crisis of its particular modernity converge here. I will suggest that the end of modernity as writ in Durkheim's paradigm will come to its close as the twentieth century closes, primarily because of the success of the paradigm as a political project in a particular global context. The strange story is that the French escape their crisis when Clemenceau gives up the Third Republic at Paris for imitating the British (Chapter Seven), and thus de Gaulle, after four decades of turmoil and indecision, is able to put the Fifth Republic in its place with great ease. If Clemenceau had not diluted his republic, neither would the dark years of the thirties have occurred to that extent, nor could de Gaulle have so easily pushed aside one republic in the name of another and instituted a quasi-Napoleonic regime.

The Third Republic as a cultural paradigm can accommodate no economic conflict; its Will is to create harmony. In *mentalité*, it allows no economy to go unrestrained as that might so easily breed conflict. Harmony requires controls on the economy. That is perhaps why state-planning was so easily implemented in France in the 1960s.[18] It was piggybacking on the remnants of the Third Republic—the social fragments left over from the state's abandonment of it—only to be transformed for the service of an imperial republic, the Fifth, thereby nullifying its Third Republic origins. For collective aspiration, national glory is here substituted for the national harmony of the Third Republic.

The third case is the story of a paradigm most antithetical to modernity.* The British imperial economy transformed the global environment up to the 1890s but also reinforced its own internal social structure, as "success" inevitably does. Yet the new world order led by the British success would better suit the managerial organizations of the Americans and the hierarchical organizations of the Germans vis-à-vis the British collegial structure. The Great War in its two phases would eventually "liberate" the world economy from the British mold. America would then prevail with its new organizational form. American

---

* Why I consider the British case as most antithetical to the French modern will be discussed in Chapter Seven.

hostility towards the British is well expressed in their language for the British whether at Yalta or later at Suez.[19] By 1958 the Suez Crisis had sent the British packing. America comes to dominate the Middle East, and the British are left to specialize in banking and finance, which best suit their collegial structure.[20] I have argued the history of the British case until the War in an unpublished manuscript. That discussion did not deal with double-contextuality but brought it to its threshold. Double-contextuality becomes operative only with and after the War, in 1945. In the post-war global context, given the radical demise of the British collegial form of organization, two consequences follow in the British Empire. One is at home. The historical solidity of the collegial form leaves no serious alternatives to emerge in Britain. At the cultural level, for example, the theatre of Osborne is most representative of a rebellion that has no alternatives other than eloquent anger. In terms of economic and social policy, whether it be the Attlee government of 1945 or subsequent Labour governments, they cannot break the mold but only seek amelioration of the crisis by mainly redistributive policies. The only semi-modernist policy that gets adopted at the time is the Beveridge Plan. The eventual reversal of the British economic decline is found in a new type of managerialism in the Thatcherite years, which is both anti-collegial and anti-modernist but best suited to the new global context. On the other hand, in the empire away from home, the rebellion is more relevant. There is more socio-cultural space for more comprehensive alternatives to rise. In India, double-contextuality is more operative. Not only has the British world economy subsided, but an internal alternative also arises in the struggle for independence generated by the white-collar middle class. It is sociologically most logical that a collegial economy would find its alternative class, in the Marxian–Lukacsian sense, in the white-collar middle class. Their affinity, again in the

Lukacsian sense, enabled them to part more radically from collegiality and to aspire to modernist solutions to their backwardness. The Indian Congress Party is quite in line with the Third Republican Radical Socialists of *fin-de-siècle* France, as was the Turkish Republican People's Party which founded the Turkish Republic in the French mold. In their Durkheimian crisis the Indians would turn to socialism and the Turks take refuge in Cold War practices, benefitting from the "luck" arising from their geostrategic position—a luck which both embellishes and corrupts like most "good lucks". As of today both are permeated by anti-Durkheimian populism of grassroots traditionalism and unrestrained capitalist *assabiyah*[21] with politics rooted in the small town.[22]

Let me conclude with brief suggestions of how "nature given" external conditions could also much set the double-contextuality. In the case of the Bolshevik revolution, the closure of the Dardanelles—Churchill instinctively so intelligent to anticipate the significance of it—and the severe winter of 1916–17 led to the total delegitimation of the Tsarist regime that no Romanov would take up the mantle when Nicolas abdicated. It paved the way for Lenin and his associates to unleash the first contradiction. A similar phenomenon occurs in Germany. The same winter in Germany, the "turnip winter", and the British blockade led to the Kaiser's regime to collapse in the midst of a perpetual revolution of a very severe kind.[23] That well scared Ludendorf to ask for an armistice on Wilsonian terms with still the German army intact in the French front. Of course, once they gave up fighting, the army mentally demobilized, and Pershing, fresh with ramblings to move to Berlin, the Wilsonian terms evaporated and a pre-draft of the Versailles treaty descended on the Germans. Finally, the revolution ended after the left collaborated with the right with Frederich Ebert's succession to the Presidency. This was as if putting the first contradiction to the back-burner, for later

Hitler to undo the first dialectic by totally turning Germany upside down with the severe brutality of the Nazi mobilization and total war. Eventually, it was once more the winter, the winter of 1941–42 which halted the German army on the gates of Moscow and led to its decimation in Stalingrad in a year.

The economic crisis of the Great Depression in Britain is again put to the back-burner by Ramsay MacDonald who plays the Ebert role of ruling a left–right coalition. The British eventually weather the storm in a direction exactly opposite of the Germans, due to strength of their deep tradition of parliamentarism. Three cheers for her patriarchal roots! (See Chapter Three.)

These examples, though much in summary, I hope, elucidate what I have meant by "historicizing the context"; and the multiplicity of these cases, I hope, validates my concepts of "narrating the dialectic" and "double-contextuality".

My method has two building blocks: Weber's Ideal-Types and a Theory of Social Paradigms.

Notes

1.   I am fully aware of the recent bad repute the term essentialism has acquired. That has mostly emanated from the current fashion of relativism, which has prevailed primarily in anthropology. Its dissemination to other fields arising from a misconstrued anti-colonial discourse that made real PC into an incorrect PC and vice versa. I think all this confusion has arisen from the loss of nerve of the practitioners of the modernist paradigm, for understandable reasons, reasons that are the subject matter of this study. See Neil J. Smelser, *Sociological Theory – A Contemporary View: How to Read, Criticize and Do Theory* (New Orleans: Quid Pro Books, 2013). This is not to forget Arthur L. Stinchcombe's majestic work, *Constructing Social Theories* (Chicago: University of Chicago Press, 1987), but for our current purposes it is Smelser's work which is the model. Stinchcombe looks at theory construction at a more general level and externally. Smelser and Parsons, in their different ways, look at theories from within. Economic Theory is perhaps the most generic milieu for rigour in the social sciences. The exemplary work in this regard, I find, is Hahn & Matthews, "The Theory of Economic Growth: A Survey", *Economic Journal* (December 1964), which has been the principal guide for my thinking here.

2.   Anthony Giddens, *Sociology* (Cambridge: Polity Press, 1989).

3.   Albrecht Wellmer, *Critical Theory of Society* (New York: Herder and Herder, 1971).

4.   Contrary to what often is suggested Marx's earlier writings, in particular his *Grundrisse*, are not different because they are more youthful, but they are different as Marx there is in the realm of what I called the historical ideal-type rather than the conceptual ideal-type of model building evident in the *Capital*.

5.   Later, in pursuit of the paradigm of the modern on its foreign travel, when we turn to the Turkish Republic in *Durkheimian Theory on its Foreign Travel*, the empirical part of this study, we will argue for a double-contextuality as the practice of the Turkish Republic in the post-1950s was taking place

in a world that had already come about in the post-Paris international context.

6. George Lichtheim, *Marxism in Modern France* (New York: Columbia University Press, 1966).

7. Alfred Schmidt, *The Concept of Nature in Marx* (New York: Verso Books, 2014).

8. Weber and the salvation of Protestant ethics. See Max Weber, *The Protestant Work Ethic and the Spirit of Capitalism* (New York: Scribner's, 1950).

9. Neil J. Smelser, *Theory of Collective Behavior* (New York: Free Press of Glencoe, 1963).

10. Max Weber, *The Protestant Work Ethic and The Spirit of Capitalism.*

11. This is most crucial to remember, and good for curbing the expansionist reductionism of the so-called Marxists of the more recent persuasion.

12. Ideologies of popular adoption, as I argued earlier, to shape the conflicts that ensue as the waves of global expansion break, like today's Islam, yesteryear's ethnicity, and nationalisms of various types.

13. In Feuerbach's and Hegel's conjunctures, Marx allows new agents to create new structures and violate the pre-existing essences.

14. Marx's two contradictions: one, the increasing irrelevance of the hegemonic class due to its successful transformation—the model I used for the British global economy; and the other, the rise of an alternative class from the pre-existing relations of production whose life-chances are constricted by the prevailing relations. In the *Manifesto*, an outstanding piece of sociological modelling, the coincidental maturing of these two contradictions in the imaginary explains the transformation of capitalism to socialism. But when it comes to the real history of the transition from feudalism to capitalism, only the first contradiction is operative but not the second. The conflict between the feudal lords and the merchant class is a matter of the emergent commercial economy, but the merchants are not as embedded as the proletariat is in antagonistic class relations. Any potential for class conflict in this latter sense would be between the merchants and the Putting-out System, and the small producer, but that is not where the political struggle would take place.

Engels identified them as the two routes to capitalism. This lacuna would later call for the brilliant Dobb–Sweezy debate about the transition to capitalism (Maurice Dobb and Paul Sweezy et al., *Transition from Feudalism to Capitalism*, New York: Verso Books, 1976) and then later, the ingenious and brilliant approach of Brenner which might be closer to what I am arguing here for its indeterminacy.

15.   Smelser, *Theory of Collective Behavior* (1963); Ralf Dahrendorf, *Class and Class Conflict in Industrial Society* (Stanford: Stanford University Press, 1959).

16.   Faruk Birtek, *Durkheimian Paradigm on Its Foreign Travel* (forthcoming).

17.   Since this was written with the closure of the Cold War, the economic dialectic of Turkey has, I think, come to the fore, carrying the seeds of the republic's transformation and demise in one direction or the other; but, perhaps *now* more favouring a town-like casting than any other, as the unrivaled American century would now be expected to elicit. Could the recent rise of ISIS be a consequence of this post-Cold War restructuring? See Faruk Birtek, "Recasting Contemporaneity – A Hypothesis in Rereading the New Politics of Localism: The New Assabiyah of the Town – Thomas Hardy Revisited", *The Post-Modern Abyss and the New Politics of Islam: Assabiyah Revisited*, ed. Faruk Birtek and Binnaz Toprak (Istanbul: Bilgi University Press, 2011).

18.   Stephen S. Cohen, *Modern Capitalist Planning: The French Model* (Berkeley: University of California Press, 1977).

19.   Serhii Plokhy, *Yalta: A Price of Peace* (New York: Viking, 2010).

20.   For the collegiality of England see Faruk Birtek, "The State and the Transition to Capitalism in England and Turkey: A Social Structural Model", Ph.D. dissertation, University of California, Berkeley, 1978.

21.   Faruk Birtek, "Recasting Contemporaneity – A Hypothesis in Rereading the New Politics of Localism: The New Assabiyah of the Town – Thomas Hardy Revisited" (2011).

22.   Small-town politics so successfully, brilliantly elucidated by Lipset

has been most helpful, has been my indispensible guideline in my understanding of the small-town politics in Turkey, notwithstanding the fact that Lipset's context is so different. Among others, Seymour Martin Lipset, "The Radical Right: A Problem for American Democracy", *The British Journal of Sociology*, vol. 6, n. 2 (1955): 176-209.

23.   A brilliant detailed and thorough scholarly work on the German revolution (Chris Harman, *The Lost Revolution: Germany 1918 to 1923*, London: Haymarket Press, 2008) would remind us the depth and the extensity of the German revolution of 1917–23.

Chapter Three

Weber's Ideal-Types

My starting axiom is that history is nothing but the history of conflicting, competing essences, of the structures that succeed or fail to transport those essences over time, and of the political economies they create in the process that often haunt them in the long run. It is only in retrospect that we can thus know whether these essences have acquired historicity (i.e. historical continuity) or not. That is the history I want to look at. That also, I believe, evokes Weber's hidden research guideline.

Each system, when understood in terms of its internal logic, its essence, is vulnerable to some kidnaps and more resistant to others; that is what the comparison of the pre-modern empires, the national empires, and the nation-states will in later discussion reveal.[1] And I shall take that as one of the "gateways" to the understanding of their historical essences.

This, I believe, conjures up one of the most profound of Weber's historical discussions and appears in ideal-typical terms, revealing Weber at his essentialist best. My logic here is a direct replication of Weber in that instance, in particular, of what I shall call Weber's "hard essentialism". Weber's "historical ideal-type" lies at the core of my discussion.

The Ideal-Types

Weber's ideal-type has confused sociologists for many years and its renditions have been extremely superficial and either they remained a poor mimicry of each other or in many times contradictory. In a careful reading of Weber one could surmise that Weber had not one kind of an ideal-type but three, each requiring a different methodology, a different level of understanding, the *Verstehen*. That might have been the source of the confusion.

Here I want to end that confusion. I suggest that Weber has three different kinds of ideal-types. It is only by distinguishing the three different kinds of ideal-types that the seemingly contradictory statements of the Weber students can be made sensible as they are each time referring to a different ideal-type. Necessary to the discussion of ideal-types is the concept of *Verstehen*, as the methodology of it always got tacked on as an addendum to the description, almost pro forma, like a disconnected tail. All good for memorizing but with little understanding—appreciation as lip service—and always vacuous.

In Weber we can thus discern three kinds of "ideal-types": I will call them, the *definitional* (e.g. status, class, power), the *conceptual* (e.g. patrimonial authority, bureaucracy), and the *historical* (e.g. the Roman Empire, or as in the example of the Protestant ethic). The *definitional* is based on naming, defining, a particular mode of action, or the identification of one aspect of a form of social behaviour. Here understanding is at the observational level. The *conceptual* is a logical construct, which, in all probability, is never found in full in empirical reality. It is a logical construct, perhaps forcing the empirical, the lived, to constantly approximate it. Here a deeper understanding is required to enable the logical construct. The third, the *historical*, refers to a unique historical case whose internal logic, its innate grammar, is best intuited and whose manifestations are related to that innate logic. Although it is probably never fully manifested at all times, it governs all aspects of that particular historical formation, gives direction to its motions, and sets its cultural map. Here the deepest level of understanding is required and *Verstehen* would here be the appropriate term.

126

The definitional is the easiest. It defines a social action: a collective action for economic ends is a class action, categorically different from Marx's theoretical concept of class. A strike is the prototypical example of a class action in Weber's terminology. Here, the ideal-type serves only as an *ex post facto* definition.

The other two types, the conceptual and the historical ideal-types, are much more germane to Weber's theory and, I will argue, central to Weber's essentialism. The conceptual ideal-type is best illustrated by, for example, "patrimonial authority". It is a system of orientation; the way actors as social beings orient themselves to authority. But it is a logical construct, never to be found in its pure, unadulterated form in its empirical manifestation, i.e. in history. It often comes in a mixture with other forms of authority and constantly tends to gravitate into one form or the other. For example, patrimonialism could more easily engender bureaucratic authority than patriarchalism would. As these types of authority are never to be empirically found in full, it is here that we need a partial *Verstehen* to understand the nature of the orientation of action deductively from the texture of behaviour. Furthermore, from the behaviour we construct the authority type, e.g. patrimonialism, in its logical totality, though it is, in fact, never likely to be found in that logical totality. This is the case even for bureaucracy, whose logic is again constructed, its principles more or less often written down, but which again is often mixed with the intrusion of other forms like patriarchalism or patrimonialism, as is evident in the endless process of nepotism and patronage that constantly interferes in bureaucratic authority. Being a logical construct but also a whole, a totality yet never to be found in total in fact. This is what I will call Weber's essentialism. Furthermore, I will call this Weber's "soft" essentialism. It is soft because the logic of the totality is clear, and the conceptual exercise in its construction makes heavy use of the empirical observation of discrete and incomplete sets of orientations of a systematic and patterned nature. The connection of the components is logical à l'Aristotle. But all this evidence is most tertiary and says nothing about its totality and never fully matches the extent of the totality; hence it is also essentialist. Its essence is to be understood and to be then conceptually constructed. I will call this Weber's "soft essentialism" as it is ultimately a logical construct.

The third is the most fascinating part of what I shall call Weber's "hard essentialism". It provides the basis for the discussion in this book. The rubric here is "historical ideal-type". It is historically unique. It might never appear in full in history, but we reconstitute it as a unique historical case. Its coherence is constructed not in logical terms but in terms of meaning; hence its discovery is not a logical reconstruction but an intuitive reconstitution. It requires *Verstehen* in the deep sense, in the sense of deep intuition: hence, my term, "hard essentialism".

Let me pursue the historical ideal-type further. For its illustration, let me recall one methodologically very important observation by Weber. Weber argues that it was the Augustan period, and not Caesar's, which defined the Roman Empire. In fact, we might even suggest that Caesarism was antithetical to the Augustan: Caesarism is populist and effervescent, the Augustan is legalistic and it is when the empire is institutionalized; in the former charisma is personified, in the other the charisma is in the institutions. It makes sense then that Brutus betrayed Caesar as Caesar betrayed the empire in Rome: two Romes—the Rome of populism and personality cult versus the Rome of laws and institutions, the Augustan. Shakespeare the clairvoyant, the magician explains it for us! Brutus was an honourable man; Mark Antony's speech was not totally in vain. In fact, when this dimension is remembered, it was perhaps more profound than is usually thought, as honour is derived from institutions, and loyalty is personal: Antony never calls Brutus loyal but calls him honourable! This I take as Weber's "hard essentialism". Here the system is constructed. It is unique yet might never have fully appeared in history, but once at least it comes very close to its ideal, the ideal state it strives for and reaches toward. Its understanding fully requires the intuitive understanding. We construct it not out of logic, as we did with the conceptual type, but in coherently piecing together its ideological and institutional components through a sociological construction. Here is where Weber's *Verstehen* is unique and key. Here Weber's "deep essentialism" is manifested.

Each system when understood in terms of its internal logic—the essence—is vulnerable to some kidnaps and more resistant to others; that is one basis of the comparison of the pre-modern empires, national empires, and the nation-states as conceptual ideal types (Fredrick Cooper, 2014). Each has a unique quality with regard to their vulnerabilities, to their hijack and kidnap. I shall make that my method, for the best way of identifying the "historically ideal cases", as well as the best way of comparing them. These innate vulnerabilities are present in all their variants, whether in their most historically representative or in the least, of the historical ideal-type cases. It is thus best to identify all the variants of the historically ideal case with regard to their specific vulnerabilities. It is through an analytical study of systematic vulnerabilities that we can penetrate the hermeneutically constructed historical case, to analyse its history, its variants and its special qualities, as each case is unique in that regard. We can now also create a category out of this unique historical case and see how its extensions and derivatives are close to or distant from that original case. Or, seeing an increased vulnerability, we can see how a particular case has deviated from the original. But its seeds have always to be found in the historically unique case (Aristotle's second cause). This indirect way of penetrating the hermeneutically constituted ideal-type is pure sociology; its rules are sociological, its concepts are sociological, its tools are sociological analysis. If logic was the indirect intellectual instrument for the understanding of the "conceptual ideal-type", sociological intuition (*Verstehen*) is the intellectual tool for understanding the historical ideal-type. In the paradigm of modernity, for example, the danger lies in the possible kidnap of practical reason by instrumental reason; its understanding—here not *Verstehen* any more but logic—is sociological, and it is that understanding that can help us to build "sociological" prohibitors, antidotes.[2]

Hence, the historical case will contain some degree of the conceptual ideal-type, which will appear in the constitution of its building blocks. In other words, we would use the conceptual ideal-type and the degree to which it was realized as the constituent elements of our mental construction of the historical case. In that language, the historical case is mentally a larger construct than the conceptual as it includes many conceptual cases, e.g. the particular rules of lineage that identify its ideal of royalty. Furthermore, that lineage rule might never fully occur, but efforts will be made to make it appear to have occurred symbolically. Its patrimonialism again might, as in the Ottoman case, be instituted by a very strong component that resembles the meritocratic aspects of bureaucracy. Hence, we would here take a patrimonial–bureaucratic structure—the synthesis of two conceptual types—as the defining quality of the ideal Ottoman case—a historical ideal-type—and once they are in the picture, change in the direction, for example, of increasing one of the conceptual types over the other was seen as a deviation from the historical ideal. The more excessive patrimonialism of the seventeenth and eighteenth centuries, for example, was seen by its contemporary critics as a deviation from the historical Ottoman case. While the patrimonial roots were conducive to the later rise of a bureaucratic republic in Turkey, patriarchal roots are perhaps more amenable to the transformation to a parliamentary democracy as occurred in Britain.

Let me go back to my original statement to adduce some historical elucidation. In this world of historical cases, history is nothing but the history of conflicting, competing essences and of the structures that succeed or fail to transport those essences over time.

There are two statements here: one, essences are distinct enough and at times rival and conflict with each other precisely in terms of their essences. What often appears purely as a conflict of economic interest, it usually is, but not necessarily, always a conflict of essences appearing as economic conflict. Let me give two examples from American history, using the now classical dichotomy of "essence vs. existence", which in itself perhaps needed to be pushed to its extinction.[3] The late eigtheenth century debate over tariffs in the US looked as if of the question of existence, but it was really about the essence: how the political economy of the new republic was to be cast, as Stephen S. Cohen and J. Bradford DeLong so well argued in their extraordinary book. Hamilton won, America boomed. On its heels, the question of slavery dawned. It looked like an issue of essences, slavery, but it was really a war about two contrary modes of labour extraction; the North and wage labour won, and the US would become the greatest world power in less than a century.[4]

Or, sometimes the reverse is the case, and both aspects are misconstrued. The Ottomans and the Venetians fight in the seventeenth century believing it to be a conflict of essences when it was actually a futile economic conflict as they were both embedded in the declining Mediterranean economy overtaken by the emerging economy of the

Atlantic. While each thought the other for the reason for their decline, both were sharing the same destiny; basically, Othello was out on the sea for nothing. Hence, sociology is to construct and build bundles of otherwise unique-appearing cases in terms of their common essences.

The second part of the statement is purely sociological and does not require much defence. It is very Marxian in nature and is about the organization of resources, whether moral resources, mobilization of individuals' volition (see Chapter Five), or material resources. Essences, of course, completely govern how, and how effectively, resources can be used by a society. As I said before, this is often the basis of "bounded rationality". This would also be the way to move from a discussion of "essences" to a discussion of change. I shall deal with that issue later (Chapter Four).

Back to essences as the mainstay of this study: I am taking Durkheimian paradigm theory as a paradigm of social action.[5] It is a world of sensibilities, of style, taste, choices, orientation to nature, life, etc., and strong urban bias. It has a coherent logic to it such that it can cope with certain problems and not with others because of its totality and urge for coherence which it cannot alter in face of challenges whether itself created or externally given. This is what is to be understood by "bounded rationality".

We shall in a later chapter (Chapter Six) construct the bounded rationality of the Durkheimian paradigm, and it will indeed be the basis of our discussion of its crises and their analytical understanding.

The Durkheimian paradigm in terms of sensibilities embodied in the Third Republicans as a cultural paradigm, can accommodate no conflict (see Chapter Six). Its will is to create harmony, and it allows no economy to go unrestrained as that might easily breed conflict. Harmony requires controls on the economy, which may be how the state planning was so easily implemented in France in 1960.[6] It was piggybacking on the remnants of the Third Republic. They were the social fragments left over after the state's abandonment of its Third Republican ancestry, only to be transformed as fragments for the service of an imperial republic, and thereby nullifying their Third Republic origins. National glory here was substituted for the national harmony of the Third Republic, formed during the Dreyfus affair and antithetical to the *belle époque*—its Esterhazy. I will also distinguish between two types of modernity in terms of Weber's third ideal-type, as modernity's two tracks: French convergent with Durkheim vs. the American—the two competing paradigms of modernity, the two cases of a historical ideal-type. (For further discussion see Chapter Seven.)

Finally, with regard to a hermeneutic study of essences, Marx is not very far from it either. In fact, Marx's capitalism in *Das Kapital* is best understood as a conceptual ideal-type. Once that is understood, it should eliminate a good deal of unfounded criticism of Marx with regard to the question of whether capitalism has ever occurred empirically in the way Marx specified. Both Marx and Weber are totally anti-empiricist in the methodological sense.

Marx's **social formation** is nothing but what we have called the historical ideal-type, except that it puts the "organization of labour extraction" at the core as its essence. But it should also be noted that two caveats exist for Marx for pre-capitalist economic formations: one, no necessity for economic maximization as it would later occur in capitalism; two, the hegemonic class is not at all necessarily the economic class in terms of definitional ideal-types. All the neo-Marxists forget these two most crucial dimensions in their developmentalist logic. The revolution of capitalism was precisely to breach both of these conditions. The uniqueness of capitalism is crucial, and that is why Marx criticizes the political economists for universalizing capitalism for all periods and societies. In terms of the above categorization of ideal-types, we can now understand Marx better and also narrow the differences to a very basic choice with regard to how to construct historical ideal-types. An example might clarify my distinction between the two ideal-types that get most confused, the conceptual and the historical. Weber has both of them put into exemplary practice in the discussion of *The Protestant Ethic and the Spirit of Capitalism*.[7] Protestantism for Weber is an historical ideal-type. It is unique and is to be comprehended by deep intuition (*Verstehen*). Capitalism, on the other hand, though constructed through a rendition of series of aphorisms by Richard Baxter and Benjamin Franklin, requires a logical construction in the fashion of geometry for its understanding, and it is universal—an example of a logically contrued ideal-type. The recounting of Franklin's aphorisms is sufficient for constructing the conceptual ideal-type of capitalism for Weber; here more logic and less intuition is required.

Finally, Weber is no dialectician but captures the fine texture of historical societies when they get transformed into their unintended ends. In Weber, dialectic is turned into irony. Weber is the student of case studies. For us Weber's historical ideal-type when rendered in essentialist terms is a *bona fide* example of a social paradigm. It is there I will search for the essentialist renditions of the contradictions.

Notes

1. Frederick Cooper, *Citizenship between Empire and Nation: Remaking France and French Africa, 1945–1960* (Princeton: Princeton University Press, 2014).

2. Faruk Birtek, *From Kant to Tristan Tzara: Unwitting the Negative Dialectic of the Enlightenment* (forthcoming).

3. That distinction was central to the 19th century epistemological debate, but when dislodged from its original abode as we, including myself, over-used it for our sociological vernacular, the distinction has become rather silly. That is the point I am trying to make above.

4. The debate over tariffs in the 18th century was in essence about what type of a political economy was to be charted for the new republic as Stephen S. Cohen and J. Bradford DeLong brilliantly argue in their wonderful book *Concrete Econonomics: The Hamilton Approach to Economic Growth and Policy* (Boston: Harvard Review Press, 2016). Conversely, the conflict over slavery in the 19th century, an essentialist conflict, had a strong economic dimension as Eugene D. Genovese so convincingly and brilliantly showed in *The Political Economy of Slavery: Studies in the Economy and Society of the Slave* (Middletown: Wesleyan University Press, 1991). In fact, the two works so well complement each other.

5. As Talcott Parsons used the term in 1937, but then shied away from it in his more Deweyesque American academic environment and turned it from a cultural system into a mechanistic systems theory with Edward A. Shils and Robert F. Bales in *Working Papers in the Theory of Action* (Westport: Greenwood Press, 1981). Earlier Parsons looked at it as a logical system since he was exclusively concerned with social theories. Here we are looking at it as a cultural system.

6. Stephen S. Cohen, *Modern Capitalist Planning: The French Model* (Berkeley: University of California Press, 1977).

7. Max Weber, *The Protestant Ethic and The Spirit of Capitalism* (New York: Scribner's, 1950).

Chapter Four

Paradigm Behaviour[*]

Toward a Partial Theory of Social Paradigms

Paradigm study will be the focus of the current chapter. My argument about paradigms is an extension of Weber's discussion of historical ideal-types. I take the social paradigm as a bona fide representation of Weber's historical ideal-type. Let me start with an extreme statement: a social paradigm is a mental cage.

The principal rubric of the following study is the Paradigm.[1] Here, I will study how social paradigms behave historically—behave in a manner peculiar to their nature but governed by general rules.

In our framework, Essentialism is the privileged domain of a "paradigm study". ONLY in essentialist terms can we fix the uniqueness of the Paradigm of the Modern, and in the dialectical method capture the vicissititudes of its history, its rise and its fall.[2]

But before an essentialist investigation of the Paradigm of the Modern let me develop a theory of paradigms.

I argue that social paradigms have their own *sui generis* history; they constitute a theoretical layer, lying in between, to use Durkheim's language, "social facts" and "social structures" to offer an intermediate

---

* I am very much grateful to Donald Black and to our numerous conversations, which were most educational for me. I am borrowing his particular use of the concept of "behaviour", behaviour which is endemic to the form. See Donald Black, *The Behaviour of Law* (London: Academic Press, 1976).

layer of determinacy. Paradigms behave. They follow their own rules to mediate the relations between social facts and processes.

I will develop here a partial theory as a subset of a General Theory of Paradigms. It is not a full-fledged theory, because it lacks closure and symmetry—more on this issue below.

To start with let me make my proposition clear. Each paradigm is unique, its nature *sui generis*, but the processes that constitute it, that is, the qualities of "paradigm-ness", are universal and amenable to generalization. Hence, we could, in the light sense à la Durkheim, talk about a science of paradigms. On the other hand, each paradigm is unique with regard to how it unfolds according to these general principles. This was the case for Marx's **social formation** and for Weber's "conceptual" and "historical" ideal-types. In this regard, each paradigm is unique and that uniqueness is in its essence. I have called my method "dialectical essentialism".

Before proceeding any further, a caveat has to be added. For the feasibility of this theory of social paradigms an axiomatic initial assumption has to be made—just like the axiom of "perpetual motion" for Galileo and Hobbes.[3] This is the assumption that paradigms are also bundles of Wills à la Schopenhauer; otherwise they wane away. Given this assumption, the great trick for the possessors of any paradigm is how to keep a razor's edge commitment to any paradigm, a commitment that does not on the one hand in its effervescence bubble over to generate hubris, or on the other lose its innate passion, in the way Bell talks about as "the end of ideology"[4] and that Fukuyama,[5] in error, celebrates. In history, millions have died or killed for their adherence to, or in the struggle for the supremacy of their paradigms.

If paradigms are systems of Wills, a cultural context, one entry to their universe might be to consider them as a context of sensibilities, what Goldmann for another yet not a very different an occasion, the world of the *intendants* and Pascal, called a "world view".[6] The more recent French historical school, the *Annales* school, called a broader phenomenon *mentalité* but without a sufficient recognition of its peaks and valleys. The latter is not valuable for our exercise, which strives also to understand the nature of crisis inherent to this universe and the lines which secure its inner coherence. *Mentalité* could only be, theoretically speaking, a cross-section, a slice in time without its inner tensions, or better, without the means to understand the way it would gravitate one way or the other under crisis—crisis generated by itself or imparted from outside. The concept of "sensibilities", in fact, best relates back to Weber's historical essentialism, and to his often misunderstood idea of *intuition*; if *mentalité* does not elevate itself above historical empiricism, Weber's intuitionism is precisely a way to oppose empiricism for an understanding of the "peaks and the valleys" of a cultural universe. Culture as a concept in itself is too insensitive to, and does not lend itself properly to, the temporal undulations which sensibilities would better recognize. In having Goldmann closest to us, what we are trying to do here is to ground Weber's historical essentialist ideal-type (see Chapter Three) in a sensibilities bundle which is best deciphered through intuition. In that context, we shall see how the *fin-de-siècle* Modern and the paradigm of sociology coincide in a single and unique context of sensibilities; and methodologically speaking, in its uniqueness, sensibilities constitute a historical ideal-type in terms of Weber's essentialist logic, and thus they have to be studied hermeneutically.

A Paradigm Story and its Methodology

This is a paradigm story; its hundred years' adventure, venturing to the hundred corners of the universe, becoming for many a population almost a creed, the basis of a knee-jerk conviction, a cause to die for, and often a cause for battling the *anciens régimes*. The definition of a paradigm however is most fuzzy. We shall tackle that question later. We shall construct that definition within an interactive, a rivalrous context, as an emergent concept, always remaining fuzzy and nebulous. Anything other would only violate the concept; its precision would only undermine and undo the concept. The most existent, extensive definition is Kuhn's,[7] and that will not do for our purposes. Kuhn's paradigm refers to the struggles in the history of theoretical debates in the physical sciences. Furthermore, Kuhn uses the concept almost coextensively with the concept of a theory, while, for us, a paradigm is defined more by a bundle of sensibilities, schemes of identity *aspirations* (not real but aspirations), a specific gestalt of symbolizations, a specific set of desires, bounded by hidden assumptions about human nature, about heaven and earth.

A paradigm contains/embodies theories of a specific species. A theory, remaining within a paradigm (compared and contrasted to a paradigm) requires consistency, specific boundaries, and internal coherence and rigour in its statements. A paradigm which embodies a particular set of theories, in contrast, is unclear with regard to its boundaries, and what is of it and what is not are only detectable by the investigation of the essence of a paradigm.

A paradigm is formed in its struggle against, and thus best understood in terms of, its rivals and competitors. For the Paradigm of the Modern, for example, this is most adamantly the *anciens régimes*, and *inter alia*, the Middle Ages, and at its margin, the medieval ludic, which continues as the contemporary "street and the circus", which the Modern has a disdain for and tries to extinguish.

The Three Nemeses

Successful paradigms are prone to various types of endogenous crises, the nemeses, which arise from their "necessary Will", as we postulated, à la Hobbes and Macpherson.*

Paradigms have three types of *nemeses*. The first nemesis is the **Paradox**. It is of two kinds. One is the inner contradictions innate to a paradigm. This paradox is lodged in the paradigm's essence and develops as the paradigm matures. This is the core of Marxian theory in the case of proletarian revolution. It is dialectics par excellence. We shall observe this paradox, in our case, in the rise of economic interests in the development of the Paradigm of the Modern. The second paradox occurs when the paradigm transforms its context but itself fails, because of its very nature, to keep up with the changes it has brought about. This is Marx's account of change from Feudalism to Capitalism and also the core of Schumpeter's theory of development. On another occasion, I have argued this case with regard to the British colonial economy when it changed the globe but itself could not adjust to it until it found itself a particular niche in international banking and insurance.[8]

I will argue later that what I call "double-contextuality" determines the historical forward motion of the paradox.

---

*   I am most grateful to İlkay Sunar for introducing me to Macpherson's political theory.

The second type of nemesis is rooted in **Hubris**. This is what happens when the paradigm in its excessive self-confidence trespasses its normative/logical boundaries. This occurs, for example, when the Modern, which is exclusively of the public realm, attempts to transform the individual as well, and thus encounters the violent response of the communal as the fount of the primordial self. In other words, paradigms in their hubris are seduced into over-extending their contextual boundaries, to delving into and trying to enforce their assumptions and logic in territories external and alien to their essences. The Paradigm of the Modern is only about the social space; it is of the public realm and not of the private. (This, I realize, is a very radical statement with regard to the conventional "un-wisdom".) The Modern is only about creating the context of opportunity for moral individualism to arise and to organically expand itself, but it is not meant to penetrate individual choices themselves; it has its own catechisms for making its adherents sustain loyalty, but it does not have the premises for making individual choices. The Modern is exclusively of the public space (please note that "public" here is not Habermasian[9] but is about Weberian rational, legitimate authority) and becomes antithetical to itself when it forces itself onto the community, thereby expanding beyond its boundaries to effectively rewrite the basis of identity.

The third nemesis occurs as **Mimesis**. This is the adoption of the practices of the modern without its core essences, without moral individualism. One example is the technicism of the modern nation-state. It is the imitation of the paradigm in form but not in essence. Below I will discuss this case in the rise of the modern nation-state, which adopts all the accoutrements of modernity in its institutions but remains devoid of the essence of the Modern in regard, in particular, to individualism and liberty.[10]

Paradigms cannot escape these rules of their unbounded Will, and only by understanding them can we know from where in their narrative history the contradictions and dilemmas arise, i.e. what is innate and what is contextual, and only then can we suggest the correct remedies for it—e.g. an essentialist grounding and/or enlightened vigilance against, for example, a nationalist kidnap. (Reminder: a dilemma is contextual, a contradiction is innate.) Sometimes essences create political economies, which in the longer run come to haunt them, conflict with them, undermine, and perhaps, when the context is right, destroy them.

To repeat briefly, paradigms for their viability inhere in Wills. Wills make them at times expand beyond where their inner logic holds. One such case occurred when the Modern expanded to intrude on the realm of the private, which I will not examine here. This is the question of hubris. At other times the "normal" activities of paradigms create changes in their external environment that undermine their own very superior logic. This is one dialectic. A third case occurs when paradigms in the course of their successful normal practice develop sufficiently to generate forces in themselves that contradict their own initial logic. The last case corresponds to what we would more often call a dialectic. This is Marx's principal case.

When the two dialectics operate at the same time, "double-contextuality" emerges. This occurs when the crisis is of radical consequence and entails an historical transformation, whereas without double-contextuality, for example, in the case of an exclusively externalities-related crisis, different forms of adaptation could occur,[11] and in the case of inner contradictions, without double-contextuality, the paradigm drifts to its even lower equilibriums, and malaise simmers, but without the consequences of a radical transformation.

A Second Layer of Determinants of Paradigm Behaviour

Every paradigm has its Devil and its Dragon,[12] and accordingly each paradigm is open to only particular kidnaps and hijacks. Kidnaps are external to the paradigm (as in the example of instrumentalism for the Paradigm of the Modern), and hijacks are internally generated, both potentially undermining, destroying, obfuscating its inner rationale, its paradigmatic logic.

All Paradigms have their Devil and the Dragon at different degrees of activity. The Devil is of a different substance but looks to be the same form as the paradigm. The Dragon, on the other hand, is of the same substance but different in form. One Devil of the Modern is "instrumental rationality", the other is "nationalism", and Dada and Surrealism are the Modern's Dragons. Paradigms are vulnerable to kidnaps when externally generated, and to hijacks when internal. All this is, of course, definitional. It does not tell us when and how any of this might take place. That is the question of a general theory. Here we shall only pursue a partial theory, which can only identify the kidnaps and hijacks, but not their timing.

The Dragon is the Yang of the Yin of the paradigm; it is its twin brother, its Ishmael. It is part of it, and for some, like Durkheim, it is more threatening in nature, while the Devil is most dangerous as it can kidnap the paradigm and take it on a "false" journey. In my discussion of the Modern, I will identify instrumental reason as the Devil of the Modern and Dada (see Chapter One) as the Dragon. Dada is what it tries to purge all the time, but can never fully succeed, and by instrumental reason, at times it is seduced for a ride to discover, only later and with much hesitation and pain, how alien that apparent friend is to its chagrin and destruction. Bauman, for example, confuses the Devil of the Modern with the Modern itself. Martin Esslin correctly noted the Dada in the Modern,[13] which Durkheim had also recognized with full understanding and with trepidation. They both, Esslin and Durkheim, in their very different ways, faced the same question and pursued the same ends: how to be reconciled with Dada, how to accept and appropriate it, to make it a source of strength and richness. As for the Devil, Durkheim deftly dismisses it with a logical parry, to end the threat by retrenching the essence that anchors the Modern.[14] It is in terms of their essences and not their empirical form nor the manifest narratives of these rivalrous states of the modern, one of the same kin, and the other of the exterminating angel, that we must seek the hidden language of the paradigm.

For these reasons, we have to tackle the problem of paradigms in terms of their essences and not their forms, as the empirical boundaries are elusive if not often misleading. It is in terms of the essences, so nebulous and fuzzy, that we have to situate the endeavour of identifying paradigms. In terms of essences, the boundaries also matter much less; hence one more reason for the essentialist methodology for paradigm construction.

Toward a Theory of Social Paradigms

To that end we have two theoretical sets of variables. One set refers to the unique nature of each paradigm and identifies, metaphorically, the *Devil* and the *Dragon* each paradigm's logic harbours as part of its necessary Will. The second refers to a set of universal categories for all paradigms, which I call the **nemeses** of paradigm practice. The two levels together constitute "a set of simultaneous equations". I call them the hazards of successful paradigm practice. The motions of the first set, i.e. the ebb and flow of the Devil and the Dragon, suggest in an *undefined manner* which nemesis is *likely* to prevail in the destiny of a particular paradigm's successful practice—this indeterminacy attests to the fact that we do not have a full-fledged theory. A *bona fide* theory would require closure and symmetry. For example, we do not know whether we have accounted for all the nemeses, hence no closure; nor do we know what brings about a possible Devil–Dragon stability, hence an absence of symmetry as we have only speculated on their possible discord.[15]

To repeat, in our theoretical framework each paradigm has its Dragon and its Devil: the Dragon is of the same substance as the paradigm but of different form; the Devil has the same form but is of different substance. For the Paradigm of the Modern, Surrealism/Dada/Pascalian-*vide* and Kierkegaardian doubt are aspects of the same Dragon; the Dragon is the source of the paradigm's inner conflict. Yet it is the Devil that is the source of its abduction. For the modern, functionalism (not sociological but architectural), utilitarianism, and instrumentalism are the Devil's different aspects. The Devil kidnaps. It is external. Paradigms also get hijacked. A hijack arises from an inner source. This is the case when the paradigm's boundaries are outwardly trespassed, often due to one type of hubris or another, and extend into domains where the paradigm is not, in terms of its essence, operative. One such case occurs when the assumption of the Ratio of the Modern is extended to the subjective, to the private, to the personal. The most obvious terrain of contention here is in the area of identity. The Modern's struggle with the communal is another example, and often is the terrain of the struggle over the question of identity.

It is in the ebb and flow of the conflictual struggle between the Dragon and the Devil that we can detect the sources of the paradigm's particular nemesis. All this is of course definitional. It does not tell us when or how any of these things might take place. That is the question of the theory. That is what I shall pursue next for the Paradigm of the Modern.

The Roots of Hijack and Kidnap

In our terminology hijacks are generated by the conflation of internal wills and kidnaps by external force(s). The curse inherent in any idea is its amenability to hijack or possible kidnap but specific only to itself. This is its soft underbelly.[16] Each idea has its own particular soft underbelly; each particular coexistence has its particular distortion of the other, analogous to Greek tragedy. The historical question is how to prevent this self-negation. In recent history, history since the French Revolution, two principal ideals, Individualism and Reason, have both signified two fundamental axes for human liberation and, equally and conversely, by their particular vulnerabilities for their own self-negation, also created equally rudimentary impediments to those forces of liberation. Furthermore, because they were hidden in the underbellies of those liberating ideals (like life and atrophy, purification and contamination, regeneration and corrosion), they remained hidden, disguised, and hence much more difficult to combat, more difficult to identify when they seemed to prevail, when they seeped into the agenda. By being so "near" the very ideals themselves, they intruded without much notice. To prevent this, essences have to be most uncompromisingly preserved; threats have to be most readily expunged. In other words, certain compromises are laden with the dangers of self-negation, certain concessions are inimical to the liberation and the ideals propounded; hence analytical rigour calls for vigilance and for the constant consciousness of the logical essence of the ideals. This is obviously a most taxing task. Because clear boundaries are by nature so alien to paradigms, vigilance about essences becomes paramount.

In Durkheim's paradigm, for the Dragon to be restrained and contained at the individual level, civic nationalism is marshalled. Its institutional abode is the republican nation-state. Yet the soft underbelly of the nation-state was that it was open to kidnap by collectivism in the name of safeguarding individualism; that was Durkheim's problem. The second danger of a kidnap is by the Devil. Atomistic individualism gravitates by its nature to utilitarianism and pragmatism;[17] and "carries in its belly" the rule of instrumental reason that Adorno later traces back to the Enlightenment, erroneously, in my view, as he did not recognize the coexistence of the Dragon and the Devil. Adorno takes the "wrong differential" of the Modern. Hitler for us is the case when the "unattended" Dragon is overtaken by the Devil, the *vide* filled with a combination of the Irrational and the Nazi will, taken over by pragmatism and Wagner, all to merge later into one in the music of Carl Orff!

For the last danger, one preventive method is to anchor the sensibilities to their original essence. Here, essentialism has to be adhered to; that is to say, we have to anchor each concept to its normative matrix and define it according to its own particular axes of aspiration, moral assumptions, and the specificity of its historical imprint.

The Hazards of Paradigm Practice: Public vs. Private

As we have seen, the inner hazards that successful paradigms face originate from the tug-of-war between the Dragon and the Devil. In fighting the Dragon, the Modern opens itself up to a nationalist kidnap; in the workings of its Devil it can fall prey to a kidnap of the functional-ist/pragmatic kind. Now let us look at these two crucial aspects of the hazards of paradigm practice.

One immediate hazard of a paradigm practice is the paradigm's transcendence of its boundaries, the issue of hubris. Compared to the category of paradox, while hubris historically has been most common, its remedy is also most readily available. The remedy lies in the vigilance of self-reflection arising from deep understanding of the paradigm's essentialist logic. A good deal of colonialist/imperialist history has been embedded in this brand of nemesis, and I fear it still very much rules the day.

On another occasion[18] I discussed how the Paradigm of the Modern extends itself into realms that are not its normative domain. A para-digm is a political project: it has a particular view of the past and a spe-cific projection of the future; it is hostile to alternatives and has a will to organize its own domain. Will is a necessity for a paradigm's survival: no Will, no paradigm history. Only with the Will inherent in it is a par-adigm a paradigm. The paradigm of the modern, by its own normative logic, is exclusively of the realm of the public, but, with its expansive in-stincts, the Will inherent in it tends to appropriate, and intrude into the realm of the private, the innate world of the individual. The Modern is meant to create the public space in which the "individual" can expand his growth potential, educate himself (*Bildung*), and strive for his own perfection, but it is not about the individual himself. It is due to the expansive Will that the Paradigm of the Modern at times transcends its boundaries. I have not yet found a satisfactory normative means at the micro-level of identifying the two boundaries, the boundary of the public where the paradigm of the modern with its logic is to expand, and the boundary of the private where the Paradigm of the Modern for its own consistency and relevance should not trespass. Let me give an example. Democracy, a quality of the public, at times intrudes on the family, which in my judgment destroys both institutions, the family and democracy. I find this to be one example of how boundaries are trespassed in contemporary society.[19]

On the above occasion, my subject matter was how the Modern presumed to organize the "inner self" of the individual, and I argued for its logical illegitimacy. In that failure, politics gravitates to "identity politics" to distort both the "public" of politics and the autonomy of the individual. These are the hazards involved when a paradigm overextends itself because of the unbounding of its necessary Will and trespasses boundaries at a cost to itself as well as to the domain it illegitimately invades. There is no dialectical process involved here. In this study I shall not look at this particular practical hazard, which after all is only the risk of having a Will that is too strong and energized introduced into the private. Instead I will look here at the systemic hazards that arise from the internal logic of the Paradigm of the Modern, i.e. not accidents but natural events.

In the next two chapters, we shall look at the vulnerability to kidnap of the Paradigm of the Modern, but let me first elaborate my point. Each paradigm, due to its internal logic, is open to particular kidnaps and not to others, and observing them in history is one way of deciphering a particular paradigm. These kidnaps are conjunctural, i.e. they do not arise from the doings of the paradigm but are external to it. But due to the paradigm's internal logic, they can easily kidnap and distort, even destroy the very paradigm with which they establish early affinity—just like viruses that invade the body and mimic its regular metabolic functions. The way to resist such a kidnap is through vigilance, often political, to ensure that the paradigm adheres to its inner core values without any compromises in the name of exigency. And for that purpose, once more Essentialism matters as a way to unearth and keep robust the inner core values of the paradigm itself.

Conclusion

We have seen that every paradigm in its successful practice faces three hazardous trajectories: the kidnap, the hijack, and the paradox—vulnerabilities all of which are specific to every paradigm—and hence paradigm study requires an essentialist method.[*] What is to be emphasized is that each hazard takes a particular form for each paradigm according to that paradigm's particular essence. Consequently, the remedy can only be rooted in the understanding of each paradigm's essence: the essentialist logic of the historical ideal-type.

I will turn next to the study of the Paradigm of the Modern (Chapters Five, Six and Seven). In its historical grounding, I will search for the elements of the paradigm's essence (Chapter Seven). In the normative chapter, Chapter Six, the modern paradigm as a construct is logically built and is logically finite. This will be a normative reconstruction of the Durkheimian paradigm. Its description demands rigour with regard to the paradigm's internal coherence and consistency, much in the way of Weber's conceptual ideal-types (e.g. Bureaucracy, Patrimonial Authority). In Chapter Seven I shall, in the most exploratory sense, situate the paradigm historically. This is not history in the pure sense of the word as the historians practise it but rather a *stylized* history. It will look at the birth of the Paradigm of the Modern in its historical con-

---

[*]   Please note, the other two nemeses, hubris and mimesis, are external to the paradigm; in our metaphoric language, they are works of the Devil but do not have specific reference to the vulnerabilities laden within the paradigm's essence.

text, which is described *only* in regard to the formation of the Modern's particular essence. It is, hence, most intuitive and exploratory and can never be finite. Here Weber's historical ideal-type is the model.

One final note on paradigms to anticipate the forthcoming descriptive chapters on the Modern: in observing the history of a paradigm it is best to start from the margin, from the paradigm's outer edge.[20] In the middle, the institutions of the old order prevail, the status groups congregate and the classes rule to obscure the changes the paradigm is enduring. When on the wane, it is on the edge the paradigm first shrinks. It is in this ebb and flow on the edge that the paradigms history is revealed and its historical itinerary best captured. A paradigm, like an ocean on its way to extinction, shrinks around its edge; its ebbs never matched by its flows, leaving behind lagoons here and there. It is the linearity of social scientific thinking which has obscured its understanding of history, which more often follows ebb and flow motions—of victory and decadence, of prevalence and recession.

Let me summarize part of my argument:

Sometimes essences create political economies which in the longer run come to haunt them, conflict with them, undermine, and perhaps, when the context is right, destroy them. And, in some other times, paradigms in their "normal" activities create changes in their external environment to undermine the very logic of the paradigm itself.[21] This is the other case of the dialectic.[*]

---

[*] I am most grateful for my discussions with Mark Cooper. Many of the insights pertaining to the collegiality owe to my most truthful collaboration with him.

The first case arises then when paradigms in the due course of their successful normal practice sufficiently develop themselves to generate forces in themselves to contradict their own initial logic. This case is Marx's case in the *Manifesto*'s discussion of the proletarian revolution.[22] In the second case, the historical context of the dialectic is transformed. When the two dialectics operate at the same time, this is what I have called double-contextuality, that is, when the crisis is of radical consequence, hence a radical crisis. Without double-contextuality, either, for the externalities related crisis, there are different forms of adaptation,[23] or, if only the first type of ordinary crisis, the paradigm drifts to ever lower equilibriums, and malaise simmers, but not as a consequence of radical transformation. Marx did not see this second case, other than the allusions to the rise of the bourgeoisie in the midst of Feudalism.

Latter-day Marxists, who dwelled in the area of the external processes, did not see the dialectical processes of double-contextuality, as in the example of Wallerstein's work.[24] They have a "theory of response" in the example of an anti-colonial political rebellion, which is neither dialectical nor often very valid—not valid since not poverty but relative affluence, I claim, is often the source of the challenge to the paradigm, and that is the process which can be subsumed under a third case.

The third case is a subset of the second case. In this third case, new actors penetrate the pre-existing paradigm and create a semblance of class conflict to replace the pre-existing elites. In a different context I called this teleologically created class consciousness *assabiyah* politics.[25]

Once more, in conclusion, we do not have a general theory since we do not know when the Devil will prevail to kidnap or hijack a paradigm to its hubris or mimesis, or when the Dragon will salvage/reinstitute the paradigm itself. We have neither the closure nor the symmetry a general theory would require.[26] *While hubris and mimesis are results of collective human frailty, sociologically more relevant perhaps is the paradox, a most captivating form of irony, and the core of Marxian theory. It is "good intentions", or what Marx saw as the necessary class action and what Weber and Parsons called "rational social action", that create the paradox.*

If mimesis and hubris are the subject of morality plays, paradox is the subject of the classical tragedy. It is part of the human condition. The remedy for it lies in the search for sub-optimization, that is, to have the Will and the un-Will at the same time in a social rational action, that is, for a project (à la Bergson) to be itself and not be itself at the same time—a very demanding political task.

Appendix I

Duality

Here perhaps an immediate methodological excursion is needed. I never say that each time, in each geography, there is only one sensibility-bundle, one paradigm, that rules. Sociology in its atemporal version necessarily does that when it has to explain "society", an abstraction with no empirical referents, and with the very hard and momentous epistemological leap it requires. It is legitimate to do so when third-order generalizations are made. For example, let us take it from Durkheim, how institutions contribute to social integration. Here, social integration or society, which Durkheim in his methodology correctly takes as interchangeable, are second order abstractions, and the causal relationship through the "latent functions" of institutions a third-degree abstraction.

My whole point is that at any one time there are at least two paradigms—thesis and antithesis—that are interdependent, that compete and at times of more rapid change a variety of paradigms compete to rule. When I take the Durkheim paradigm to rule after the Dreyfus affair, I am only suggesting that it becomes the source of the *obvious*, of self-confidence, of the limits of politics. Other world views, of other definitions, concurrently flow but are nowhere of the importance of the Modern in its Durkheimian, Third Republican form and substance. The rest are marginalized and seen as such and the followers indeed define themselves as such and at times indeed become a source of attraction for some precisely because they are deemed marginal and extreme, archaic and "antique" yet always outside and disconnected from the prevailing Paradigm of the Modern. Yet it has to be emphasized that this is not the margin of the Modern but outside of its reference point. The margin that will arise on the edge of the Modern, part of it yet antithetical to it, is what I shall later refer to more extensively as Dada and Surrealism. They are the new margin, and they attract individuals as such, and have to be distinguished from the marginal that the Modern as a rule leaves behind more for nostalgic or archaic longing unless it is rooted in the depths of the countryside, where, as we observed, the affair had already been brought to an end. These are the moralist, Ultramontane movements that will surface later when the Modern wanes, as I shall show in the later period of the Republic. They might be hostile, rivalrous, competing with the Modern but not antithetical to it in the Hegelian sense. As I have shown above, they are not of the same substance, they might be reacting to it, to the Modern, but are not a true challenge once the Modern has already turned the world upside down—I am borrowing the metaphor from Christopher Hill. My concern is how paradigms are challenged by their own "other" (what I have called the Dragon of Dada, the *vide*, the Surrealists), how they create problems they cannot solve, i.e. economic conflict, and how they go beyond themselves to create categories that they can neither absorb nor understand, i.e. the Hardyesque town, the countryside, the harbinger of the new when conjecturally coupled with a new global process to turn into what has come to be called the post-modern without the clarity of self-identity or the directionality of a singular aspiration as had existed, for example, within the rise of the Modern in 1889.

Appendix II

The Paradigm and Its Adversary

What puzzles the sociologist with the heuristic device of assuming a singular society is that every geography comes with two histories that are inseparable and intertwined, yet rivalrous and at times most antithetical. Revolution in its true sense is not to change this equation but to change that totality; it is to annul both of these histories, to replace them with a totally new simultaneous equation. It is thus tantamount to changing the geography.

History will soon come to realize that every geography has a central matrix with two interdependent but rivalrous, separate but coterminous, deadly conflictual but mutually necessary, histories.

One cannot be fully told without describing the other. One ascendant, the other *all* present subterraneanly. The histories of any particular geography start with one of these matrices setting the mold of the narrative, and the rest follows in the tracks of this innate conflict. The Biblical metaphor of Cain and Abel, of course, predicted this grammar of history for the rest of the human society. Matrices change with what we call a revolution to cast a new matrix. Not all apparent revolutions have managed to do that, of course. The Soviet, it seems now, has not; nor did the French manage to do it if one takes de Tocqueville seriously, as I am inclined to do. A historical epoch may really be defined as what happens when a matrix changes to be replaced by another but still contains the duality. Politics, or to put it differently, what agents do, is to manifest the rise of one of the histories at the expense of its twin sister, which had until then been relegated to subterranean status. In other words, agency operates in terms of what happens to the Yin–Yang, i.e. what happens to the relative strength of each of the two histories, either fully repressed or at times much more coming to the surface to challenge, and perhaps to replace, its rival, the other. The Bosnians have the ethnic matrix, which is really the matrix of communities—the reasons why the EU so identifies it will become clearer. Either there are interdependence and intermarriage in inter-communal coexistence, or there are inter-communal strife and attempts at obliteration. The history of the region was severed from its Ottoman past. Ottoman rule was built on an inter-communal game of backgammon. The two communities had to be preserved for its success, hence kept apart and together at the same time. That is why it is not an ethnic or a racial or even essentially a religious conflict. It is a conflict of communities, however, they may be defined, and it is this Ottoman historical matrix that still continues in the geography, and both stories are valid. "Agency" is to make one history superior to the other, to make one the defining grammar, and the other to remain purely subterranean and not capable of emerging. That is what politics is about. Not far from Bosnia, in the north, the same matrix is often defined by the interdependent and inevitable rivalry of the Rhine and the Elbe, each necessary for the other but each signifying two radically different histories. One recent example of historical agency has been to move the capital from the banks of the Rhine to the Elbe, and with it, I think, unrecognized consequences will follow. This agency question, which past historians have both praised and condemned, operates exactly in this manner, and that might be why, in centuries to come, without the knowledge of this paradigm of mine, they will mark the move of the capital from Bonn to Berlin as the beginning of a new period in the German geographical matrix. French history, if we were to read de Tocqueville once more, is the history of central authority and communalism as two rival histories; England, perhaps, the histories of the City of London versus the North (Manchester) and industry, the two bases of privilege that, for example, Thatcher and the Labour Party in their very different ways constantly tried to marry as a way of overcoming that tension. The extension of citizenship,[27] which in sociological parlance has come to define the recent history of Britain after a revival of fifty years, is most apt, because it is exactly how the North can be incorporated into the definition of citizenship, i.e. privilege, read London and the submergence of the North.

The matrix for the USA is one of immigration and conquest. The Yin–Yang has been the cerebral trend toward inclusion versus an emotive yearning for exclusion.[28] The history of the USA can be read according to this matrix, that is, when one looks at the history of the last two decades, one is hard put to say what happened to "racial integration". A lot has been achieved, yet a lot has gotten worse, just like the two histories of Bosnia, a Yin–Yang, most separate but most intertwined, forever puzzling us as to the "true" history of its geography. Once I suggested that if we give up our search for a single history but understand the Yin–Yang involved in the histories that jointly define a particular matrix, then we can be more conscious of the results of our endeavours and become more responsible in our political choices, i.e. more aware of their consequences with respect to which side of the matrix, which of the two histories, our role as "agent" is going to affect, favour or submerge. Whether we can face the challenge of such knowledge, which puts our political efforts in the forefront of history is, of course, another question that nobody can answer. The history of both is ethnic. When multiple streams coexist and flow together, the antithesis of each has a weaker force, but when one stream suppresses the others, singularity is obtained, and then the alternate, the Yang of the Yin, bursts forth in a most forceful attempt to annul its counterpart.

Notes

1. Three masters of "paradigm study" provide us with guidelines for telling their paradigm stories from the inside. They are Christopher Hill, C. B. Macpherson, and Richard Hofstadter. Their brilliance is unmatchable. Lucien Goldmann guides us—though at times confusing the macro and the micro analyses—in the study of historical paradigms from the outside and in comparative terms, in the footsteps of Marx and in the company of the early Lukács. But none of the above theorists has developed a dialectical historical theory of paradigm-change of the brilliance of Marx's *Manifesto*. Yet his dialectical rendition is too broad and too non-specific to qualify as anything more than shorthand for a theory. Marx's *Kapital*, on the other hand, is more of what I would call a conceptual ideal-type. In either case, Marx's dialectics is a brilliant methodology for historical research. Here, I will take Marx as my point of departure and work toward a theory of paradigm motions. Yet it will not be a full theory as, in its current form, it lacks the closure and symmetry that a general theory would require.

2. In reference to Oswald Spengler (*The Decline of the West*, New York: Knopf, 1970) and Pitirim Sorokin (*Social and Cultural Dynamics: A Study of Change in Major Systems of Art, Truth, Ethics, Law, and Social Relationships*, London: Owen, 1957), who fail to raise this issue because they both lack an analytically rigorous framework in their quest of similar questions.

3. Crawford B. Macpherson in *The Political Theory of Possessive Individualism: Hobbes to Locke* (Oxford: Clarendon Press, 1962) brilliantly demonstrates that Hobbes, inspired by Galileo, assumed a "perpetual motion" for his theory to be possible.

4. Daniel Bell, *The End of Ideology: On the Exhaustion of Political Ideas in the Fifties* (New York: Free Press, 1965).

5. Francis Fukuyama, *The End of History and the Last Man* (London: Hamilton 1992).

6. Lucien Goldman, *The Hidden God* (New York: Taylor & Francis 1981). Goldmann in his various works, Hofstadter in his various works, and Élie

Halévy in *The Growth of Philosophic Radicalism* (Clifton: Kelley, 1972) have been my models.

7.   Thomas S. Kuhn, *The Structure of Scientific Revolutions* (Chicago: The University of Chicago Press, 1962).

8.   Faruk Birtek, *Structure and Transformation*, (Vilnius Academic Publishing, forthcoming); (Ph.D. diss., University of California, Berkeley, 1978).

9.   Jürgen Habermas, *The Structural Transformation of the Public Sphere: An Inquiry into a Category of Bourgeois Society* (Cambridge: MIT Press, 1989).

10.   Not to increase complexity I did not here include the amalgam cases. One most common amalgam case is the overlap of mimesis and hubris, evident in the expansion of the "modernizing" authoritarian state to the internal dynamics of the family in its attempts to "form" the individual's personality by "scienticized" child rearing to create "useful" citizens. Historically there have been attempts to create the Modern's essence teleologically through attempts at extensive mimesis, an example of which was the Kemalist travails of the Turkish Republic (1923–38). This is a version of what one might call "behaviourist optimism". On the whole, this does not foreclose an occasional optimist outcome. This putting the cart before the horse might at times work but that only when an appropriate "double-contextuality" is present. However, the hubris this project entails is pregnant with its reaction especially when the suitable "double-contextuality" wanes away. I have discussed this case in Chapter Two as the crisis of the Turkish Republic after 1950s, on the margins of a waning Western modernity.

11.   For British specialization in banking and insurance, see Faruk Birtek, *Social Structure and Transformation* (Vilnius Academic Publishing, forthcoming).

12.   The inspiration for the term Dragon comes from the 1963 song, *Puff the Magic Dragon*, sung by Peter, Paul and Mary.

> For our construct of the Devil it is best described by Shakespeare in *Hamlet*:
> "The spirit that I have seen
> May be the devil: and the devil hath power

> To assume a pleasing shape; yea, and perhaps
> Out of my weakness and my melancholy,
> As he is very potent with such spirits,
> Abuses me to damn me." (Act II, Scene 2)

13. Martin Esslin, *The Theatre of the Absurd* (NY: Overlook Press, 1973).

14. See Durkheim's critique of Dewey in Dennis Rusche and Rick Tilman, "The Aims of Knowledge: Emile Durkheim's Critique of American Pragmatism", *The European Legacy*, October 2007.

15. That is, the independent variable is less specific than the dependent variable.

16. Talcott Parsons, *The Structure of Social Action: A Study in Social Theory* (New York: Free Press, 1968).

17. Rusche and Tilman, "The Aims of Knowledge: Emile Durkheim's Critique of American Pragmatism".

18. Faruk Birtek, "Structure and Transformation", Ph.D. diss. (University of California, Berkeley, 1978).

19. I find this to be often an endemic American problem due to the deep equalitarian streak in American culture; however, it might also be what led to its phenomenal history of technological and economic innovation, see Everett E. Hagen, *On the Theory of Social Change: How Economic Growth Begins* (Homewood: Dorsey Press, 1962). Democracy axiomatically presupposes the more or less equality of all opinions and assumes further that in large enough numbers this presupposition does not entail too heavy public costs. Whereas a family as an institution requires inequality of opinions, if socializing the young accepted as the functional goal of the family as an institution, then some members necessarily have to have opinions assumed to be superior to others.

20. That is why I have chosen Alexandrine Dalida to represent the demise of the Modern as she expires in Paris. In *The Durkheimian Paradigm on Its Foreign Travel* (forthcoming), I take up the Turkish Republic for the contradictions—the paradoxes, to use the language of the chapter—that the Paradigm of the Modern harbours in its construction.

21. This was the case, for example, with the medieval church and the riches it created, or as I will argue below was the case with the Paradigm of the Modern with the depth of economic interests it created. In the modern case, we shall discuss (Vol II), will have the two cases of the paradox/dialectic consecutively. The first case to be enveloped by the second case, the case of the externalities—whether self-generated as it was with England or externally given as was the case with the Turkish Republic in its ascendance or its later demise—to create the case of double-contextuality.

22. Karl Marx and Friedrich Engels, *Manifesto of the Communist Party* (Chicago: Kerr, 1915).

23. Faruk Birtek, *Structure and Transformation* (Vilnius Academic Publishing, 2018); (Ph.D. diss. University of California, Berkeley, 1978).

24. Immanuel M. Wallerstein, *The Modern World-System* (Berkeley: University of California Press, 2011).

25. Faruk Birtek, "Recasting Contemporaneity – A Hypothesis in Rereading the New Politics of Localism: the New Assabiyah of the Town – Thomas Hardy Revisited", *The Post-Modern Abyss and the New Politics of Islam: Assabiyah Revisited*, ed. Faruk Birtek and Binnaz Toprak (Istanbul: Bilgi University Press, 2011).

26. We do not have closure since we do not know whether we have accounted for all the possibilities of the paradigm; we do not have symmetry since we have more dependent variables than independent variables.

27. T. H. Marshall, *Citizenship and Social Class* (Cambridge: Cambridge University Press, 1950).

28. This was written six years before Trump was elected.

Chapter Five

The Paradigm in Its Practice: The Modern and Its Hazardous History – Nationalism

To illustrate the propositions of the previous chapter, here I will discuss some of the cases from the past of the paradigm of the modern, arising from one or another aspect of its nemeses, each laden with its particular historical crisis.

Above all else, nationalism is a social practice for *extraordinary* mobilization of human and material resources. Nationalism was Modern's best friend and the nation-state was its instrument. To begin with, much of Modern's progress was built on nationalism's unusual élan. Yet, because of its particular effervescent nature nationalism eventually also became modern's worst enemy—too often to corrupt the modern, to undermine and to destroy it in its mimicry. Nationalism became the embodiment of the hubris of the paradigm of the Modern, when the Modern took the belligerent track. This of course was not what Durkheim had foreseen.[1]

Leaving Durkheim aside for a moment, in history the greatest crisis of the modern occurred when the Devil kidnapped the paradigm. The paradigm's own Devil was pragmatism, which seduced the paradigm away from its base; it was its kidnap. The paradigm kidnapped, the Dragon was left unattended. A wayward Devil, not the paradigm's own, abducted the Dragon. I will call it Satan. It was intergalactic, not of this earth but a most alien substance, a horror that no human species could comprehend. That was the case of Hitler. It was an archaic force arising from the tension between the desire for modernity and its un-permitting context.[2] I will discuss that later. This was a clear case of abduction. It had no connection with the inner nature of the paradigm of the modern, perhaps with the exception of its vulnerability, compared to other political systems, to satanic intrusions from outside. Yet this can only be the subject of another study.

Kidnaps and the Paradox

Before all else let me start with a common knowledge. The nation-state was the best friend of the modern, yet historically it was also its worst enemy. For that adventure, a most thorough and brilliant discussion at a more immediate level with contemporary relevance was recently best raised by Claus Offe.[3]

Let me now discuss the two *kidnaps* the paradigm of the modern had been victim of: **functionalism** and **nationalism**—very different yet at times convergent as I shall briefly discuss below.

The recent history of the modern, with nationalism on the one side and capitalism on the other, has only amplified the paradigm's vulnerability to kidnaps—capitalism, however, arising from its innate particular paradox. That is what I shall focus first.

For the kidnap of individualism by capitalist accumulation, via the institution of the market and the idea of freedom founded exclusively in and through free exchange in the market, the task becomes how to safeguard the fundamentals of the modern while embracing capitalism as the basic rule of production.

Nationalism, on the other hand, threatens the individualism of the modern with an incipient notion of collectivism that seeps in via the institutions of citizenship to subvert its roots in individualism, and to compensate for this loss through a notion of equality founded in and through a desire for an imagined solidarity. Citizenship demands individualism to be now expressed in self-sacrifice for the nation in moments of national crisis.

Both nationalism and capitalism refer particularly to two different modes of labour organization and intensification of resource mobilization, and each maximizes within different modes of economic organization. The former maximizes responsiveness, adjustment, possibilities of novelty, and a potential for refinement and fine-tuning, while the latter achieves massive tasks, continuous movement and gigantic results. They are two different parrying strategies.

Capitalism and Weber's Instrumental Rationality: The Paradox

Capitalism is a subset of a larger orientation: pragmatism/functional efficiency as Weber had observed. In its success, the paradigm of the modern enabled applied science and technology to progress in a most overwhelming manner, devaluing in its anti-traditionalism all pre-existing symbolic values (a point that is most central to Weber's critique of modernity and part of Marx's critique of capitalism). In this world, all considerations could be reduced to efficiency and all symbolic attributes militantly purged, without of course noticing that efficiency is also a value of a radical kind, and conservation of energy—which efficiency is all about—a fundamental value that prioritizes material resources over others. Durkheim successfully challenges this version of pseudo-modernity in his critique of Dewey, Bentham, and the Economists.[4]

One serious challenge, and the reason in some cases for the relative demise of the modern, was due to neither the Devil nor the Dragon but to the modern's own natural expansion, its own success, its own paradox. This was the case of the rise of social classes. In some sense, historically speaking, it was a consequence of the paradigm's "forward" motion. There is little to add to Marx's incontestable theory on this matter. This economically induced contradiction would only become nascent with the paradigm's successful practice. It was not part of its essence but its rules were most conducive to the rise of capitalism. Innocent of any economic theory, it elicited measures that would conjure up to curb the free reign of accumulation reminiscent of Hobbes and Rousseau which were also indirectly appealing to Durkheim.[5]

Thus, Durkheim's modernity could not account for the rise of antagonistic class interests, or, better, the rising hegemony of one class over another. That was Labriola's astute critique.[6] Durkheim had ignored Marx by dismissing socialism for its leveraging of fragmented society.

Yet, the paradigm of the modern with its four humours (see Chapter One) was most conducive to the maturing of the capitalist paradigm. It was its twin brother. The question was how capitalism would not become a Cain to its Abel. If the Modern entailed the danger of its expanding "hubris", for capitalism accumulation as its necessary dynamo would hijack capitalism's modern context. I have mentioned some of the ingredients of that phenomenon above. That question underlay Hobbes's central issue, "How is social order possible?" Rousseau's solution was to categorically curb accumulation.[7] Marx demonstrated that only a total revolution could salvage the principles of the modern paradigm, but he left most uncertain how that would be realized once capitalism was radically overthrown and the class nature of society eliminated. *Manifesto* was an incomplete text as Dahrendorf astutely argued.[8] Durkheim's solution on the other hand was reminiscent of Rousseau's "volonté générale" which could only be upheld by limiting appropriation.[9] In Durkheim's scheme, the power of professional organizations would curb the power of capital—what is not clear is whether Durkheim is suggesting something of a cooperative ownership of the means of production by each professional organization—and, most importantly, they would also curb the power of the central state.[10] Durkheim was thus not very clear on the economic issue. His primary aim was to create the solidarity of civic society. In my view, Durkheim's solution was not far from the medieval guild structure.

The Nationalist Kidnap

The second most damaging kidnap of the modern was by nationalism. In Durkheim's century, nationalism was the mood for serving the modern and serving it fully. Nationalism was there to destroy the old divisions and open up a venue in which moral individualism could blossom. In the service of Enlightenment individualism, nationalism and the nation-state would eradicate the *anciens régimes* and their feudal remnants. Nobody thought that in "eradicating primordialism" nationalism itself might be kidnapped by a sort of "retooled tribalism".[11] The nationalism of the early nineteenth century should have already alerted the intelligentsia to this threat by its adoration of the native, its praise for the hard-labouring yeomen, as in Thomas Gray's *Elegy* and for the purity of the countryside Wordsworth's *Daffodils*, or for its beginning Mme de Sévigné and Mme de Staël.

But the problem was not in the origins of the nationalist mood. Nationalism and the modern had become sufficiently urban and politically powerful that the peasant had been reduced to a symbol of the innocent native only to be celebrated and dismissed; the fault line was in the modern's later practice—a collectivist practice that relied on the popular will, a will that injected self-confidence and righteousness into its upholders. That was most tricky for the modern's "individualist" ends (writ large in the 1789 *Declaration of the Rights of Man and of the Citizen*). Durkheim hoped that the civic morality to be taught in school and the more participatory venue of the secondary organizations could prevent the politics of Caesarism.[12] It might have worked if constant reflexivity (Kantian self-reflection) had been omnipresent whenever the nationalist mood was mobilized. But diplomacy and daily politics, the self-interest of what Gramsci called the state class(es), would find the philosophical habit of self-reflection inimical to their aggrandizing nature, and the new politics the modernist paradigm marshalled at the expense of the amateurism of the *ancien régime* and its aristocratic *noblesse oblige*, would only make social mobilization the most viable source of political power, especially in the context of democratic competition without aristocratic barriers as de Tocqueville in his customary brilliance so insightfully had anticipated. Durkheim was naïve about power and politics. The French–Jewish emancipation emulated Kant and distanced itself from Machiavelli—perhaps also necessary to counter the latent anti-Semitism of the time. So did Durkheim, so later did Léon Blum, and so did Mendès-France later in the Republic. Once they had distanced themselves from the Talmud, they had to take the moral high road to disallow all the politics of cynicism and instrumentalism. (It is not ironic that Sarkozy, who had "escaped" the Lycée and the Left Bank, would turn it all—Dreyfus and the modern—upside down as if to extol Esterhazy's delayed comeback!)

Alien Romanticism of the Positivist Modern

Early in the nineteenth century, the world to some appeared to be ridden only by too much a concern with the "form and style", which the Romantics resented in earnest in their passion for the rustic. At the tail end their challenge was more profound; it was the class resentment of the new middle class trying to walk over the old cadres with an extra-earnest anger against form and style. Later in the century, the rise of Nationalism can be seen as a streak of latter-day Romanticism, stronger now as the marching song of the new, upwardly mobile classes.

Yet this march was not only Romantic! However, charged by Romanticism and disdainful of the "form-centredness" of the earlier elite of the epoch, compared to the dawn of the century, the intellectual trajectory at the end of the century would turn into Positivism. Positivism was both a rejection of form and etiquette of the earlier century for their assumed disutility but also was against the folkloric bubble of the early Romantics. For the Positivists, the future lay not in the rustic sentimentalism that the Romantics had adored, but in the geometry of the urban setting. These two polar rejections of the turn-of-the-century elite ideology, led to a very strange combination of a most unstable kind. What I would call "Romantic positivism" was epitomized in experimenting with one's life in order to scientifically and experimentally understand the process of dying. Positivist disdain of form and sentiment recalled Cromwell's Roundheads. Puritanical in temper, they made the modern depict itself in grey and beige. Eksteins, otherwise most miscued, correctly takes Stravinsky's *Firebird* as the overture to the modern.[13] A new mold to sever music from the music of Mozart and Beethoven.

This innate contradiction between the Romanticism and the Positivism embodied in the rising ideology of nationalism would play funny games with the history of the rising classes. It would resolve its inner tension in one of the two ways: either by totally dissolving the geometry and positivism by a romantic rustification of the modern, making technology appear as the chariots of Wagner's Valhallic gods and technology part of the might that is subsumed under the Romantic will and the purity sought in the racial mythologies of the pre-Classical past. The other would be by totally ridiculing the Romantic, as in the hyper-positivism of Soviet drab and grey. Hitler's was not a nationalism of Republicanism but a mad search for the archaic, for the fundamentalism of pre-civilization. Stalinism was positivism turned into technicism. Both were radical solutions to the temporary, contextual interdependence of Romanticism and Positivism at the turn of the century when nationalism was the credo of the new middle-class rebellion against the old order. Yet this unstable combination was not in the normativity of the modern but it was in its contextuality. Fascist mobilization was a way to gloss over this contextual tension by constant mobilization.

This "latter-day" Romanticism would set the context for the modern's essence to meet one of its dialectical hazards. It made the contradiction arising from its success more consequential. It is in this "double contextuality", connecting its content to its historical context that the narrative can underscore our idea of dialectical motion as emphasized in Chapter Two.

Positivist normativity would require two wars to cleanse itself of its contextual involvement with Romanticism, to eventually find itself in its true form, in the ultimate normativity of Weberian disenchantment, which Daniel Bell has called "the end of ideology", and which Fukuyama erroneously celebrates.[14]

Varieties of Nationalism

Historically, the nation-state has been the modern's best friend and worst enemy, making "enlightened vigilance" most necessary. The intimate relationship between the paradigm of the modern and nation-state was historically most significant, but it has to be understood clearly since so much error has already been committed in that analysis.

I will start with the nationalist narrative and then, in unearthing its essentials, identify two different paradigms of nationalism. Rogers Brubaker in his seminal work has alerted us to that confusion and identified the two types of the nation-state.[15] Here I want to go a step beyond Brubaker's distinction and unearth the sociological essence of the division in terms of the type of nationalism each embodied, so they can be more clearly kept apart. Notwithstanding that in their origins the two types of nationalisms shared the same discourse. In historical and essentialist terms, we can decipher the differences between these two antithetical kinds.[16]

Ethnic versus Civic Nationalism

Let me further pursue in their historical context, the contrast between the two paradigms in which the nationalist narrative would be molded, both at times succumbing to their *mimeses*—the civic and ethnic kind.

As we saw above, nationalist discourse in its early stage had two incompatible streams running through it: for the modern it was the political form of the nation-state that would be the enabling context for moral individualism as it countered the primordialisms of the *ancien régime*. To have any chance historically, this stream required a bourgeois transformation. We shall review that second, under civic nationalism (*below*).

History in Broad Brushes

This is a "stylized history". It is not a history as practised by the historians. The narrative here will select some facts over others according to the logic of the paradigm in the manner of Marx and Weber as harbingers of comparative historical sociology. What validates the selection is the explanatory value of the paradigm. For our methodology not all facts are relevant for the particular issue in hand. My stylized history is grounded in the nineteenth-century Hungary. At this conjuncture, I must apologize to my most valuable Hungarian colleagues and friends for my shortcuts, yet I should not be forgiven for my errors.

Looking at Hungary at the turn of the nineteenth century, one can detect the two nationalisms coexisting—the first, the ethnic nationalism of the petty nobility characterized by a belief in the sanctity of consanguinity and ruling in the countryside with a socially dependent peasantry. They are immersed in ethnic nationalism of a Romantic rural kind with the strangest symbolisms dating to an imaginary, thousandyear-old nomadic past. Even today rural nationalist symbols emerge in full on national holidays with headgear made of horns and animal heads and costumes made of animal skin, which, from a distance and to the anthropologically ignorant, bear great resemblance to some of Native American ceremonial dress.

Ethnic Nationalism

In the Romantics' mold, the question was different from the modernist nation-state as the historical challenge for its inception was different. Here, the idea of the nation constantly drifted into communalism, only to lose its universalistic mission, often privileging one segment of society over another and breeding intense hostility and at times, and even worse, internal terror (the Holocaust is one example). Historically, this was the path most convenient for societies that had not purged their local—national is a misnomer here—nobilities, as evidenced in Eastern Europe (e.g. the Magyars). Marx's point about the absence of the bourgeois revolution and the continuity of late feudalism in Germany is relevant here. A most powerful belief in consanguinity, which also typified the defensive nobility of the Magyar kind, provides congruence between the two cases.

By defensive nobility I have in mind the example of Hungarian minor nobility. The name Magyar identified them before that word came more recently to identify all Hungarians. Small in landholding and many in number, consanguinity was their way of protecting their class interests against the rising middle peasantry who might have come to possess larger lots and more affluence. Exaggerating the importance of consanguinity might have been their struggle for "boundary maintenance". The deep, all-powerful belief in consanguinity as an explicator of character that still exists today, extensively but subterranean, in Eastern Europe, making the past history of Dracula so germane.

Nationalism of this type had Romantic origins, finding its source in a particular folklore that adulated nature and the native, often the peasant. This was the version that flourished in parts of Europe where the minor nobility prevailed and a distant extraterritorial power ruled. Here the local elites were trying to wrest power from the extraterritorial authority with a new ideology of "independence" that secured them relative popular support. This was the case especially when the peasants were feeling the brunt of the new fiscal demands of the central authority, which itself was facing a fiscal crisis arising from the needs the new war technology had introduced into inter-power competition. This was the story for most of the Balkans and Eastern Europe. This version of nationalism, however much new technology it might have used, is anti-modern, and its only relation to the modern is its animadversion to the values of paradigm of the modern.

This was akin to the narrative of Hitler's march, which had different but not very different origins. It was rooted in Germany's unfinished feudalism.[17] It had nothing to do with the modern except a hatred for it. It is thus not even a kidnap of the modern, which both Bauman and Eksteins miss in their different ways because of their empiricisms/historicisms. They looked at symptoms and not into the essences. In our terms, this is a clear case of an abduction: abducted by an external force and externally consummated with none of the modern's inner core, without any of the modern's essence, and antithetical to it. It saw the values of the modern as its principal adversary. The explanation for this abduction could, I believe, best be found in Marx's perhaps most outstanding essay, in English translation, "The Critique of Hegel's Philosophy of Right". For Marx, the German polity, in contrast to the French, could never uproot itself from its medieval past. In the double-contextuality of the interwar context, the buddings of modernity were thus quashed by a most archaic form of ethnic nationalism.

Let me continue with my brief historical excursion to underscore my points about petty nobility as the carrier of ethnic nationalism. Especially for Hungary but also for parts of the rest of Eastern Europe, the Ottomans and later the Habsburgs might bear a lot of the blame for this phenomenon. By "freezing" all the local customs in their various *kanunnames*[18] and preserving local habits and hierarchies to optimize political stability for the ends of their fiscal empire, the Ottomans as a consequence allowed the minor local nobility to survive for a long time, thereby retarding any future chances of a bourgeois revolution.[19]

The Ottoman "freeze" was ingenious. It incorporated the local nota-
bles, big and small, into its administrative machinery, even employing
the Catholic clergy for its administrative posts (e.g. *timar*) to the great
annoyance of the Habsburgs as the defenders of Catholicism across the
border.[20]

Later, the Habsburg rule continued in a similar manner, though to a
lesser extent.[21] Yet, the Habsburgs—as I have argued above—were still
no better than a fiscal empire, hence not conducive to a deep capitalist
transformation, and thus had little to add to possible local bourgeois
development in the countryside. The late Hungarian transformation
was the work of the Hungarian upper nobility, the aristocracy, whom
Habsburg rule had elevated at the expense of the local gentry. The bourgeois transformation did not affect the countryside: it was late, it was
urban, and it was mostly Jewish. Both the Austrian and the Hungarian aristocracies, who were the ruling classes *par excellence*, were large
landholders and derived their prestige, position and income from that
fact. The Hungarian upper nobility by then had more land, prestige
and power than its Austrian counterparts. They also had a symbiotic
relationship with the local small landowners, and none wanted much
change in the countryside. Any urban change and urban industry
would come in the second half of the nineteenth century with the legal
emancipation of the Jews. It was the large concentration of Jewish population in the Carpathian region that would come and transform urban
Hungary and create Pest anew to be annexed by Buda: annexed by an
aristocrat who must have owned a good part of Hungary, Count István
Széchenyi. Next to the bridge that Széchenyi had personally built is
the Hungarian Academy of Sciences—a monument to the "humanistic
tradition" which the nineteenth-century Hungarian aristocracy upheld
in their own self-legitimation. No doubt some Hungarian aristocrats

were visionaries. I believe the universalistic vision of the old aristocracy and ethnic localism of the country petty-nobility still clash in Hungary today, even when they are now represented by different groups![22]

Whether it was the earlier struggle against the Ottomans or the later struggle against the Habsburgs, on the whole local mobilization was for the protection of local custom and folklore, which was seen as lodged in and identified with the "national" nobility, meaning the local gentry. The struggle of the minor local nobility was dominated by folkloric nationalism.

The greater nobility had different strategies: either to collaborate with the extraterritorial powers, (e.g. Thököly with the Ottomans), or, later, in the nineteenth century, to seek alliances with the urban population in universalistic terms under the aegis of the Habsburgs to whom the aristocracy became well integrated. The locals remained local to safeguard their consanguity, Hungarian aristocracy waltzed in Vienna. The Opera and the Waltz integrated the imperial elites. The Budapest opera built much later than in Vienna brought the upwardly mobile Budapestian middle class into the imperial élan, this was after 1867. The distance between the aristocracy and the country nobility would never be bridged. Latin as the language of the Parliament kept the country nobility relatively disenfranchised, but privileged the new urban professional classes who owed much of their status to education.

In the 1860s Széchenyi, a most *bona fide* aristocrat was left stranded by the minor Magyar nobility when he prepared the Habsburgs for a deal on Hungarian autonomy that would have eliminated much of the bloodshed that would later follow. Instead, an alternative deal that perpetuated the local political power of the minor nobility was struck with the Habsburgs in 1867 after much bloodshed. Budapest as we know it today was built then to house the new middle class in boulevards modeled after Haussman's Paris, and "hôtels particulier" or the urban residences of the aristocracy, both excluding the petty nobility. Horty regime of the 1920s and 1930s well represented this resentment and the first ethnic laws were promulgated in Hungary to exclude Jews who had already become secular and the mainstays of urban Hungary.

The Beginnings of Hungarian Civic Nationalism: Budapest in the late 19th Century

The second articulation of modernity with nationalism occurs when the modern with its inner logic feeds on nationalism of the second kind, the nationalism of the bourgeois urban middle class. In its "pure", unadulterated form this is what we would call civic nationalism. It is grounded in the four humours of the modern and in the service of expanding moral individualism. This is Durkheim's historical agenda, i.e. understood in essentialist terms, that the paradigm of the modern when articulated with urban nationalism is antithetical to the nativist nationalism.

Civic nationalism of the Durkheimian kind, which totally over-shadowed the ethnic, is to be found in Budapest in contrast with its population, over one-third of whom were urban middle class, mostly secular Jews who refused to follow their compatriot Theodor Herzl, in the conviction that they had already found their Zion in the Hungarian capital.[23]

Budapest with its cosmopolitanism was perhaps the location where Durkheim's civic patriotism was most evident. They had the advantage over Paris for not bearing the burden of a Great Nation illusion, over Vienna for not being dominated by a thick aristocracy, and over

Berlin for not having an ever-present Kaiser. Although they considered themselves culturally second to Vienna, and although they were mesmerized by the intellectualism of Paris,[24] in retrospect, in the two or three decades before the War, Budapest was indeed a most vibrant and productive intellectual city, a showpiece of modernity though not with any nominal awareness but as a natural consequence of the age, which in fact might be its great historical attraction! What I find most exemplary in that historical episode is the civic nationalism, civic patriotism à la Durkheim, that found its expression in pre-war Budapest with its one-third Jewish population.

At the end of the War the victors in Paris, in grand insouciance and ridden by ignorance of the "little matters" of the little people, remained oblivious to the complexities of redrawing the map of Europe formed over many centuries.[25] The great powers had a colossal task, which I am not sure they fully understood. They had only preconceived notions about anything beyond the narrow confines of Western Europe, nor did they listen to their junior staff who were doing their homework.[26] It was not enough for them that post-Habsburg Hungary selected a pacific, anti-war leader, Mihaly Károlyi, to lead the country as a new republic. The contempt of the victors, especially of the French, for the Hungarian leadership, eventually totally undermined its credibility. Károlyi, left-leaning and a socially progressive leader with great aristocratic legitimacy, might have been a good candidate for holding together the different segments of Hungarian society in the civic mold.[*] But Hungary was perhaps one of the worst treated nations after the war. In the midst of the tremendous economic shortages that ensued, mostly of the Entente's doing, and its leadership contemptuously undermined,

---

[*] My Hungarian friends today on the whole do not share my views on Károlyi.

Hungary succumbed to a communist/socialist-led revolution of Budapest's making with a strong Jewish intellectual component. Horthy came in with the support of the victors and the countryside to take revenge on Budapest. The regime was well-suited to ethnic nationalism in both ideology and practice.

The Horthy regime of nationalist fascism with its anti-Semitic laws, first in recent history, could be seen as a natural outgrowth of this background, as could Béla Kun's earlier contrasting road to modernity, which in its extreme ruined all its possibilities and paved the way to Horthy. Horthy came in and brought Budapest to its knees. I do not think that Béla Kun's path would have succeeded without a good deal of bloodshed. Even if they had defeated the Rumanian armies invading in the north, Béla Kun's party would have had to face the countryside.

Again, it is no accident that it was eventually the Jewish population of Budapest that made a mark on history by being the harbingers of the great intellectual ideas of the twentieth century and winning numerous Nobel Prizes on behalf of Hungary. That cosmopolitanism of Budapest, making it the seat of civic nationalism, must have played a role in their ability to "conquer the world", to make the monumental Hollywood films sometimes with subject matter so distant from that of Budapest. Here I have in mind Michael Curtiz, both for *Casablanca* as a monumental film which nonetheless could easily be perceived from a Budapestian perspective, but much more in particular for the *Robin Hood* films, which were obviously so alien to the urban Budapest experience.

Among many other "cosmopolitan tap dancers", Joseph Kosma is one other example among many of the products of Budapestian civic culture. Joseph Kosma was again of Jewish origin, again secular, studied at a gymnasium in Budapest, went to Berlin on a musical grant. He met and worked with Brecht until 1934. He escaped to Paris with no penny nor a word of French. He became friends with Jacques Prévert, wrote to the scores of many films of the best of French cinema including part of the score of *The Grand Illussion* and the pantomime of Jean-Louis Barrault in *Les Enfants du Paradis*. He wrote jazz as well as rendering Jacques Prévert's poem into the music of one of the most sensational melodies, *Les Feuilles Mortes*. He died in France and buried in the Montmartre Cemetry.

It is my belief that only Budapest of the turn of the century could produce so many artists and intellectuals of such cosmopolitan versatility. I think the intensity of the intellectual debate of the decade earlier, provided the leitmotif for artists of the next generation.[27] All that Horty could not destroy in Budapest, Eichman would later put an end to it all.

Double-Contextuality

In celebrating Budapest's past, we have to put it in a historical perspective. The ascendance of the Budapestian civic society was another example of what I called "double-contextuality". The global historical context was most opportune for the cosmopolitan universalism that the four humours of the modern issued. Between roughly the *fin de siècle* and the First War is the period of the effervescence of cities. This is the period when city culture reaches its apex, with its diversity and multiethnic demography and with much travelling population in this gay era of dancing, reading and debating, and of no passports. While Paris wore the crown, the other traditional urban centres like Vienna and Berlin were living their great years. But for us what matters are new cities, new not necessarily in history but in habit: This is when cities from Baku to Budapest, from Smyrna to Beirut, from Odessa to Alexandria, St Petersburg to Johannesburg, from Shanghai to Buenos Aires are glowing in their festive lives: tolerant, multiethnic, with an intermingling of languages and people and a good deal, relatively speaking, of interethnic marriage, or at least unconventional living habits, with a multilingual population, multilingual calendars, multilingual advertisements, and a diversity of newspapers in many languages, the breakdown of city quarters and the prevalence of an urban totality, in Durkheim's language, a new society. This is the double-contextuality, the urbanity of the several decades before the war, which situates the great effervescence of Budapest. What distinguishes Budapest from the others however is the civic nationalism and civic patriotism that came to define her. We may have different theories about why Budapest was so unique. But we have to remember that Budapest's unique qualities could only come to fruition in a global context that strongly encouraged a new urbanity. Again, we may have different theories about this global phenomenon, one of which, I am sure, would be the world economy at the turn of the century. Yet this was not the first time the economy turned global, nor was it last. It is during this time that the modern figured so prominently in peoples' collective aspirations—some were able to achieve it, others were not. What is most universal, however, is that the nationalism the war engendered destroyed this urbane excitement and consciousness of urbanity.[28] As for nationalism, the victors used it, while the defeated instrumentalized it to overcome their post-war predicament. If urbanity punctuated the *fin de siècle*, the small town sets the grid for the twenty-first century and embeds the post-modern.

What distinguished Budapest among all these centres of new urbanity was perhaps its extraordinary intellectual prowess and the outstanding educational institutions that laid behind it. That is how the local and the global meet to make a different history possible, the uniqueness of Budapest's civic nationalism in the sea of rising urbane aspirations at the end of the century. Eventually it was Horthy's heavy hand that became necessary to bridge these two incompatible nationalisms until the Nazis destroyed them both for a murderous ideology of blood purity, the ideals of consanguinity—ethnic nationalism taken to its extreme.

Civic Nationalism in Jeopardy: State Nationalism

Still, the nationalism of the new age after the First War could become the curse that the paradigm of the modern could not easily resist. In one case, Turkey, not only the ideals of the modern but also the desire to "skip stages" on the road to the modern took its sway. The true kidnap/hijack of the modern by nationalism occurs in this later version of nationalism. Here all four axioms of the modern—Chapter One above referred to it as the four humours of the paradigm of the modern—are fully operative, but the core value for which these axiomatic fundamentals of the public realm are created, i.e. individualism, is eclipsed.[29]

In between the two types of nationalism, a third type emulating one of the two paradigmatic types, often oscillating between the two, is the nationalism of what Gramsci called as "the state class". It is like a tree with roots in the sky and branches in the earth. Without roots, it can go ethnic or civic, or oscillate between the two in its confusion. Because it is created for the state's centric functions of economic mobilization and struggles for territorial unification which the post-war treaties left in askance the historical circumstances privileged the "state class" to take over.[30]

When a true combination of ethnic nationalism with state nationalism occurred, horrors ensued. This was the case of the Nazi regime. In trying to bridge the historical gap between an archaic form and an industrial state, in trying to synthesize state nationalism with ethnic nationalism, most heightened social mobilization was required to collate the two paradigms into one "unnatural alliance". It required the utmost bellicosity both within the nation and without.

Closing the Discussion: The Paradigm of Modernity under Civic Nationalism

Now a critic is called for to conclude the discussion. After the above praise of "civic nationalism" we have to draw attention to a fundamental source of possible instability that civic nationalism might engender in its practice—once more underlining the need for constant vigilance.

Is there not a dialectic of instability inherent in the historical imprint of universal individualism? The historical crucible of universalism in the French Revolution also had to battle privilege and mobilize manpower; the former required radical egalitarianism to couple with collectivism for the broader struggle of universalism that the revolutionary mobilizational circumstances called for. "Citizenship" is the lynchpin of its public universalism, and individual rights are lodged in the political society and political society assumes logical and temporal antecedence. The French Republic since the Revolution had to go through five constitutions. The British have a different historical trajectory. Individual liberties were the rights of the nobility and had existed as their inviolable privilege. In their extension to the rest of the populace servility was gradually displaced by the innate nobility of all individuals.[31] Hence, individual liberties become universal so far as they are severed from privilege. Liberties is antecedent to political society and political society is created to safeguard the liberties. This process is historical and not logical. The British need history and not a logical constitution. Durkheim is obviously in the French track.

Universalism ought to be the equality of the "differents" and not only of the "sames",* requiring a dialogical and not only a monological discourse; the question is how much differentness even the most civic of all republics allows, and how well it encourages a robust self to thrive?

In theory, it is a demand to allow differentness as a minimal common denominator: this is Durkheimian universalism which is to be constituted via a national society. A national society, by tearing asunder pre-universal primordialism, would create the bases of eventual universalism which would be obtained by transcending national society. This halfway position of national society is explicit only in one place of Durkheim's writings but could be shown to exist even more clearly as a logical extension of his theoretical paradigm. This universalism, however, is at the level of a "rational being", i.e. anti-primordial. Leaving aside how much identity is constituted in the realm of the primordial and assuming that all we want to obtain is "legal universalism"—hence the definition of "minimal universalism"—the question of how much primordialism the republic tolerates still remains at bay. This is both an empirical/phenomenological point, perhaps exclusively grounded in the formational context of each republic, and a normative point grounded in the essentialism of the logic of the republic. Leaving the first issue aside, let us look at the second and for us the more fundamental issue. Even if and when the republic tolerates the primordial differentness as

---

*   I owe much to Seyla Benhabib for this critique. Without her alert, this crucial point would have remained amiss. I am most grateful. The final formulation above is mine.

embodied in the realm of the private (whether that is the case or not has to be further ascertained), nonetheless the republic cannot build safeguards to protect this aspect of the private. Most optimistically it tolerates but does not protect, i.e. it has a one-way tendency unless the legal institutions are so instructed often by a constitution. That need for such an instruction is an evidence that such protection of individuality is not sufficiently engrained in the logic of the republic, however civic it might be. In other words, however the civic republic provides the space for moral individualism to expand, it does not sufficiently protect individualism from "assault".

Republic has the innate essentialist capacity to resist primordialism at the level of its own essences, (i.e. when primordialised it is departing from its own logic), but the aspects of the private self that are not within the bounds of legal universalism, is in constant jeopardy under the republic and thus is the reason why republics so easily gravitate to monologicalism. The private in essence, however, cannot be assumed to have universal rationality as its founding premise—i.e. when individuality is not erroneously reduced to atomistic individualism. In its search for differentness which can only, by definition, be created at the not rational level: individuality needs universalism, to develop and flourish, but itself emerges by nuancing away from the rational that is universal to all under conditions of non-pathology.[32] This is what the modernist republics however democratic they might be fail to recognize due to the innate biases arising from their paradigmatic—the modern—anchors lodged in its universalizing concept of citizenship. Citizenship, the bedrock of civic nationalism is a "double-edged sword". It could become both inclusionary and exclusionary. It underwrites republic's universalism but shrinks when "self" challenges its all-embracive impulses.[33]

Democracy is best defined in relation to the distance available between public persona and individual identity.[34]

Notes

1. Robert N. Bellah, ed., *Emile Durkheim: On Morality and Society* (Chicago: The University of Chicago Press, 1973).

2. I find Marx's essay, (in English) "Critique of Hegel's Theory of Right" as his most brilliant piece of writing. In that essay Marx most brilliantly argues why German polity could never shed its feudal moorings. That is what I am referring to as the "un-permitting context". Weimer was one context that feudalism was attempted to be eradicated. It did not last to be destroyed by the Nazis. I think perhaps because of that history the present German Republic is the most proto-typical modern state as it exists in the global order today.

3. Claus Offe, *Modernity and the State: East, West* (Cambridge: Polity Press, 1996).

4. See Durkheim's critique of Dewey in Dennis Rusche and Rick Tilman, "The Aims of Knowledge: Emile Durkheim's Critique of American Pragmatism", *The European Legacy*, October 2007. Another example of this extension of the modern into a realm not innate to it is in architecture. In finding the Baroque too excessive and ornate, i.e. wasteful, recent architecture has gone for simplicity, efficiency, and functionalism as in Lloyd Wright and Le Corbusier. In our paradigmatic language, this trend is antithetical to the modern—contrary to the existing usage. In its innate expansiveness, this trend in function turns simplicity and functionalism first into the aestheticization of simplicity and then into the easy solution of the colossal. The colossal is the Palais de Chaillot, built for the 1930 Paris Exposition, across the river from the Eiffel Tower whose construction I take as the beginning of the Modern.

5. Émile Durkheim, *Socialism and Saint-Simon* (New York: Collier Books, 1962).

6. Faruk Birtek, "The Turkish Adventures of the Durkheim Paradigm: Does History Vindicate M. Labriola", *Il Politico*, Volume LVI, Number 1 (1991): 107-146.

7. Crawford B. Macpherson, *The Political Theory of Possessive Individualism: Hobbes to Locke* (Oxford: Clarendon Press, 1962).

8. Ralf Dahrendorf, *Class and Class Conflict in Industrial Society* (Stanford: Stanford University Press, 1959).

9. Crawford B. Macpherson, *The Political Theory of Possessive Individualism*.

10. Émile Durkheim, *Professional Ethics and Civic Morals* (Illinois: Free Press, 1958).

11. Faruk Birtek, "Emergence and Limits of National Political Identities", *Identities, Affiliations, and Allegiances*, ed. Seyla Benhabib, Ian Shapiro and Danilo Petranovich (Cambridge: Cambridge University Press, 2007).

12. Durkheim, *Professional Ethics and Civic Morals*.

13. Modris Eksteins, *Rites of Spring: The Great War and the Birth of the Modern Age* (New York: Doubleday, 1989).

14. Daniel Bell, *The End of Ideology: On the Exhaustion of Political Ideas in the Fifties* (New York: Free Press, 1965).

15. Roger Brubaker, *Nationalism Reframed: Nationhood and the national questions in the New Europe* (Cambridge: Cambridge University Press, 1996). So much most valuable literature on nationalism but I believe my discussion in terms of typifying varieties of nationalism in terms of both their history and ideology is new. The absence of such distinction, for example, leaves Ernest Gellner's work *Nationalism* (London: Phoenix, 1997) most one-sided.

16. In this culture of folkloric nationalism, the much-admired Béla Bartók could perhaps be explained somewhat differently, as could Franz Lizst, who came to Budapest only to learn Hungarian late in life. The differences between the two composers notwithstanding, they equally share the same Museum of Music History in Budapest today. They represent the two different Hungarys, one celebrating the rural, the peasant and the folklore, the other the urban, the cosmopolitan and the international; both housed today in the same museum.

17. Karl Marx and Friedrich Engels, *Manifesto of the Communist Party* (Chicago: Kerr, 1915).

18. Ahmed Akgündüz, *Osmanlı Kanunnameleri ve Hukuki Tahlileri* (Is-

tanbul: Osmanlı Araştırmaları Vakfı-OSAV, 1996). Again, as Mark Lilla (in "How the French Face Terror", *The New York Review of Books*, Volume LXIII Number 5) refers to Montesquieu for the issue of where *les lois* (legal order) ends and *les moeurs* (traditions) start and where they are embodied, let me give the example of the Ottomans. They had two sources of law: one was the cannon clearly created by the state for the purposes of administration, the other the common law expressing the customs of the people. It was yet essential that *les lois* would not too much violate the custom. When Ottomans wrote the laws of Budin—today's Hungary—for the first two years they registered the pre-existing local practices as travelling inspectors recorded them and then submit them to the cabinet *Divan* for them not to violate any Ottoman principles. Then the *Divan* established the law of Budin with only after minor changes from what that had locally existed. The Ottomans had different cannon *Kanunname* for each of their regions, different for Budin than, for example, Syria. I feel that procedure was one reason for the Ottoman rule to survive, notwithstanding its growing weakness in terms of its economic capacities—which of course also held those very regions economically retrograde over the long run.

19. Balázs A. Szelényi, *The Failure of the Central European Bourgeoisie* (New York: Palgrave Macmillan, 2006).

20. It is perhaps no accident that after four centuries, Ottoman administrative terms like *sipahi* and *timar* still survive as street names in Buda. To the retrospective surprise of all Hungarian and Austrian historians, the Hungarian small gentry were fighting with the Ottomans at the siege of Vienna in 1683, and it was the Crimean Tatars, the ancient vassals of the Ottomans, who betrayed the Ottoman army for Austrian gold to enable Jan Sobieski and his cavalry to fill the gap thus created and save Vienna from Ottoman conquest. In the long run, this Ottoman incorporative policy and what I have called the "Ottoman freeze" not only perpetuated the local hierarchies but in consequence also left all the Balkans economically most backward.

21. This discussion of Austria-Hungary, of the Habsburgs in particular, has to be put in perspective so not to ignore an alternative view. Let me mention one contrasting view among others. One such example is the radi-

cal denigration of the Habsburgs found in Geoffrey Wawro's book, *A Mad Catastrophe: The Outbreak of World War I and the Collapse of the Habsburg Empire* (New York: Basic Books, 2014). The book is a diatribe describing the incompetence of the Austrians in the Great War, which might have been the case but which it then attributes largely to Franz Joseph's senility. The concern for etiquette and hierarchy is for the author the sole source of Austria's extreme incompetence without his recognizing that it was precisely the emperor's prestige and imperial legitimacy that had the magic to hold the otherwise increasingly untenable empire together. To quote Charles I's dictum, "no lords, no bishops, no king", for the Habsburgs no monarchy, no empire would be the rule. Loyalty to the emperor was a basic ingredient of good performance as portrayed, for example, in the character Sonnenschein in István Szabó's 1999 film of the same name, a traditional, affluent Jewish lawyer, whose pride in having been decorated by the emperor was the reason for his selfless attitude during the War. The author does not recognize that Austria-Hungary had relatively no industrial base for fighting the war amidst the industrially advanced nations. Like the Ottomans, it was one of the last empires trying to wage war like a nation-state in the face of the recently emergent, real nation-states. As I will argue later, empires are far inferior to nation-states in mobilizing resources, because their political system impinges on their ability to optimize stability and not total mobilization, which nation-states, given their means of legitimation, can do much better. As proof of Franz Joseph's incompetence, the author stoops to mention that at a younger age the emperor would visit his youthful mistress every morning at eight before taking up his office work at nine, as if that would in any way explain the Austrian disaster of 1914–1918. I take this as the view from a small Ukrainian town in Galicia incubated in north Texas a hundred years later. Moltke in the west was no better a tactician than Hötzendorf, and Wilhelm, though he engaged in no indulgences along the lines of Franz Joseph, he was certainly no better a monarch than the latter in running his state. It was more relevant that selling fezzes and Thonet furniture to the Ottoman Empire was no basis for waging a modern war when compared with the railways, Ruhr coal, and the iron of Alsace-Lorraine. In short, Austria-Hungary never became an industrial power to challenge the other powers in the First War. It was dependent on German coal and steel and remained mostly a rural country. That, I believe, is the main reason for the Austrian weakness in the war and not Franz Joseph's obsession with etiquette. In fact, it was the decorum and the waltz that held the empire together. It is really superfluous to write that Franz Joseph visited his twenty-year-old mistress every morning before going to work at nine to explain the Austrians' easy defeat. Wawro's closing sentence, "The great war has justly earned a dark place on our historical map, and Vienna, no less than Berlin, was the heart of darkness" (p. 385), leaves no doubt where author's heart lies, nor does the last paragraph, which is punctuated with a celebration, "In July 1914, the emperor drew his sword for the last time ... as the blade was parried, reversed, and driven back to his own gut" (p. 385). A lot of data, so many archives, so much painstaking and impressively extensive research, so many diverse people to thank abroad including librarians and friends who shared their homes, yet I would not call this history writing! I had to mention this work as it stands in such opposition to the views expressed here.

Obviously, a good part of history writing is like the seven blind men and the elephant, each historian writing from a different angle and referring to its own correct facts. However, the talent of good history writing is to see the total picture in its historical depth, to understand the grammar of things, in other words, to benefit from a sociological instinct. An exemplary work, in contrast, of this caliber, again coming out of Texas in 2014, this time from Rice, is Kristian Coates Ulrichsen's *The First World War in the Middle East* (London: Hurst, 2013) a superb work, which, I believe, is one of the very best of this hundredth anniversary crop.

22. This divide between the countryside and Budapest, the latent hostility between the two, I believe, still persists and shapes the very politics of today although contemporary Hungarians themselves are reluctant to admit. The Orban regime of 2015 still thrives on the countryside's revenge over cosmopolitan Budapest.

23. The central synagogue, built in the mid-1850s, recalls in its architecture the Jewish intellectual glory of the cosmopolitan Andalusian *convivenza*. Dohány Street Synagogue was finished the year the New Synagogue of Berlin

was started. The Berlin synagogue also exhibits similar Moorish lines, again referring to the same period in Jewish history. I do not know the relationship between the two synagogues, and I do not know how these Moorish lines came to dominate at the time. The later American version was obviously an imitation of the European models. In contrast, the Ottoman synagogues do not have the Moorish influence. It was the Ashkenazi intelligentsia of the 19th century who yearned for the Andalusian *convivenza* and not the Ottoman Sephardim bankers. Dohány, the street in Budapest after which the synagogue is named, is a word of Arabic origin, from the Arabic *duhan* meaning "smoke" or tobacco. The street is called Tabakgasse in German. It could have come into Hungarian with other Arabic words already present in the Ottoman language; but, I remain to be corrected on that.

24. Joseph Roth, *Report from a Parisian Paradise: Essays from France, 1925–1939* (New York: W. W. Norton, 2005).

25. Margaret MacMillan's *Paris 1919* (NY: Random House, 2003) is most insufficient the minute we turn our gaze to the smaller players in Europe.

26. Its American context notwithstanding, Arthur Walworth's *Wilson and His Peacemakers: American Diplomacy at the Paris Peace Conference, 1919* (New York: W. W. Norton, 1986) is still the best book for a discussion of Paris in 1919.

27. Mary Gluck, *Georg Lukács and His Generation, 1900–1918* (Cambridge: Harvard University Press, 1991).

28. Philip Mansel, *Levant: Splendour and Catastrophe on the Mediterranean* (London: John Murray, 2010).

29. This is the situation, as we shall see, that the modern often encounters in its travels, and we shall discuss one such case, Turkey, in *Durkheimian Paradigm on its Foreign Travel* (forthcoming). But the later crisis of Turkish modernity was not due to this kidnap but rather to an economic paradox of the inner logic of the Durkheimian paradigm, which runs into crises because of its own success. This happens specifically in two crises, both of which arise from the paradigm's success, making the Durkheimian theory's assumption unviable due to the changes the theory engenders by its very success. In both

cases these crises are exacerbated by the global context. This double jeopardy, one internal and self-created, the other external, gives us the situation of double-contextuality to verify the inner contradictions of the paradigm when its sphere of relevance—note, not irrelevance—has expanded, i.e. expanding the self-boundaries—hubris—to the domain of irrelevance. It is in that gap that the inner assumptions of a model are often best revealed.

30. In Turkish case it was a strictly French model in theory, with fascist overtones that the doldrums of the 1930s had made globally fashionable. Notwithstanding the adherence to the modernist paradigm and its universalism, some ethnic discourse seeped into some of the state's practices. The ideologues of the regime did not understand their crises and compromised on its ideological core. In the waning of the civic modernist paradigm later, the state became diluted in its ideology and distanced from its realities—I once called it the "hovercraft state" in Faruk Birtek and Binnaz Toprak, "The Conflictual Agendas of Neo-liberal Reconstruction and the Rise of Islamic Politics in Turkey: the Hazards of Rewriting Modernity", *The Post-Modern Abyss and the New Politics of Islam: Assabiyah Revisited*, ed. Faruk Birtek and Binnaz Toprak (Istanbul: Bilgi University Press, 2011) only to be kept afloat with much pressure onto below. That was the tragedy that came forth for the modernist Turkish state after the 1980s to 2000. It had become modernism without ideology, kidnapped by the state's use of its class.

31. T. H. Marshall, *Citizenship and Social Class* (Cambridge: Cambridge University Press, 1950).

32. In the pathological social space, this nuancing for individualisation is often attempted at by psychopathology such as Ronald D. Laing and Aaron Esterson, *Sanity, Madness and the Family* (London: Tavistock, 1964) and the works of Ed Lemert, Thomas Szasz and Thomas Scheff.

33. On the other hand, in general I think empire, when properly defined in terms of a modern context, can write in more readily the protection of the primordial as a part of its "social contract". Thus, the private can be better protected in its heterogeneous logic, but perhaps weakens at the very point of individualization of the private instead of its primordialism. In other words,

while the republic is not at ease with "voluntary associations" that capture the individual in some less than universal groupings, the empire is at ill at ease when the individual refuses to be defined in terms of any kind of voluntary sub-groupings. The end of the nineteenth-century aporia—in the positive sense of this word—in allowing a double identity and skilling itself in the fine-tuning for the two (see Birtek, "Emergence and Limits of National Political Identities"), created more space for the individual virtuosity and creating more a private space than the republics; the nemesis of the republics and their downfall then has been for the republics to so easily gravitate to an ever-expanding space of the universal, and that expanding through monologizing the otherwise potentially dialogical discourse; in this sense republic in its opportune contextuality "retribalizes" while it is trying to universalize; this I believe had been the problem of the Turkish Republic mostly due to its historical context of inception, for which both the victors of the War for their dismemberment project, and the defenders of the "realm" for their survival legitimacy are jointly responsible; the empire—empire in the social qua political contract—is precarious when public participation is enhanced without being able to restrain or balance-out primordial voluntary associations, by a public realm of unified voluntary association of a "political class" (Gramsci) the example of Magyar Habsburg and the non-Muslim political elites in the Ottoman Empire; i.e. a need for a balance between participation and the minimalist definition of a "political class" identity. I have called this political universalism and elite-limited socio-political participation—however the elite is defined—imperial universalism. Historically what I have in mind are the Habsburg and the Ottoman cases of the 19th century. The Habsburg instrument was the Waltz, whereas the Ottoman was the Parliament of 1876. See Robert Devereux, "The First Ottoman Constitutional Period: A Study of the Midhat Constitution and Parliament", *The Johns Hopkins University Studies in Historical and Political Science* Ser. LXXXI, NO. 1 (1963): 310.

34. Faruk Birtek, "Emergence and Limits of National Political Identities", *Identities, Affiliations, and Allegiances*, ed. Seyla Benhabib, Ian Shapiro and Danilo Petranovich (Cambridge: Cambridge University Press, 2007).

Chapter Six

Flowers bloom in May to transcend their Solitude,

Their blossoms carry the seeds of their species being,
Each blossom the uniqueness of its individual scent[1]

The Paradigm in the Normative: Durkheim's Sociology

The *bona fide* modern was Durkheim. He was the Modern's theorist, its warrior. It is in Durkheim, and *inter alia*, in the sociological paradigm in its origins, where we will search for the promises and the weaknesses of the paradigm of the Modern.

Durkheim's principal concern is the fragility, the precariousness, of the emergent modern society. While Marx is optimistic about the historical outcome of his dialectical motions, Durkheim is most apprehensive about the endemic dangers of change, which he otherwise wholeheartedly supports. For Durkheim, contemporary society's forward motion only engenders the danger of chaos: "Thence are formed currents of depression and disillusionment emanating from no particular individual but expressing society's state of disintegration. ... a sort of collective asthenia, a social malaise... Then metaphysical and religious systems spring up which, by reducing these obscure sentiments to formulae, attempt to prove to man the senselessness of life and that it is deception to believe that it has purpose. New moralities then originate which, by elevating facts to ethics, commend suicide or at least tend in that direction by suggesting a minimal existence."[2] Hence, notwithstanding the linearity of his thinking, which I have called the "curse" of Durkheim's thought, Durkheim has brought the dialectic in through the backdoor to permeate all other questions. He is akin to Hobbes and shares with him the same fundamental question: *How is social order possible?* This question lies at the heart of Durkheim's search for his new science, Sociology. This is also why Durkheim, in a narrow perspective, has been erroneously accused of being a conservative thinker.

For the modern and sociology, we have to "get into the mind" of Durkheim, in Weber's sense of the *Verstehen*, for a gateway to the modern and sociology. He best represented this paradigm of the sociological modern because he was the best who reflected on it to save it from its possible slumber. He also had a personal interest in saving it as the son of a rabbi who turns lay notwithstanding his father's profession. He personally was one proto-typical stories of Jewish emancipation so consequential for my story of the nineteenth century.

Durkheim's paradigm is about harmony, about how to found it. Harmony is so central for the modern as the modern is so innately precarious, precarious because of the tremendous inner tension between the emergent self—what Durkheim called the cult of individualism, its unassailable particularism, its unbounded subjectivity—and the need for a social order which cannot—and should not—be founded on any primordialisms whether religious, tribal, or even familial, as social progress in its own momentum would require. This solution to that tension furthermore could not be partial, segmental, which also eliminates a socialist solution for Durkheim as it privileges one element in society over the others. This harmony has to be universalizing and totalizing as individual freedom requires reciprocity inlaid in social solidarity.

For Durkheim, it is this merger of particularism and universalism that has to be resolved simultaneously, in the same act, at the same time. That is the challenge of Modernity.

I have used "Dada" to identify the individual because of its essentialized subjectivity—as opposed to, for example, Kant's reason—to signify the particularism that arises when nature, tribalism and all types of primordiality are transcended in moral individualism.

I find Durkheim's intellectual contribution of monumental importance. His mental innovation made sociology possible. For Durkheim's sociology, I have two principal works in mind for departure: *The Rules of Sociological Method* (1895), and on its heels and in its practice, *Suicide* (1897). *Suicide* is the book in which Durkheim's epistemological leap occurs, the epistemological break that makes sociology as a discipline possible. A sociology close to Marx, but certainly not to Weber. In *Suicide*, subjectivity and intentions are dropped and the logic of the argument is sealed against them. This is a tremendous epistemological leap that at times even Durkheim cannot get accustomed to, and at times he slips back into the more conventional view. The suicide rate is what society yields, and it has its sui generis history! This is a very difficult leap, and it is extraordinary to forget about the individual when talking about individuals collectively. For example, Durkheim, in one of his backslides, wonders whether the suicide rate for a particular society is equally represented in each individual of that society. Again, he questions whether the rates of each type of suicide, i.e. altruistic, egoistic, anomic and, of course, the neglected fatalistic, are represented in each one of us to the same degree. These speculations are, of course, contrary to his methodology. The suicide rate is what it is, and that is that. It is *bona fide* social. As the Rules clearly state, we cannot logically go from society to individuals or vice-versa! Society behaves according to its own rules![3]

The Interdependence of Dada and Rationalism

In the broadest terms, from the Enlightenment through the French Revolution to the *fin-de-siècle* and twentieth-century modernity, two interdependent, two intertwined streams, the Yin–Yang, of modern thought emerged; each seemingly necessary for the other, both sharing the same intellectual–epistemological rupture, first of Hume, then of Kant, and each the diametrical opposite of the other: Rationalism and Dada. Dada the surrogate to fill the space, the *void* that the emergent "Doubt" of the Enlightenment would have created. Durkheim's was an effort to bridge this fundamental gap with his sociology.

In terms of his politics it was to build on Rationalism, without any concessions, without any relativism, but with full awareness of the ever-presence and fundamental reality of Dada itself. This is why for Durkheim political rationalism—the meaning of which will be clarified below—is only a choice, and a choice essentially and exclusively construed for the public sphere: neither ontologically innate nor psychologically inscribed or necessitated but an almost existential choice quite in the stream from Pascal through Spinoza to Kierkegaard and yet certainly more public and less individualistic than it had been for them, especially for Kierkegaard. For Durkheim, political rationalism in this instance, as a matter of collective choice, can tolerate no concessions and no moral relativism, because it is a construct. And nothing but an insistence on its purism could secure its viability and salience. Because it is a social construct, its charisma can withstand no compromises, and because it is the basis of new political morality, its power lies in the consistency of its principles.

If political rationalism was a choice, a necessary utopia for civilization, this was not in order to fulfil the imperatives of man's innate reason or to satisfy his need for order but rather for the survival of the "Dada" that modern individualism had brought about, for safeguarding the "doubt" that inevitably abounds in the modern individual once the omnipotent god is removed as the source of his certainty. (Note

Durkheim's similarity with Hobbes in their search for a social order in which individualism and its attendant strife, which is essential for civilization, are to be preserved without the danger of chaos at the public level.) Otherwise, without the rationalism of the public sphere, Dada for the individual is totally in jeopardy. It is only with public rationalism that Dada can survive and become the source of the individual's creativity, survival, and natural being, in short, its *raison d'être*.

This is the interdependence of Dada and rationalism as the two principles that define the private and the public spheres. Their strict separation is necessary for each, and the joint presence of each safeguards that of the other. Furthermore, the sociological bases of each are ensured by the normative separation of each sphere. This irreducibility of the two spheres, or rather their normative separation, which enables each sphere to flourish without distortions and in mutual safeguard of the other, was perhaps why Durkheim put so much emphasis on the analytical separation of the social from the individual.

The central component of Durkheim's solution to modernity was the creation of national society, and its safeguard of last resort the nation-state. Both national society and the nation-state were new and had to be created; they differed radically from their pre-existing namesakes. In contrast to others, Durkheim's national society was to resolve the three issues of the modern age as it evolved from the Enlightenment and was shaped by the French Revolution. If these historical vessels had not been institutionalized in the form of national society, and if the nation-state had not been created, these achievements, historically, might only would become unstable.

The three achievements were, first, the legal-rational order that universalized individual rights, second, individualism as the source that gave purpose to all social arrangements, and, third, public rationalism, which did not necessitate individual rationalism nor could be reduced to it. Hence, a triangle that can survive by the interdependence yet at the same time clear conceptual separation of its corners: individualism, universalism, and public rationality. The lynchpin of this arrangement was national society, and its instrument of last resort the nation-state. Hence Durkheim's nationalism was a necessary vessel for universalism, for the sustenance of the universalizing concept of humanity. It was to reconcile moral individualism with a rational public sphere and individual particularism. It was very different from other nationalisms, for example, from German *Volksgeist* nationalism, which prevented, and was contrary to, the establishment of individualism and universalism.

Durkheim's nation-state is the ideal-typical public realm for the emergence of universal individualism. Yet the history of the nation-state is the history of universalism and citizenship checkered by a most hazardous past, a hazardous past of collectivism that absconded with the nation-state's universalist ambitions to prevent the individualist ends of universalism, about which we have written so much above, from emerging. It is for that history that I have chosen Dada as the kernel of individualism to be recognized, and collectivism as the hazard to be purged.

Equally, the limits of the liberal state are best defined by the non-public sphere, in which *Dada* prevails. It is the existence of these very limits that save the state from distortions, from purporting to be what it is not, from claims that would weaken its premises by undue extension. Dada helps the state to define its boundaries, safeguard its premises and curb its excesses, which would otherwise undermine the liberal state.

Clarifying Some Concepts

Let us briefly review the emergence of the public in the form of the modern Durkheimian nation-state to see why it is that only with an undissolvable, unsociable Dada can it fulfil the ends Durkheim ascribed to it.

It is an axiomatic necessity for a normative "public" to be underpinned by a transcending reason à la Kant which underlies the public realm but not the realm of the private.

Durkheim put Kant's notion of practical reason at the centre of his concept of the "public" sphere. It is a consciously "constructed" public sphere of formal rationality, i.e. neither an extension of man's innate reason nor a developmental/evolutionist history of rationality à la Hegel. It is built on "false naturalism", and that "falsity" lies at the core of its very strength. It is that notion of the public sphere that I want to present as the context in which the "Dada-laden" individual is best safeguarded.

Hence, for Durkheim public-rationality is a created world, a world of Pascalian "as if" in which the recently emergent individualism can survive. It is the world of Kantian practical reason. But it is not a derivative of any innate qualities of man, nor is it a naturalistic rationality à la the Stoics transposed to the public. It is an axiomatic necessity only to separate the created world of public rationality from the subjective/the private/the irrational.

I can now "fill" my public realm to prevent its kidnap, or to prohibit transgression at its boundaries. For that we have to fill it with its proper texture, just as we prevented the kidnap of citizenship with its proper kernel, universalism.

For that purpose, after setting up our categories à la Durkheim, we now have to do a little more of Weber to detect the "texture" of our categories before we embark further. We first have to specify the realm of the public in terms of the nature of its legitimation and the texture of the "proper" code of socially rational action, in the way Weber would look at these questions from his "ideal-typical-forms" methodology. First, we should briefly see, again à la Weber, what it is not, see how it contrasts with the world of the private in terms of its socially rational action. In the private, instrumental logic is only pathologically available.[4] Impersonalization undermines it; ascription is the legitimate norm. Prototypically, the family is the seat, and procedural correctness refers to an assumed substantive realm (e.g. love, kinship, friendship, collegial loyalty) and not to legal-rational indifference, i.e. indifference to ascriptive qualities. In this realm of the private, charisma is constantly assumed for otherwise ordinary persons.

Just as reason could be kidnapped and forced into instrumentalization, the republics and nation-states that Durkheim pushed for the creation of a new space for the self to develop freely, and for it to gain its freedom from primordialism, are also ridden with the danger of the demands of "self-less-ness". The mobilizational capacities of the new order could win the battle for Dreyfus, but in the same terms shrank the space in which identities could be founded. When Republics build the counter-space to primordialism, they also limit the avenues in which identity is to be safeguarded for a robust notion of citizenship and for self to be constructed.

But in all these purported solutions and quasi-solutions, the republican/Durkheimian solution to identity is to squeeze it into the republican space, which was however intended only to be the means of creating and forming identities. An ambiguous under-definition would bring the problem to a standstill, until the Republic for some reason or other braces itself to mobilize. Then this "spacelessness" becomes real.

That is the kidnap of the Republic to which the republican form is most prone. And the reaction of virtually reinventing the old primordiality is perhaps a response to this and an effort to carve out a new space in the construct of modernity.[5] Yet this is for Durkheim, only a "cowardly" solution. For Durkheim there is an implicit assumption of a Nietzchean heroic self. A self which has to construct a will in the midst of the *vide* without any recourse to any primordialisms.

Otherwise, the question we thought we had answered remains unresolved. We had argued that "individualism" in its truest form would be a check on the state, on the national society of Durkheim, just as self-reflection is the hope of reason against instrumentalization. Yet in both cases this at times only pushes the problem a step backward. Reason in itself cannot generate constant self-reflection when assailed with such force laden with human interest. In other words, self-reflection is a given capacity, part of reason, but under kidnap hard to reinvent. The same holds for republics: Dada is to save them from excesses against the self, but it is also vulnerable to a particular kidnap, i.e. mass mobilization, at which point Dada is nowhere to be retrieved. Modern revolutions single out gays, artists and poets as their first targets, as was demonstrated even in the most modern of all revolutions, the Soviet, even in Lenin's time, i.e. before Stalin. The struggle is how to keep Dada available when republics are so easily seduced into their own mobilization.[6]

Bringing Dada Back

Can Dada as we have construed it parry the radical question Weber asked? Weber's world of the modern was also checkered with rationalization, bureaucratization and austerity. Let us listen to him: "[...] ascetism descended like a frost on the life of 'Merrie olde England'." Later in the text he would continue, "For of the last stage of this cultural development, it might well be truly said: 'Specialists without spirit, sensualists without heart; this nullity imagines that it has attained a level of civilization never before achieved'." And, a few lines earlier, "No one knows who will live in this cage in the future, [...] mechanized petrification, embellished with a sort of convulsive self-importance."[7] Was the modern's animosity toward the *belle époque* no different from Puritanism's hatred of the theatre? Is the modern rooted in a Protestant past?

Is Weber reading too much into Protestantism and bringing it up to his times through capitalism and its requisite bureaucratization? Is Weber so imbued with the sadness of his times as to miss the modern itself as a chilling effect? Or is it that in the German cultural paradigm the modern comes through as a grafting onto the already existent Protestant revolution? If Weber were right, logically, we would have the unfortunate, i.e. logically weaker, argument that the modern is really Protestantism/Puritanism in its final stage.

I will not concede that for two reasons, but first let me state my belief. My conviction, based not only on intuition, is as follows, using our earlier language: the modern has Dada as its alter ego and the Dragon is written in its inner grammar, whereas Puritanism has Sin to manage and has the Devil as its companion.

Less intuitively, sociologically speaking, I reject the hypothesis that Durkheim's modern might be lodged in a Protestant past for two reasons: one, the background to Durkheim's struggle was Catholic France. His aim was to purge France of Catholicism but was never a purge as radical as what Protestantism sought in other parts of Europe. Protestantism secularized the world but never extinguished religion from the public sphere. Protestantism only displaced Catholicism, whereas

Durkheim wanted to repress it. He sought ways to accommodate Catholicism only in privatized form and thus only as a separate sphere. The Christian dogma helped him in that task (Render unto Caesar what is Caesar's, unto God what is God's); second, the French modern, by expunging religion from the public sphere, would become the avenue on which the emancipated, secularized Jews of the French Republic came into their own and shaped it to a good degree on their itinerary of emancipation. Their emancipation was the emancipation of the world—the way Lukács and Marx thought of the working class.

Durkheim is embedded in his period, a period that stretches from the Dreyfus affair to the Great Depression—though he personally stayed out of the Dreyfus struggle.[8] The Third Republic comes into its own only in the 1880s and 1890s.[9] The Dreyfus affair in its conclusion does very little to Captain Dreyfus but makes its greatest impact through the struggle waged in getting there, the struggle between the first court ruling and the retrial that absolved Dreyfus. This approximately eight-year period is the Procrustean bed of the Third Republic, and of the Modern as we celebrate it today (see Chapter Seven).

Durkheim rebels against the baroque and the kitsch in the *belle époque*. The austerity of the modern is moderated by reflections of Art Nouveau, and the newly discovered Far East enters into the aesthetics. The Far East has no right angles, and the Eiffel Tower has none either, and yet it is the great celebration of steel as a medium of aesthetic expression. Industrialism's victory cries tamed into an aesthetic monument, it soars into the sky as the great moment of the modern age with steel as its infrastructure, austere yet with the hidden contours of Art Nouveau.

The Paris Exhibition of 1889 is as *belle-époque* as its end. The Eiffel Tower is *belle-époque* in its conception but expresses itself in the Modern.

The hidden Art Nouveau embedded in the tower is the ambivalence. The Eiffel Tower rebels against the austerity that the Modern might involuntarily admit. The tower puts steel—the arch-symbol of the new industrialism—into an organic form. Its curvilinearity gingerly embraces the sky, its steel aestheticized forever.

Durkheim is as modern as the Eiffel Tower, but he is more. He not only represents that moment, which he shares with the tower, but he also very much detects the future of modernity for its real crisis, the crisis that is endemic to the modern and not external and oppositional to it. Durkheim in his intuitive genius anticipates the true modern of the twentieth century: the Existentialists, the Expressionists, and Dada. He has more in common with Max Ernst than with Renoir. Durkheim sees and worries about the *vide* that the modern is pregnant with. Just as Marx anticipated the Devil in capitalism right at the beginning, so Durkheim anticipates the Surrealists, before they were even born, in the great inner threat that the modern is to face in its future. Renoir is *belle-époque*, with which Durkheim has absolutely no patience. It is Esterhazy versus Dreyfus. On this road fraught with the dangers of the *vide*, Durkheim arrives at the nation-state and argues for building the institutions of civil society as if he had sensed even the more distant catastrophe of the 1930s.

The state of the 1930s is no longer the modern state Durkheim advocated. His is the Third Republic. It is that state and that national society—totally antithetical to the primordial and the tribal and thus anti-ethnic—which had not been possible in Germany, and which France had to a great extent abandoned by the 1930s. It was thinned and flattened by the very heroes of the Third Republic in their hubris when Clemenceau at Paris exchanged the Republic for the pretence of an imperial power, as I will later emphasize (see Chapter Seven). Soon after Versailles, the Republic is only a flattened surface that everybody can ride and hence has become defenceless when the Devil beckons in the distance from the land where a regime antithetical to the republic prevails.

Durkheim's Theory of the State

From these concerns let me now construct Durkheim's theory of the state. It requires a teleological construction that, I hope, will eliminate a lot of unnecessary talk about Durkheim's étatism, talk that stems from taking a snapshot and then trying to build on that two-dimensional picture. It is only in these roots, in the anticipated crises of the modern, that we can construct Durkheim's model of state and society. It is part of Durkheim's effort to construct the modern so that harmony prevails and social order is sustained, as Hobbes suggested on a slightly narrower plane.

The problem for Durkheim is how to rein in the Dragon. But one has to be careful not to exaggerate here. It was less the Dragon that Durkheim feared. The danger he saw as most immediate was the *vide* and Beckett's Godot and Malone. The Dragon was there in the paradigm but only in its distant, secondary nature, perhaps to fill the space left between receding primordialism and the non-participating *vide*. The ultimate question is how to survive the *vide*. Thus, to repeat, I can be justified in claiming Durkheim's perfect anticipation of the Surrealists, even of Beckett's Godot and Malone.

So how does Durkheim arrive at his nation-state and national society all epiphenomenal to his more rudimentary question of self and society?

He starts from the turbulence of Dostoyevsky and, following Pascal's way, seeks the tranquility of Kant. Weber, driven by Nietzsche, can hope either for an aestheticized charisma or for the dullness of bureaucracy as solace. Plato is too distant to find the basis of charisma in aesthetics. Weber is stuck between bureaucratic dullness and the abyss, and sinks in the latter until he can convince himself to do a little gardening—i.e. liberal politics—in the last stage of his life.

Contrary to what has often been suggested, I believe that Durkheim is much more Kantian than Weber. Durkheim's central concern was to make "moral individualism" a viable credo. That, for him, fundamentally defined modernity. Yet no fundamental basis could be found for it other than a history of its gradual construction in an almost evolutionary manner:[10] fully agnostic and without ontological foundations *per se*—as was perhaps implied by Descartes and Kant. Durkheim is agnostic, and if any "evolutionarism" exists in him it would be the postulate of sociability—as a process of "getting away" from nature, from the original abode of humans, that is, perhaps as a process of evolutionary adaptation *not* to nature à la Spencer,[11] but away from nature to a socially constructed world. This is a socially constructed process, a society, so to speak, interacting with itself, as well as a process of individuals distancing and differentiating themselves both from the natural abode and from the nature within themselves—i.e. the instincts and the sensory world, both extensions of the natural environment within the individual. Consequently, the precarious nature of this existence breeds a desperate need for social institutions.[12]

Without nature, which is objective and always salient—an eternal pedestal—there is always a danger in the evolution of the development of "moral individualism" that this process will be left in "limbo", in the *vide*, the abyss of meaninglessness. Hence, moral individualism, totally à la Kant, is the destiny of western society in particular, and of societies in general, and since the basic driving force behind it is human interaction within society (division of labour), it is also a cause of separation from nature. It occurs with most hesitant steps. It is precarious and bound to endure long periods of institutional adjustment to the inner-driven process of social evolution. Because of its necessary institutional matrix, these steps are bound by the institutional stages of crisis and irregular movements forward. Institutional nature is necessary because—and this was our point of departure—self in its liberation from its external, and hence internal, nature requires socially provided supports for its project of emancipation. This can only be done socially through varieties of social phenomena, all of which can be summed up as "ritualization and symbolization" of recurrent "dense" interaction and reciprocal bonding. Progress in civilization is then mirrored in the development of moral individualism. But owing to the absence of any ontological and/or *a priori* pedestal onto which to rest this growing phenomenon, which is an absolutist moral position à la Kant, institutions are most essential, institutions that will let "moral individualism" float, vibrant and fully meaningful. Durkheim sees this institutional matrix as possible only in national society—from this it should be clear why Durkheim is antithetical to ethnic nationalism—with a type of nationalism that totally negates ethnic, tribal, familial bonds since they are bonds that restrict, constrain and contradict individualism. National society has to be such that it would be indifferent to the individual's primordial origins, yet sustain his/her individuality, subjectivity, and particularisms. Hence, there is a necessary quality to the space in which the individual can best develop, express, and appreciate his/her individuality. The space for providing this optimal ground for particularism is a universalist public space, a public space governed by universalism, and for that, as the most universalist and human-free, the principle is reason, i.e. it has to be a rational space. The way reason is sustained requires ritualization and symbolization, which obviously connects us to the Revolution and its Enlightenment roots.

This is how Durkheim arrives at his national society. National society is for social harmony that at the same time constantly supports moral individualism. For this ultimate concern with self and its precarious existence in the social world of civilization, some see Durkheim as a social psychologist. I leave it to the definers of the term.

Hence Durkheim's project is to create a harmonious civic society, for upholding full freedom for the development of individualism and of the particularism of individuals, thereby enabling them to find their moral shell, as well as a social space external to it, to be maintained by rational, i.e. sociological, processes of collective rituals and symbols, and yet governed by reason.

Hence, civic society and the nation-state as the defender of civic society are for Durkheim a necessary institutional matrix for the development of moral individualism, which in turn identifies civilization as the end point of our emancipation from nature. Yet all this is most precarious because of the non-ontological basis of moral individualism. What Durkheim is doing here is putting Kant into a sociological context by making practical reason a viable, self-sustaining proposition that in itself is not contrary to what Kant stipulated. What is to be done is at times an open question for Durkheim; at other times, it has the implication of a sociological intervention, quite in the Jacobean tradition of the revolution.

In any event what underlies all this harmony and "happy self" is civic national society. This is Durkheim's paradigm, and it lies at the core of the paradigm of modernity.

Durkheim and Kant

Here I want to underline some aspects of Durkheim's Kantianism. The purpose here is to analytically ground Durkheim's Kantian predilections in several ways: how Durkheim formulated his "new science", much in the manner of the "Kantian revolution", and did so most consciously; how he also tried to go beyond Kant and solve Kant's "ontological" riddle to make that solution the necessary postulate of his new science and yet at times failing at it—in his own terms—only to drift back to a pre-Kantian materialism; and, finally, how, in these efforts of absorbing Kant into a "new reality", he thereby, *inter alia*, transcended Kant for a presumed better epistemology. One can readily reconstruct Durkheim's paradigm as a straight imitation of a simplified model of Kantian ontology. My logic here will be, as I declared earlier, analytical. That is, I shall only try to unearth these in part (often) hidden structures in Durkheim's theory—which I shall claim as the Founding Paradigm of sociology—by logical deduction. But these strengths and weaknesses in the Durkheimian paradigm, as the Founding Paradigm of the discipline of Sociology, will, I suggest, also necessarily permeate the overall logic of the analyses in the field. Other "rebellions" in the field can be read either as intellectual frustration with these unresolved epistemological issues inherited from the Durkheimian founding, or as unconscious efforts to resolve the issue. My effort here then, albeit only analytical and deductive, is modest in its scope. It harbours, however, a loftier hope. By logically unearthing these hidden lines of constraint on the Sociological Paradigm at its birth—in the manner of a systematic process of self-reflection—one hopes to open up avenues of building consciousness to dispel the latent frustrations and thereby enabling some of that rebellion to turn into a more conscious effort of "paradigm change", or, better, a more conscious effort of "paradigm reconstruction".

Here, Durkheim's Kantianism is obvious. Yet I shall for a moment or two elaborate some of its aspects in order to begin the argument. I will suggest that Durkheim, and *inter alia* sociology in general, is anchored in the question of Kant's practical reason. Hence, modernity for Durkheim, if it is to be a "harmonious" state, requires a conscious construction. The fragility of the paradigm of modernity for Durkheim was due to its being inherently more unstable than any earlier "cultural system". This was the case because individualism had to be socially constructed and maintained when the individual found its kernel in his/her particularism, and in that pursuit the road was most hazardous since particularism could so easily gravitate to asociality.[13] Previous cultural regimes were not ridden by such tensions, but historical evolution constantly replaced the natural in man with the social and the intellectual, best represented in the world of the modes. (Note the confusion in the two aspects of man!) Furthermore, the social order of the rational, Kant's practical reason, was nowhere to be anchored in the normalcy of society. It had thus to be created a priori, with a Kierkegaardian leap of faith, and to be upheld by a hidden consensus of norms that would only survive by their social collective celebration—nothing innate.

In Weber, a cultural system is forthcoming of itself; it might inhere in a Will to ensure its perpetuation. Weber's system is much less problematical, and its social theory is solved tautologically—a cultural system of moral individualism with its appropriate Will—and hence a cultural system is nothing but the reflection of a Will with a particular bent and orientation. When the Will thins, the cultural system atrophies. Weber could only be pessimistic but not problematizing. Durkheim is optimistic but most problematizing. He is worried and he sees society as most fragile and precarious, yet he is optimistic that it can be "scientifically" mended. Only in this optimism can Durkheim be called a positivist. Durkheim has the self-confidence of a total agnostic, Weber the pessimism of a believer. Durkheim sees chaos lurking behind each social act but is confident of his science to keep it at bay. Weber sees the danger in the anti-Christ but not in the *vide*; Durkheim is worried that the *vide* might allow the anti-Christ to steal the day. "Flattening" of culture is what worries Weber, the emptying of the content of the future Will. For Durkheim the problem is the everlasting possibility of "Willlessness". Durkheim is Kantian in aspiration and thought, Weber perhaps in methodology.

Durkheim gave the republic its creed, its way to chart its political itinerary when that word also means—as it should according to the classics, i.e. Hobbes—the social order that is envisioned.

As an exemplary child of the French Revolution and the Enlightenment, the Durkheimian theory as a whole could become a most effective paradigm for a modernist program of nation-building. It contained the basis of a political summary of the rationalist side of nineteenth-century intellectual achievements, and thus set the political parameters of twentieth-century modernity. Here is not the place to repeat in detail how the end of the nineteenth century stood on the threshold of the modern age, laying its basis and setting its conceptual parameters. Yet in order to recover, for the forthcoming discussion, Durkheim's contribution to political modernity, it might help to underscore some general aspects of Durkheim's "science" in relation to his intellectual context.

Varieties of the Modern

The ideas of the modern penetrated all walks of life in Europe on principle starting from the Enlightenment, whereas the modern, as a social system, a system of social action, would only gain momentum with the French Revolution and become established socially in France and Paris by the end of the nineteenth century when sociological ideas were adopted by many thinkers in Europe. Weber, for example, was a theoretical sociologist but not a paradigmatic sociologist. Ibn Khaldun was a paradigmatic precursor of historical sociology and Marx a true paradigmatic thinker who shared with the sociologists many methodological premises, e.g. the idea of totality, the idea of institutionalization, and the concepts of labour and ideology, but the true sociological paradigm was Durkheim's. He made a deliberate, conscious effort to build the sociological paradigm. It was also a very turn-of-the-century French effort: anti-Descartes, Pascalian with a strong Kantian grid, St Simonian in its futurology, and Rousseauesque in its politics with restraints à la Montesquieu.

The four humours of the modern public domain are: universalism, legal-rational political authority, scientific outlook, and laicism. These are the preconditions for the exercise of moral individualism. The problem however is how to sustain moral individualism as the anchor of practical reason. Three problems arise. The first is with regard to the means for the creation of the public domain necessary for moral individualism to expand. The instruments, political as they are, require collectivist means to achieve individualistic aims. This is a problem of individualism being overshadowed by its instruments. It was, for example, part of the Soviet problem and is very much part of the weakness of the Marxist theory of revolution. Marx creates a world in which moral individualism is to be unchallenged, hence all structural sources of economic power are to be eradicated, but the means undermines the ends. This is a challenge to the practice and not the content of the paradigm.

The second problem is the kidnap of individualism by its illogical extension: the Devil problem. Here, individualism, when disconnected from its moral roots, can be taken over by instrumental reason. This is the atomistic individualism of Bentham and the pragmatism of Dewey, both most radically and successfully eradicated by Durkheim, and hence the roots of the economism of the Neo-classicals. The final and third danger is the endemic alter ego of individualism, which is the *vide*. In this view, Surrealism is the alter ego of individualism, and Max Ernst is Durkheim's Cain. It is against this danger that Durkheim builds his paradigm of the modern, and the Will, as long as it is vibrant—à la Bergson—can keep it from gravitating to its alter ego. The Will is grounded in one of Durkheim's "axiomatic presuppositions" for the science of sociology. Durkheim has three axioms of this nature, explicated in his monograph on methodology. One of the three is the critical idea of totality. Only through the drive to totality can society, in its modern form (i.e. organic solidarity—the mechanical is not really society for Durkheim), survive. It is only thanks to this drive that the individual is kept from drifting to asocialness, one of whose forms is egoistic suicide. For this "totalness" to prevail, any divisive presuppositions are to be shunned. In other words, divisiveness destroys its foundation. This is why, for Durkheim, "class society" undermines society because it is structurally segmented. This is a major problem that will wag the dog. Harmony is necessary for society for this purpose—for moral individualism to be possible and thus to remind us that all these problems are what make moral individualism possible and that moral individualism remains the defining quality of practical reason. Durkheim in this way is most Kantian. The individual, for example, best expands and strives toward its self-realization—always an unending process—in the universalism of the public domain, not in institutions, i.e. no family, no tradition to shackle this "expansiveness". The problem is how to create this totality of universalism, non-segmented, non-familial, non-class, non-tribal, and non-Jewish. In this sense Durkheim's project is Jewish and anti-Jewish at the same time. In one sense it is the Christianization of Judaism, in which Durkheim sees the origins of both individualism and secularism. Durkheim's project coincides, reflects, depends on and furthers the Jewish emancipation, both without and within. It is a part of the "normalization" of French Judaism, normalization in the double French sense, which contrasts with "naturalization" in the American sense. It is a precursor of Léon Blum and later of Mendès-France, the former a failed architect of the modern, the latter the failed curator of the modern. Both are the end points of the Durkheimian modern.

•   •   •   •

Several parenthetical points have to be made here. Both Eksteins and Bauman totally miss the point. Bauman confuses the kidnappers with the victim. Hitler is totally anti-modern, though he used the new techniques of science that the modern inadvertently helped to create. We must be careful to distinguish the contemporary from the modern, technology from civilization, and obsessive punctiliousness from geometry. For example, the problem of using collective means to achieve individualistic ends is again not to describe Hitler. Hitler uses collectivist means to achieve collectivist ends, the *Gemütlichkeit* of community, of communalism. That, I believe, is a sufficient test for distinguishing the individualism that shapes the modern from technology that seeks nature and community. It is not appearances but essences that tell us about paradigms; otherwise the analysis succumbs to the crudest form of pragmatism, which gives us at best a superficial, virtual taxonomy but not science. That is what Bauman and, in his own small way, Eksteins were both guilty of. (For a detailed discussion, see Chapters One and Seven.)

For our logic, on the other hand, the Soviets are an exaggerated extension of the modern, an extension in which the modern turned against itself and against its individualistic logic. The Soviets used collectivist ends to found a community in which moral individualism could for them to be best achieved. Contrary to the use of the term communism, it clearly is anti-communitarian when compared with the Hitler project.[14] In regard to capitalism, Durkheim is not too friendly with it as he presupposes necessary checks to unbounded capitalist accumulation insofar it disrupts social harmony and creates sources of unwarranted power to subvert harmony and the naturalness of progress in the process of society being distantiated from nature.

Yet the paradigm of the modern helped to create the replica of the instrumentalization of capitalism in the practice of Sovietism. It helped to create it because the modern has an innate call to control nature. But this is nature within, and not outside of the individual. It is the capitalist version of the modern that equates the two, to control nature embedding the individual and nature within the self. A true kidnap is not Hitler but the Soviets, a logical extension of the modern in which the instruments take over. This dualism is confusing. With regard to the modern's innate drive to control nature within, this is not anti-*vide* but rather to make the individual, and hence the *vide*, possible. Durkheim, too, is confused by this issue in 1897. He confuses the drive to extricate nature in humans with the need to fill the space against gravitation to the *vide*. These are two contrary processes, and Durkheim in his two different discussions of individualism confuses the issue.[15] Only the expurgation of the natural self makes the *vide* a problem.

The Crisis, the Kidnap,
and the Demise of the Modern

One reason for the demise of the modern was due to neither the Devil nor the Dragon but to its own natural expansion, its very success. A contradiction specific to the paradigm of the modern made it vulnerable to this abduction. That was the case of the rise of social classes. In some sense, historically speaking, this was a consequence of the paradigm's "forward" motion, and the measures it would conjure up were reminiscent of Hobbes and Rousseau. i.e. curbing the free reign of accumulation.[16]

Durkheim was trying to subdue an inner conflict central to the paradigm, a conflict that lay at the core of the paradigm of the modern. This was the conflict between "reason" and the "unreason" the surreal represented. Whereas the economically induced contradiction would only become nascent with the paradigm's successful practice, it was only a potential contradiction. It was not a contradiction within, not part of the essence, but rather an aspect that only became endemic and penetrated its roots when the modern—innocent of any economic theory—found its capitalist practice. There is little to add to Marx's incontestable theory on this matter. For Durkheim, socialism was not a viable proposition since it assumed a segmented, a class-divided society. Socialism could not offer a solution since it was the "totality" in its practice that could hold society together and ensure the participation of individuals. Socialism in its divided position could lose society for the sake of remedying the ills of the economy. Durkheim's solution to the problem was to put restraints on the power of capital and not allow economic power to become social power, which would only result in an even worse type of segmentation.[17]

Dilemmas and Contradictions:
Nationalism and the Paradigm of the Modern

Dilemmas are contextual. They are external to the paradigm. Contradictions are internal. They are part of the essence of the paradigm. Both arise in the paradigm's successful practice.

In its historical practice, nationalism became the nemesis of the paradigm of the modern although it did not have to be, nor was it for Durkheim. It was a solution to a particular dilemma in the face of an internal conflict—not a contradiction, but a conflict between Dada and "proper grammar". It laid the groundwork for a dilemma of the "social order": how to create continuity of social action when God was dead and traditional rationality had lost its sway, how to keep individuals participating, how to make society possible, how to keep Beckett's "Maloneism" at bay. Nationalism was Durkheim's solution. Nationalism as a collective ideology of "society building" is a version of this dilemma, a subset of a larger collective application: how to induce sacrifice, extract surplus labour, and impart unity of direction to the wills of individuals.

That special relationship, the dilemma posed by individualism and the infinite possibility of "non-participation", is one of the key equations in this study.

In Durkheimian vision Civic Nationalism would short-circuit both the danger of Dada and the rise of social classes—two theoretically very different problems, one part of a dilemma, the other the result of a contradiction. Nationalism was a remedy if it could be kept under control, kept from exploding, but even then it had a fundamentally contradictory aspect. It was collectivist, and a collectivism worse than socialism. Since in the latter, collectivism was assumed to be only a passing phase until economic inequality in terms of economic power could be eliminated, at which point individuals could emerge in their full moral individualism, whereas the individual in any form and any time frame was antithetical to nationalism. That was the contradiction: nationalism as an instrument both for purging the primordial to enable individualism to arise, and for offsetting the reign of Dada and the conflict of class-divided society as a collectivist solution through and through, and hence unable to recognize the legitimacy of the moral individualism it was meant to serve.

Durkheim's paradigm—compared to Freud's, for example—could not in its rigour extend itself to the individual psyche, and hence was left with the catechisms of the modern à la Weber—free press, legal rational authority, limits on accumulation—which civic nationalism could provide but with one great danger, namely, that it obfuscated the individual and dismissed its morality. Furthermore, nationalism, civic or not, had no inner limits to its expansion without constant vigilance and self-reflection. It could only have external restraints: one of which would be communalism, which harboured an identity most incongruent with Durkheim's modern individualist universe, and the other Sovietism which destroyed the self by absorbing it into a collectivist ideology of a dictated "volonté générale!"

Dilemmas and Contradictions: Putting Civic Nationalism in the Service of the Modern and the Durkheimian Dilemma

For earnest practitioners of the modern like Durkheim, the greater danger the modern faced was rooted in what I have called the Dragon. The Dragon is the *vide* that the modern harbours at its core. It is its own doing and inherent to it, whereas nationalism arises from a particular vulnerability but is not part of modern's necessary logic; it is external to it in its origins. The Dragon appears to be of different form but it is of the same substance; it is not antithetical to the paradigm but is its extension into its negative. This is why Pascal and the *vide* are more modern than Descartes and geometry. This is what makes Ionesco so modern, Beckett so apt, Malone such a big threat,[18] and this is also what Durkheim was writing about in *Suicide*, in egoistic suicide, which, I believe, is the most representative of his work and the best manifestation of his sociological paradigm. T. S. Eliot in his conservatism best describes the unredeemable *vide* at the heart of the modern. It is for the challenge of that *vide* which made Durkheim to take the road of Kant's practical reason and Pascal's "as if" to not to eliminate Eliot's insight but to overlay it with "make belief". Durkheim's embracing the Dragon would have been a more substantive remedy which Durkheim also recognizes. He is split in his own language, at times in the same paragraph of his writings.[19]

Durkheim's fundamental question, and the *raison d'être* of his theory, the very reason for Durkheim's gigantic edifice, the sociological paradigm, is however "how to keep the Dragon at bay" for the social order to be maintained and the individuals' participation is unabatedly forthcoming. It was Durkheim's great virtue to understand that the Dragon can never be destroyed as long as the modern is alive since it is an intrinsic part of it. It is the main ingredient of "moral individualism". It is of its own substance, unlike the Devil which can be destroyed, beaten to extinction.[20] So the ultimate task is to tame the Dragon and enable the modern to live with it.

This was not an issue of psychology but a trademark of his new science, sociology. Durkheim's great wisdom was to recognize that questions of identity and psychology lie outside the realm of his sociology.

Durkheim never issues "correctives" for individual identities, nor is he concerned about the question of identity; he is exclusively concerned with the social space at the end of the nineteenth century when new identities emerged and psychologies ran amok.

The Surreal lies at the heart of the Modern. That was Durkheim's great discovery. In recognizing the limits of the paradigm of the modern, instead of trying to deny the surreal he tried to tame it; he thought sociology gave him the charter to do that. His new science would give him the rules for expunging the surreal from the social, an effort that, in the end, brought nationalism, albeit of a soft civic kind, in through the backdoor to nonetheless ultimately throw "moral individualism" overboard. Essences brook no compromises!

The more immediate and "essential" for Durkheim was to subdue an inner conflict central to the paradigm of the modern, a conflict that lay at its core. This was the conflict between "reason" and the "unreason" that the surreal represented.

A moderate "civic nationalism", which Durkheim saw as an antidote to Dada, to subdue the Dragon of unreason would later in others' hands become an instrument for fighting the politics of class divisions. The discourse of the modern would be hijacked to counter the threat of working class revolution. This hijack was equally practised by the capitalist societies and the so-called communist societies. Communism would become a shorthand, an imaginary vehicle for the modern compressed in time—the metaphor of skipping stages—for achieving its ends, yet so compressed that the individualism that defined the very premise of the modern would be squeezed out. Communism in the name of the modern left out, if not fought against, the very reasons for the rise of the modern. The modern was for establishing the groundwork for the constant *Bildung* of moral individualism, whereas nationalism and communism were collectivist instruments for these ends and hence projects whose means would constantly undermine their very ends—ultimately undermining the very basis of the "good life" in trying to pave the way to it, the expansive well-being of moral individualism, moral as free and choosing individual.

Conclusion: Allying with the Dragon

In the face of Durkheimian dilemma the only way to offset the *vide*—ever-present in the project of the Modern once man is so radically severed from nature—would be through the workings of Dada for the humour it interjects. Durkheim in his linearity instead took "civic nationalism" as the way to overcome the *vide*. Theoretically speaking, that was not a wrong track, but "civic nationalism" faced two hazards in its practice. One, it had no natural, innate limits and thus could easily get "carried away" in its unwarranted hubris to "legislate the good". Secondly, at worst, it could be hijacked to nullify all the liberal (J.S. Mill), individualism-expanding premises of the modernist paradigm. If Durkheim had been sufficiently dialectical, he could have cast surrealism in a beneficent role to safeguard his paradigm instead of trying to purge the modern of its innate surreal—which he had been so perceptive as to note—through the guardians of the republic, however selfless they might be. From my perspective, the *vide* in Dada is to be celebrated for its "system-maintaining"[21] qualities. Is not Charlie Chaplin, or even better, Buster Keaton with his "expressionless" expression, the savior of the paradigm of the modern?

For Durkheim the best way to battle the Devil, I suggest, would be to ally with the Dragon, to appropriate it as part of the unrecognized essence.

Durkheim's Inadvertent Hijack

For Durkheim, every society needs solidarity (moral coherence as I roughly translate it here), and some need it more than others. The paradigm of the modern needs it more as it is the result of social individuation with moral individualism at its core. Moral individualism flourishes in a solidarity secured by a moderate civic nationalism akin to the civic patriotism found in Classical Athenian democracy à la Pericles.[22]

Durkheim, as I said before, was naïve about power and politics. His choice of civic nationalism, however innocent and benevolent, still harboured the seeds of the modern's possible hijack!

This Durkheimian political project inadvertently involved the possibility of a double jeopardy. Nationalism of any kind was a collectivist instrument, and once checks were not in place and vigilance was relaxed, it could, in its effervescence, undermine moral individualism with the aid of the political classes and their antithetical interests. Secondly, nationalism could crawl out of its bottle in a crisis and be kidnapped by the Devil to destroy the very thing it was intended to serve, moral individualism. This is what happened in 1914 to undermine Durkheim's paradigm; and the war, in defense of moral individualism—as Durkheim saw it—took away Durkheim's son as well. Durkheim must have been a sad man indeed when he died soon after, in 1917.

Nonetheless two questions remain to be solved for Durkheim's desired social order. The first is the economic contradiction which remains inescapably nascent when modern is lodged in capitalism. I will not deal with that question here but refer to Marx and Claus Offe.

The second question more ever present within the Durkheimian perspective, and is more phenomenologically innate as it pertains to a more fundamental, a priori, issue of how social is to be all-salient. This is yet not an essentialist issue. It is not laden in individual's "nature" but only a question which pertains to the practice of the paradigm hence theoretically its cure—to use Durkheim's own medical language—is socially possible. This relates to the issue of participation, or the reproduction of the will to participate without shrinking the space for a robust self-identity. Let me conclude with that discussion.*

Instability in the Paradigm of the Modern: The Question of Reproduction of the Will

How the "will" to socially participate is secured and how a robust self is sustained remains ontologically a question in the backroom of even in the most democratically constituted civic societies. The question is how much "self" can develop in participation? In other words, if universalist citizenship is the cradle of a developing self, whether the same citizenship allows a robust self to aggrandise itself or it does at times get threatened by that citizenship, especially in times of crisis. In that sense citizenship is a very tricky concept, certainly double-edged: it is all giving and yet at times all demanding. That balancing act is key to the success of the modern liberal regimes.

---

*   I am most grateful to Seyla Benhabib to raise that critique. The final formulation is mine. It is an attempt to account for Benhabib's challenge, within my theoretical framework.

235

Notes

1. This is my rendition of Durkheim's essay, "The Dualism of Human Nature and Its Social Condition" in *Emile Durkheim 1858–1917*, ed. Kurt H. Wolff (Columbus: Ohio State University Press, 1960), pp. 325-40.

2. Émile Durkheim, *Suicide: A Study in Sociology* (New York: Free Press, 1997).

3. Donald Black, *The Behaviour of Law* (London: Academic Press, 1976).

4. R. D. Laing, *Sanity, Madness, and the Family* (London: Penguin, 1964).

5. It might also be what Pierre Birnbaum observed, in *Sur un nouveau moment antisémite: "Jour de colère"* (Paris: Fayard, 2015), as the rise of anti-Semitism in France: this is new and not the old, and it is part of the rebellion against the pax republicana as Islamic fundamentalism in Turkey is; it is not the old thing but new (see Nilüfer Göle, *Modern Mahrem: Medeniyet ve Örtünme*, İstanbul: Metis Yayınları, 1991). Thus, what is important here is that these new realms of primordialism, though we are trying to call them old, are nevertheless very different. They are different because they bear the radical marks of modernity. The old primordiality was ascriptive, quiet, often subterranean and open to some type of juggle and negotiation. The new realms of primordiality are self-created and socially generated, they are adoptive and find their existence in their expressivity, in their assabiyah (see Faruk Birtek, "Recasting Contemporaneity – A Hypothesis in Rereading the New Politics of Localism: The New Assabiyah of the Town – Thomas Hardy Revisited", *The Post-Modern Abyss and the New Politics of Islam: Assabiyah Revisited*, ed. Faruk Birtek and Binnaz Toprak, Istanbul: Bilgi University Press, 2011). Hence, the new primordiality and the old that the new tries to recall are radically different. The new is due to modernity's embrace of the old and its transformation without recognition. Now, of course, the unresolved question is to what extent identity has to be constructed within the exclusivity of primordialism, and to what extent civil society, without taking on the even more restrictive nature of the new primordiality, can provide that realm.

6. Faruk Birtek, "Emergence and Limits of National Political Identities",

Identities, Affiliations, and Allegiances, ed. Seyla Benhabib, Ian Shapiro and Danilo Petranovich (Cambridge: Cambridge University Press, 2007).

7. Max Weber, *The Protestant Work Ethic and the Spirit of Capitalism* (New York: Scribner's, 1950).

8. Different views on that but my logic compels me to think that Durkheim chose a studied public indifference.

9. E. Tiryakian, "Durkheim, Mathiez, and the French Revolution", *Archives Européennes de Sociologie,* Volume 2 (1988).

10. Émile Durkheim, *Division of Labor in Society* (London: Gardners Books, 1993).

11. Ibid.

12. Yet Durkheim is inconsistent about this issue: sometimes it is nature in us that is to be suppressed, and sometimes it is the problem of the lacuna created by nature receding within us and the ebb and flow of the "self" filling that space—ebb and flow because it is not the natural self but the socially constructed self. I am taking the second version because it fits the paradigm, as I shall show below, and not the former, though dates oscillate.

13. Durkheim never uses, for example, language or linguistic capacity to ground a rational practical reason in ensuring the rationality of the public space, as Habermas later does so admirably.

14. Mussolini is a strange combination, always confused, ambivalent and intellectually opportunistic, with a Sorelian understanding that puts the Will ahead of the idea. Perhaps that is why Mussolini succeeded to instill more voluntarism than either Hitler or the Soviets. All these are perhaps responses to the rise of individualism. Hitler identifies the individual in his communion with community, a communion based on purity and naturalness of power. The Soviets mechanize to free the individual from nature and eradicate the source of economic power that would undermine the rise of moral individualism. Mussolini has his corporate structures to secure the rise of the individual in the immediate every day and work environment, perhaps close to Durkheim via Sorel, but more Sorel and the instrument of the Will than

Durkheim. The infusion of the Will destroys the Durkheim project as there is too much Will and not enough of the moral of moral individualism. We must be careful here to distinguish the term modern from contemporary, also capitalism from modern. They all overlap but refer to different phenomena.

15. Émile Durkheim, *Suicide*, p. 214.

16. The French solution went even farther than that; it was Napoleonic. The Swedes and the Germans more brought labour in as co-partner with capital. How much this is a continuation of Sorel on the one hand and Italian fascism on the other I cannot judge! The state would come in as the collective economic interest through ownership. Even today the French state's ownership of industry exceeds fifty per cent of major companies. That would eliminate potential conflict on a small scale, but then it totally turned the state into a major area of class conflict over issues of importance. Classes then had to fight no more at the level of industry or the shop floor alone but for hegemony. In that context, the politics of the left would be to elevate all issues to major issues by implicating the state: a system of stability in the short run but a cause of major instability in the long run.

17. Émile Durkheim, *Socialism and Saint-Simon* (New York: Collier Books, 1962); Faruk Birtek, "The Turkish Adventures of the Durkheim Paradigm: Does History Vindicate M. Labriola", *Il Politico* Volume LVI Number 1 (1991): 107–146.

18. Samuel Beckett, *Malone Dies: A Novel* (New York: Grove, 1977).

19. Robert N. Bellah, ed., *Emile Durkheim: On Morality and Society* (Chicago: The University of Chicago Press, 1973); Durkheim, *Suicide*, p. 214.

20. Robert N. Bellah, ed., *Emile Durkheim: On Morality and Society.*

21. David Lockwood, "Some Remarks on the Social System", *The British Journal of Sociology*, Volume 7, Number 7 (1956): 134-146. I am grateful to İlkay Sunar for this reminder.

22. Robert N. Bellah, ed., *Emile Durkheim: On Morality and Society.*

Chapter Seven

A Stylized History of the Modern*

Defining the Modern

Here I will turn to the study of the Paradigm of the Modern in its history. In its historical grounding, I will search for the elements of its paradigm's essence. I shall in the most exploratory sense historically situate the paradigm. This is not *history* in the pure sense of the word as historians practise it. It is a stylized history. It will look at the birth of the Paradigm of the Modern in its historical context, which is described only in regard to the formation of the Modern's particular essence. It is hence most intuitive and exploratory and can never be finite.[1]

Before I begin I must emphasize that the definition of the Modern is no less contentious than in the case of the elephant and the seven blind men. From defining it in terms of the revolutionary advance of technology to the enhanced rationalism of the human project, hundreds of authors have marshalled hundreds of definitions, at times at odds with each other.

In regard to the question of "What is the Modern?", leaving the seventeenth-century origin of the word aside, axiomatically, as my concept of paradigmatic essences (above) would require, I insist on one definition. The Modern is the social organization of everyday life for the ascendance of moral individualism—a definition I take as most loyal to Durkheim. The four pillars of the Paradigm of the Modern are universalism, laicism (not secularism), legal-rational political authority,

---

*   For a definition of stylized history please see Chapter Five.

and the rationalist/scientific outlook. They were extensively discussed in Chapter One.

The protagonist of the Modern predates the Modern by three centuries. It is Hamlet—Shakespeare the-great-clairvoyant. The art form of the Modern is cinema, not only for the Lumière brothers, but also for its great illumination of the spirit of the age.

Let me now turn to how the conceptual/normative essence of the paradigm connects with its narrative. The Modern, originating in the world of ideas of the Enlightenment as a social paradigm directly descending from the French Revolution, found its ultimate practice in the Third Republic. Many ideas of the Modern were disseminated to various parts of the Continent in the century following the French Revolution. Voltaire and his iconoclasts sat at the helm. There were many ideas of the Modern, for example, in Germany, some trickled and crossed the channel to Britain, the Italian Risorgimento was based on many of its borrowed promises, and, above all, Napoléon took many of its principles across the continent. Germany on each side of the Elbe would have different histories because Napoléon had established himself for a short duration in the West, on the Rhine but not on the Elbe.[2] One could talk about the degree of modernity and gauge it by the intellectual distance from Paris.

Russia probably would have had a different history if Napoléon had not been defeated on the doorsteps of Moscow and the "modernization" of Russia had not been aborted. The Soviet Revolution perhaps might then never have had the reasons it had for its radical inception. The Soviet Revolution in this language was nothing but an extreme political feat to institutionalize, in the extreme, most of the aspirations of the Modern, and with a vengeance, as the initial "modernization" could not succeed. This is not to say that Count Witte and others did not bring modern institutions to Russia, but they were restricted to the economy and were most superficial and partial—"habits" of the Modern but not the paradigm itself. The Soviet Revolution was possible because that introduction had already been made; yet it remained unfulfilled and superficial. The Soviet Revolution was to complete the picture with a vengeance and hence in excess of the Modern in the name of the Modern.

If Bonaparte had spread the ideas of the Revolution, the final coherent practice of the Modern, as a universe, as a paradigm, as the true child of the Revolution, would prevail only a hundred years after the revolution in France and more precisely in Paris—as France as a totality experienced more of an ebb and flow motion with regard to the Revolution's institutions: the Church and the peasant resisting in the countryside and the centre imposing itself on the countryside with uneven movements. The Paris Fair and the Eiffel Tower, I suggest, best expressed the Revolution as the paradigm of modernity in 1889, which I take to be the beginning of its hundred years.

The Dreyfus affair totalized it to make it a world view with a collective Will. It was the latent opposition to the *ancien régime* which led to the Dreyfusard mobilization that the Modern needed in 1895 to establish itself as the dominant paradigm. It then had its cultural hegemony. It shaped the sensibilities, the desires, the aspirations. It breathed certainty into its actors and bred self-assuredness in its practitioners. It became the dominant world view.

The early ideas of the Modern had penetrated all walks of life in Europe starting from the Enlightenment, but the Modern as a social system, as a system of social action, would only gain momentum with the French Revolution and become socially established in France and Paris by the end of the nineteenth century, in the world of the *fin de siècle*.

Earlier, the ideas of the Modern would penetrate the existing universes, challenge them, and find a place for themselves in the interstices of the existing world views. Many individuals had gone out on a limb for its anticipatory practice, but before 1895 the Modern had not been a collectively reinforcing practice with the bonding mutuality of its practices among the actors. Before 1895 it was not a basis for a new solidarity. For Durkheim as a sociologist his fundamental concern, the concern that made him build, develop, and methodologically, put his sociology on a high intellectual pedestal, was how to make the Paradigm of the Modern the social dogma of the *fin de siècle*. It was to make it a viable and lasting proposition notwithstanding its fragility with a dead God and the individual put in his stead. It was the Dreyfus affair that gave it that impetus. I take the social mobilization of the Dreyfus affair as the benchmark for the beginning of the modern as a social paradigm.

Only a sophisticated modern like Durkheim would think that it was not enough that the content of the ideas was more valid—in whatever sense one means—but rather that there were other social ingredients to secure their salience. Sociology for Durkheim was a science in systematic theory construction for understanding and devising ways of securing the prevalence of the "dogma of the Modern". The sociology of the Modern had to be the Modern itself in practice, in process, in application.

The Modern was to create a life-space for the individual to best develop and expand himself/herself for his/her *Bildung*, a *bona fide* Enlightenment project. That, of course, also lies at the core of the Hobbesian question of order: how to maintain individualism and still have the social context for that individualism to be fulfilled in its aspiration and volition. Marx had the same question: how can we create a context—now economically defined—in which all the promise of individualism can be fulfilled without the hazards of its practice destroying its premises? How to save the ideals of individualism from self-destructing in their practice?

The practices of individualism are, of course, very much present in the Renaissance. Machiavelli is almost Benthamite in his pragmatism yet by his genius escapes Bentham's innate confusion. Castiglione's courtier is most individualistic in his drives, and Boccaccio in his narrative is indeed most individualistic in his escapades, and so cynical about tradition and religion. Yet in all these individualisms, including a proto-modern like Laclos's, the individuals are only two-dimensional. They have all the behaviors and the attitudes, all the freedoms and liberties, of individualism but without its purpose. The Enlightenment brought the purpose to individualism that the two-dimensional individualism of the Renaissance had not had. In the Enlightenment it is self-expansion, self-education, self-growth. In fact, here now individualism could be God's creation, and it is in appreciation of God that individual self-expansion would be practiced. Kant is the best example of that. God is relegated to heaven. He is there only as the first cause. Nietzsche's dead God is about the individual "cannibalizing" God in the totemic sense, anthropologically speaking.[3]

For the Modern and sociology, we have to "get into the mind" of Durkheim, in Weber's sense of the *Verstehen*, for a gateway to the Modern and sociology. He best represented this paradigm of the sociological modern because he was the best who reflected on it to save it from its possible slumber. He might also have had a personal interest in saving it as the son of a rabbi who turned lay when sent to Paris for his rabbinical education. He personally was one proto-typical story of the Jewish emancipation so widespread in the late nineteenth century and so crucial in shaping the period. The secular Jewish contribution to modern European thought is immeasurable.[4]

Dating the Modern as a New Paradigm

The birthplace of the Modern was *fin-de-siècle* Paris. Concurrently but separately three mental historical processes ruled the day to set the broad matrix in the development of the Paradigm of the Modern, in the midst of the torrential expansion of industrialism and the consequent urbanism in the second half of the nineteenth century. They were nationalism, the emancipation of European Jewry, both within and without, and the undisputed hegemony of the scientific outlook. Each process gave tremendous fuel to the advance of the Modern but each also made it so unstable in the middle run. Let me explain.

Nationalism, which took up a good part of our discussion of the Modern's instability, at the least constantly pulled the Modern to collectivist solutions for the ultimate end of moral individualism, a theoretically non-contradictory yet in practice a very contradictory process (see Chapter Five). The scientific outlook at times made the Modern transcend its public domain boundedness and extend in its excessive hubris to delve into the world of the private. Lastly, the Modern as the venue of Jewish emancipation often developed into logically unsustainable critiques of the *ancien régime*. Their definitive place was the new-urban context after the industrial revolution. In terms of the Jewish emancipation, the urban, anti-*shtetl* nature of the context was of most crucial significance.

The Paradigm of the Modern was strictly and exclusively hatched in the new urban context—a bias, I will argue, that had an immediate consequence for the later challenges to the paradigm. Durkheim's theory's urban context could not accommodate the question of the traditional village. When it tried to intrude, the paradigm got paralyzed, and when it succeeded in the intrusion, it energized the village to find its radical defeat.[5] This exclusively urban context of the Modern thus played funny tricks on the Paradigm of the Modern.

In this new urban-centredness, "country" acquired a new definition! The new urban had the hustle and bustle of the new city, with individuals running in a habit hitherto unknown, and there is a lot of smell of cheap coal and smog that burns the eyes and the nostrils; the weekend in the country was now an extension of the urban. It is its imagined antithesis, and meaningful only with that urban foul air and mist that citizens escape from. This is, of course, neither the country of before nor the country that survives alongside the urban's own countryside, often unbeknownst to the urbanites themselves.

The Modern created by France in its different ways structured the globe between 1889 and 1989. It is a social paradigm with a political vision, and with a clear purpose in its political practice, i.e. it is not utopian. Its practice is very much at its core. My claim is that there is no Modern other than the sociological modern, i.e. the discipline of sociology and the Paradigm of the Modern are coterminous, nay more than that, they have a complete overlap as they are the same thing.[6]

For us, chronologically speaking, the Modern starts with the Dreyfus affair, between the first court ruling and the second. It is the "affair" that makes the Modern—the Modern as a social paradigm—the paradigm to rule, the paradigm that becomes the "obvious", the root of "common sense". Gramsci's is a chicken and egg problem.[7] Gramsci is a brilliant observer yet often theoretically confused. Is it common sense that makes the ruling class or the obverse? Gramsci certainly implies the latter. I am not sure that that has been the best analytical track. It loads history with too much conspiracy, and with too much instrumental intention. Here my position is that common sense, which the social reproduces, confirms and substantiates the "ruling classes". We can know that only retrospectively, notwithstanding the brave efforts of Lukács and Goldmann.

Returning to the Dreyfus affair, it was the Affair that matters for my analysis, and not the court case or Dreyfus himself. He eventually gets exonerated and reinstated but with little ado, just a brief ceremony at Champ de Mars, that was all! By then the Affair was over. But it had then established itself. Here is what I read into the "affair" to make 1889 the starting point for the Modern and not 1870 as Stuart Hughes had done in his still seminal work, seminal for his insight and intuition. The Affair is the final establishment of the "urban". To be part of it was to be part of the urban, the urbane and urbanity. This mattered psychologically—i.e. identity-wise—for many educated young men of the provincial lycées who had come to Paris. It made them part of the city, part of the new, part of the progress, *l'avenir*, and crucially perhaps, it made them march with Zola.

This was the victory over the *ancien régime* which certainly had not been tucked away even after a century of the Bastille. The 14th of July could only come to be celebrated a few years before 1889, in 1883. My argument is that the Dreyfus affair created the movement within which the new identity as urbanite and Parisian could be so readily constructed with euphoria. This euphoric dimension is of ultimate importance as Durkheim in his sociology reminds us on other occasions. Zola gave the assurance for the new self-esteem that the movement created for its adherents. After Dreyfus, urban hegemony is finally established. The country is now the rustic for weekends, picnics and the outings. It would later become a source of solace and tranquility, a desired absence, an abode of escape, in a way no men of the country would or could talk about. The notion of the "campagne" is created with the Dreyfus affair when the provincial *lycéen* had become Parisian. This is why I take the Affair as the crucible in which the Modern was forged as a paradigm, as a cauldron of sensibilities, as the source of the new common sense, of the new Will, the new collective mentality.

The Essentialist Fixing of Culture: Paris

Let me start with Paris to demonstrate what I mean as the "essentialist fixing" of the sensibilities, which I shall here identify with the cities they best represent. I will take the city as the embodiment of that particular sensibility. Paris reacts to its *belle époque* in the form of extreme cerebral rationalist individualism. I take Paris at the turn of the century as having eventually come into its own and having left its imprint on the movement to modernity at that moment. Paris in 1900 is at the height of its own definition and not a "gare"—a metaphor Eksteins uses to dismiss Paris's modernity at the end of the century.[8] Indeed, if Paris is a "gare", it is because it is the most international, the most cosmopolitan of cities, and that is what underlies its superiority and marks its centrality in shaping what, in retrospect, I would call the ultimate "Modern".

I believe a good contrast would be the Secession Building in Vienna. This extraordinary building—a gift by the Wittgenstein family of the secular Jewish population ("community" would be a misnomer)—was to envelope the individual, to provide it with a new abode but only as a recluse. Klimt was most traditionalist in his temper notwithstanding his extraordinary individualistic techniques. Nolde could be seen as an artist panicked by his sudden discovery of individualism, whereas in France individualism is optimistic, and self-confident to the degree of arrogance, which is perhaps what made Durkheim worry about its innate fragility. It indeed impacted the world exactly with that sensibility, and impacted it most profoundly and enduringly with a fatal hubris. I claim the Modern is not about Nietzsche but about Kant's moral individualism juxtaposed with Bentham.[9]

Eksteins takes Berlin after 1930 and Hitler as the representative of the Modern, whereas I take Durkheim and Paris and the Third Republic as the *bona fide* modern. In my categories Hitler is neither the Modern nor a rebellion against the Modern—I take rebellion as a response from within, like Dada and the Surrealists. Hitler is a reaction to the threat of the Modern and not even to the Modern itself. The Modern had not come to Germany, only its extensions were appearing on the horizon in the form of the Weimar Republic.

In terms of art forms, I suggest Impressionism is the way the Modern transcends itself to redefine itself. Impressionism is both the harbinger of the Modern and its antithesis. Impressionism is a search for a remedy for the Modern's cerebral hubris, which injected so much fragility into the paradigm. On the other hand, at a later period the appearance of Expressionism and Dada are rebellions against the Modern at its very core, which the Modern desperately and brutally represses through Art Deco, which I claim is a true betrayal of the Modern. It is the form carried to its extreme and the abandonment of the spirit of the Modern. The Modern in its maturity had become an "iron cage" (Weber) for the tormented emergent self. The Bauhaus is the purging of the self, a tool of repression that murders its subject. Art Nouveau, on the other hand, beautifies the Modern without touching its essence. It is the self-confidence of the Modern which enables it for such a dance of seven veils. The Eiffel Tower is the Modern with a touch of Art Nouveau without any right angles, thus contrasting so well with the Art Deco of a later period.

Fin-de-siècle Paris was the centre of the universe. Every artist, every intellectual had to experience it. To understand the centrality of Paris in the world imagination, roughly from the *fin de siècle* to the decade after the war, one should go to the visitors to Paris in that period.[10] If today Paris glitters, it is no different from Dubai or Singapore in the current imagination of the outsiders. *Fin-de-siècle* Paris was the magnet, and other big cities were refashioned after Paris in habit, lifestyle, and urban architecture. A million examples could be quoted but one out of many is Joseph Roth.[11] Roth tells in his biographical book how mesmerized he was by Paris though he had spent his entire youth in Vienna and Berlin. Paris's exceptionalism is striking in his writings. But I want to go to the extreme. When the Nazis occupied Paris, one is struck to note how much the Germans had been in awe of the city and felt somewhat inferior to its citizens. This attitude contrasts well with the way they viewed the Ukrainians and the Russians as Jewish and Bolshevik, and hence unable to, they thought, fight German might. How they abused and massacred them with self-righteousness only later to face their great disaster at Stalingrad.[12] One example of how different their attitude was in Paris is evident in an episode. When a madam of a salon visited the commander of the German occupying force to tell him that she would not allow the German officers to visit her establishment in their uniforms, the same officers would come the next day in their finest civil attire.

Hitler visited Paris only once at a very early hour of the morning for only a few hours in a motor car that took him to Trocadéro. The photograph of Hitler overlooking the Eiffel Tower, I feel, captures Hitler at a unique moment of reserved modesty and perhaps awe. The last commander of Paris, General Dietrich von Choltitz, did not obey Hitler's orders to blow up the cathedrals of the city as he exited—most extraordinary for a German general to violate an order from his superiors. Paris was saved for today.

This discussion should show what I mean by the "essentialist fixing" of culture in the particular sensibility of a cultural capital. In identifying these sensibilities with their cities and comparing them in these terms, it should be understood that empirically other currents also coexisted. My point is that at a particular time, for a period, a particular sensibility clearly comes to prevail and shape all others to various degrees, and, in this homogeneity, it influences the world. What Eksteins (1989) and his earlier art critique had observed was not the decline of Paris as evinced in her cosmopolitanism. It is exactly this sensibility that defines the period and homogenizes all else and rules France.

Paris's sensibility represented the Modern, the future, the way the new would be cast in the institutions of the Third Republic, its individualism. Durkheim's is the great feat of making that individualism a social phenomenon as opposed to the version of Bentham and Dewey, which Durkheim so successfully destroys in a critique for it being atomistic and socially disconnected.[13] Durkheim creates the science of society with individualism at its core, at its pinnacle. That is so majestic of Durkheim, making a science by synthesizing two seemingly opposed phenomena. Paris is as modern as its total rejection of the *ancien régime*, with its middle-class egalitarianism, its impatience with decorative form, with its secularism, its laicism, and its focus on the self rather than the forms of social etiquette. Here once more I completely disagree with Eksteins. He sees Berlin as the harbinger of the Modern, whereas for me it is an archaic revival and a reaction to the Modern until Berlin fractures into black and red after the war. If he is correct and Hitler represents the Modern, what then of Marx's brilliant reading of the German question, "Critique of Hegel's Philosophy of Right", in which he sees Germany as incurably ridden with its unpurged feudalism and only donning the instruments and utensils of modernity? Finally, for us, the Germans had already reneged on the Modern when they burned down the Leuven library for punishing a few snipers in 1914.

Eksteins in his critique of the Modern is more rustic and in line with early nineteenth-century yearning for the primitive and the native, indeed without any seeds of the Modern in it. Nietzsche, who is very different from the pursuers of the pure and the spirit in the rustic, is the critic of the Modern but also its most astute adherent. Nietzsche is tormented by the Modern, hence very much in it, and is fragmented, or better, his soul is fractured. Nietzsche is the alter ego, the other side of the Modern, and German spiritualism[14] is an authentic reaction to the Modern. Until Berlin fractures, for us, Berlin embodies the militarism and efficiency that are pursued in the archaic mode of authoritarianism and paternalism that the Kaiser so well personified. Berlin is not modern until it fractures and the Red is the Modern at its "beyond"; the Red—the Left—is the Modern of the future. The revolution of 1920 and the Spartacist movement are what epitomize the Modern in Berlin eventually, perhaps because they are so anti-modern in sensibility that the Modern in Germany could only come at its extreme and at its margin. The reaction once more, in the black, is reaction in the form of the archaic. Finally, in the Weimar Republic, the Modern settles in Berlin but only to remain unstable.

Mood in *fin-de-siècle* Paris

When we move to the close of the century, Paris as we know it today had already been built. This is the period of the end of the grand illusion: grand ideas and common people intermingling most comfortably. Background mattered in some circles and not others, and these found a way to cohabit. In England, the old school prevailed far more *en rigueur*, but in France the urban middle class had replaced it all. Clemenceau most typified the French conscience; thus, as Romanticism had completely died out, and a new consciousness, tormented more deeply but also better managed, had become more the core of things, minds had become fully accustomed to their innate yawn. Rimbaud's shadow had grown bigger than him.

Paris and the *fin de siècle* "fix" the Modern in its paradigmatic mold, the mold that *defines* this text. The Lumière brothers had just opened the cinema, which would soon become the major vehicle for shaping the sensibilities of the urban population *en masse*, to accompany the new poetry and fiction. Transport is still the train, cars will start to make inroads as the mode of transport of the bourgeoisie, but the tram is still the vehicle of this period, and the airplane as a means of intercontinental transport will need half a century to prevail. Photography is still only an extension of picture painting and clearly in the realm of the artists and professionals and not an instrument of the ordinary household.

This relatively small transformation in the technologies of everyday practice notwithstanding, in ideas the epoch was most radical. The new ideas constituting a mindset are epitomized in the city of Paris. By the end of the century, Paris as we know it today had just been built—it is not the Île Saint-Louis that today represents Paris but it is the boulevard and the majestic residential buildings that represent the Paris of the postcards. The Arc de Triomphe is the lynchpin of the new understanding of the power of the French state, and in its midst sits a totally new sentiment of patriotism, the flame that rekindles the spirits of the war dead. This is novel as it puts the common man as the war hero at the centre of the common conscience, and not the church but a pagan public monument to house the flame. In contrast to the Arc de Triomphe, Sacré-Cœur is a pudding for the weekend. What is, however, to surpass the hilltop Sacré-Cœur is the Eiffel Tower, which I take as the defining structure of the period, and the events of the Dreyfus decade, the process that transforms the minds and fits them to the new mold. Durkheim is unthinkable without the victory of the Dreyfusards, and the universalism, anti-primordialism, individualism, and publicness of reason as the four components that make up the Modern are pumped to every cell of the paradigm by the Dreyfusard mobilization.

Unequivocally, the Radical Socialists are the political party of the age of the Paradigm of the Modern, and the professional classes the carriers of the new ideology. The rise of the party to overwhelm its rivals is, to my mind, dated by the first celebration of the revolution as Bastille Day in 1878, its hero is *le soldat inconnu* and the poet is Apollinaire, and its two sciences are Medicine and Sociology, the two aspects of the "human condition". The representative scientists of the age are Mme Curie and Émile Durkheim, the thinkers André Gide and Paul Valéry as one. Underlying their rationalism, always ever present, is the fear of the universal *vide*, reminding all of the narrowness of the limits of geometric reason and the dream-like aspect of each individual (Nerval), the capacity for the *synthetic a priori* embedded in the fleeting mind.

At the two ends of this limit sit Art Nouveau and Surrealism. The Eiffel Tower typified the age because of the Art Nouveau, so secretly yet so much of the essence, it embodied in its huge steel trunk jutting into an abstract sky.

Sometimes paradigms survive, almost as a knee-jerk, although their constituent ideas partly wane away, as their conscience thins out, their judgments become erratic, their self-awareness spotty, only some of their actions, some of their Will appear in the correct direction, but only contradicting their earlier premises. When we cross the river from Eiffel and its hidden Art Nouveau and the Paris of 1889 to Palais de Chaillot built for the Paris fair of 1937 with its adulation of post-Art Deco classicism, we are struck by one such contrast. The Modern here is expressed by the geometry and massiveness of its power, of its annihilation of the individual, extinguishing the autonomous spirit and injecting cement in its stead. Classical figures appear in their de-spiritualized nudity as if representing the scientific de-sexualization of the human body in the petrified freezing of the aesthetic. The Modern in the 1930s in the weakness of its conscience is thus sandwiched between the Art Nouveau of the Eiffel Tower and the unashamed monstrosity of the Palais de Chaillot. In one, one sees the gushing forth of the twentieth century at the end of the nineteenth, in the other the dark side of the twentieth century and the partial betrayal of the Modern by the Modern itself. Without knowing how much is betrayal, how much is real, or rather too disconnected from the categories of the Modern, Place de Trocadéro in its ancient classicism as if too embarrassed by such close association, with such unnatural proximity to the unabashed giant, leans to associate with Avenue Balzac, or at times even tries to sneak away to Rue de la Pompe.

The essence of the Paradigm of the Modern can be unearthed in *fin-de-siècle* Paris by observing the radical mood change that occurred in that particular time and space. I have taken the Eiffel Tower as the symbol of the Modern, of the processes that the Dreyfus affair had brought about. It is the new Will projecting itself—Magritte's finger—oozing self-confidence in its new logic and capacity.

In being two years antecedent to the Dreyfus affair, the Tower anticipates the optimism that the Affair cultivated in its adherents, in the new Parisians, the new citizens, the citizens of the new Republic. The Third Republic in its true form, a true form only twenty years after its inception. A unity of will is displayed in the Tower. Only then could the archaic challenges to the Third Republic be tossed into the dust bin of history. By the time this unity is fragmented the Will has waned, its élan fizzled out, and then the *trahison des clercs*, then the hesitations, then all the older elements—from the anti-Dreyfusards to the rural Romantics, from the religious peasantry to the threatened industrialists, a motley array of otherwise disconnected segments—come to the surface.

Every Parisian knows that each district is another cultural sub-context, each very different from the other, albeit some districts are too large to signify only one, e.g. the Eighth, or some too small to signify one by itself, the Fifth. The Modern adjoined the Fifth to the Sixth, the hegemonic norm, and on the Avenue Gay-Lussac two modest nineteenth-century hotels stand side by side, Hôtel de l'Avenir and Hôtel du Progrès. This is by the heart of the clercs' Paris, off Gay-Lussac, only a few minutes from the Avenue de l'Observatoire on the way to Jardin du Luxembourg, where the professors of the Sorbonne, those Mandarins of the Modern, *les hauts fonctionnaires*, the famous writers, and the eminent scientists reside, by the Lycée Henri IV.

The glitter of the Modern is the inherited Empire of the Champs-Élysées, the Petit and Grand Palais, where the bourgeois dwell, carving themselves a new but more neutral territory. The President at the Élysée is closer to this *grande bourgeoisie* and the *Parlement* at the edge of the Left Bank and its *éminence grise*. The Odéon and Montparnasse of the Modern's *éminence grise* are to replace the Montmartre of the *belle époque* and the "street". The Modern speaks in the name of the "street" against the *ancien régime* but never for the "street" speaking for itself; the Modern is afraid of the street as was Marie Antoinette's naiveté a century earlier. The Modern, if allowed, would despise the street, the circus, Montmartre and the *belle époque* for its *gaieté*. The Modern comes on the heels of the *belle époque* to displace it; it is its social nemesis. The Modern is serious and somber, it is the haven of the new professional classes and their norms of hegemony, their way of holding onto power, their way of eradicating the past, the street, the rabble, the proletariat. The Third Republic's clerks are leftist in temperament but rightist in political practice. They take their creed from the Revolution, but embalm it in its institutions.

The Champs-Élysées expands toward the Bois de Boulogne and Neuilly, transforming the village of Saint-Cloud to its immediate luxurious *banlieue*. The *éminence grise* of the Left Bank expands to Vincennes and to the east along the river for its scientific institutes. In the middle, the Île Saint-Louis remains as the untouched bastion of the sixteenth century, as if to control everything at its core while all the recent elites dance *à la ronde* on the surface. It is Molière, Racine, and the great Chancellor, Colbert, who remain as the hidden font of it all, sitting on the Île Saint-Louis facing north as the south of the island is taken over by the post-Napoleonic *cadres* and the *haute bourgeoisie*. The north of the island is aristocratic and the south *grand bourgeois* and *cadre supérieur* with the church in the middle. Given the pure power orientation of these two wings of the elite, that most cynical of religions, the church stands on the island as if it were a monastic organization of the countryside, a stone's throw today from the island's pocket theatre. But the heart of the Modern is not there; it is across the river, on the Left Bank.[15]

The credo of the Third Republic and its modernity was theoretically formulated by Émile Durkheim. The Third Republic arose when the Jewish population represented the new middle class with its natural laicism, progressivism, anti-traditionalism, republicanism, and anti-clericalism. The old *haute bourgeoisie* would either adjust or be replaced by the new wealth, wealth now in the service of education and the public good, self-sacrifice for the ethics of responsibility and not for the gallantry of form: philanthropy replaced charity,[16] Masonic lodges replaced the conviviality of the *hauts salons*. A strong concept of society would emerge with its naturalness much in question. It required attention and care, for its care required its theory and its science. Social tranquility and the normalcy of social conduct were under a constant hidden threat. The social order was fragile and a good part of society was based on a belief in it. It was practical reason that had to be constantly and vigilantly defended, cultivated, and most importantly, instilled through universal education.

With this replacement of a weak concept of society by a strong concept of society, the middle class charted its course of politics: the politics of normalcy, homogeneity and harmony; a strong animadversion against a political vision of division, of partialized interest and of fragmentation, to end up with a weak concept of politics and a weak idea of history. In this regard, the economy was to be controlled so that social harmony would not be disrupted; politics was a reactive sphere only to protect, and at times, actively intervene to safeguard the desired harmony. These parameters, a strong concept of society and weak concepts of politics and historicity, would be the source of the strengths, and later, the weaknesses of this Third Republican paradigm of modernity.

Rivals of Paris: Vienna and Budapest

At the end of the century the real competing paradigm to Paris was Vienna and Budapest. In Vienna, the *Waltz* assimilates the bourgeoisie into aristocratic ways. It is the *ancien régime* retooled for a middle-class accession. They are keen to be modern but cannot adjust to modernity until the Horthy regime descends on the Hungarians. Only then does Budapest find its Modern in counter distinction to the hegemony of the petty nobility. No more bourgeois affection for the styles of the country squire; no more Jewish emulation of the gentry but rather solace sought in urban Paris or Vienna. Horthy, as their antithesis, urbanizes the self-image of Budapest Jewry—no more country estates aspiring to emulate the aristocracy, now the palatial apartment is the abode. It was the proto-fascist Horthy Regime that cleansed the Jewish Budapest bourgeoisie of their habit of donning the role of country squirearchy. It urbanized them: From emulation of country estates they moved to villas by Hösök Tere and Ligetpark and the grand apartments of Andrassy by the Opera.[17]

In Germany, Weimar republicanism remained the alien corn as evinced by its tumultuous, unstable ten years. In France, Clemenceau compromised on the republic for a politics of colonialism in Paris, which, I will argue, opened the gates to a weakening of the republic at home. Vichy could only arise in that softened, disorganized republicanism after Clemenceau at Paris, and that regime rightly gets no rank in the Republican series of French history. Vichy is simply "le gouvernement de France" but a part of neither the Third nor the Fourth Republic.

Paris at the turn of the century was the centre of the universe: all emulated French ways. From the Ottomans to Brazil, they named and framed their institutions after it. The Ottoman Party of Union and Progress borrowed its mottos about this time, as well as the Brazilians their flag. Vienna to Budapest chose Paris to follow suit but only in habit, not in essence. Berlin, a distant third, could only build the avenues, but not *gai Paris*. Berlin did not have the bourgeoisie asserting itself with a radical disdain for the aristocracy. Berlin remained more of a Spartan power to attract the more military-authoritarian political aspirants of the period; Paris the true middle class of the new civil society. Vienna recreated the *belle époque* over and over again, slightly behind the times but fitting for its class alliances. The middle classes of diverse ethnicity found the Habsburg solution much more hospitable to their more fragile condition, and the Habsburg practice of creating a *noblesse de robe* made them adhere to *gaie* aristocratic *embourgeoisement* through the *Waltz*. The French rejection of the *belle époque* could not be theirs, their *fin de siècle* could not take French form. Their rejection, their *fin de siècle*, was to internalize the torment of separation, a separation from the *belle époque*, but not to institutionalize an alternative. It was the secessionists, Klimt and Schiele, and not Émile Durkheim who pointed to a new avenue out of nineteenth-century Vienna.

Budapest, while being shaped by the Viennese temper, and while the Habsburgs invested so much at the end of the century, could have also emulated some of Paris behind Vienna's back, to create a middle-class society to compete with Schnitzler's Vienna. The Danube had a bridge for each, one for the French, as if built by the Eiffel Company and at a careless glance one thinks one sees a capital N on the crown of each of its arches, and the other named after Franz Joseph's daughter, Elisabeth. It is not sure that the Budapest bourgeoisie split between emulating the aristocracy and the new middle-class rejection of the Habsburg *ancien régime*. One hopelessly imagines that the latter would rival the other by looking up to Paris; and the Jews of Budapest would best represent this aspiration.

Budapest did not split; it was the times that were splitting. Budapest on crossing the Danube bore the dualism of its period, but politically, to one's great surprise, Budapest does not bear the conflict of its times. Maybe it was this absence of a modernity-wedded bourgeoisie that eventually led to the split that would come about with the sudden rise of the Communist Party, which possessed power even in the turmoil following the Great War. The Government of Béla Kun had György Lukács, son of a Jewish banking family, to serve as a cabinet minister of high rank. Béla Kun brought about the reaction of Admiral Horthy and his fascist-like rule for twenty-four years until the Nazis threw him out of office for "insufficient collaboration". On the heels of Béla Kun's defeat, Hungary in 1920 was passing the first anti-Semitic laws to prohibit Jews from attending university. The Napoleonic bridge alone could not bring the Paradigm of the Modern, and Hungarian nationalism had the history of being dominated by its prestigious nobility.

The Habsburg lands escaped the Paradigm of the Modern. Egon Schiele best represented the intensity of an enormous split, his was the Modernist's agony but without an abode; deeply steeped in the Modern's pain without the paradigm in which to lodge himself, it is so deep and yet so hesitant. His was a double agony; he could never be imagined in Paris. If T. S. Eliot so well represented British modernity without the paradigm, Schiele best represented the Habsburg context of the Modern's pain without the paradigm. The intensity of its pain would not be possible in Paris. Closest to comparison might be Van Gogh. Van Gogh's pain is expressed differently; his turbulence finds a home on his canvas. Van Gogh was in Paris.

Crossing the Channel:
Paradigmatic versus non-Paradigmatic Modernity

Paradigms are best depicted through a discussion of their contrasts (see Chapter Four). Crossing the Channel, for the British deep down, the enemy is the Modern in ideas, not in name, and France is the example for that "archaic mindset" as the British would view it. For the British, for a long time the Channel tunnel was not to be built so the French would not be coming, whether that be Napoléon or his later surrogates. Not Agincourt but Edmund Burke had shaped the British mind forever. The French, of course, never failed to respond as evinced in de Gaulle's shabby response to the British wish to enter the European Union, then the European Community. De Gaulle was fundamentally correct, and he was right to reject the British as the British view of Europe was not of the French and thus not of Europe itself—not of Europe at its core. The British were totally against the Revolution, and the Continent was totally of it. In England, thus, the story is very different! The Modern is never a paradigm; nor was it ever intended to be. Here, the ideas of the Modern cross the Channel and not the paradigm itself; it is a trickle, but yet appears in its novelty and innocence. Conversely, this is the case when modern ideas come without the paradigm, until the paradigm as its false copy arrives without the ideas themselves.

The Modern in England is about novelty, about rebellion, nay more a rejection of the old, but always partial and more of the erudite middle class, affluent and connected with the well surviving aristocratic elite.

The Modern in England, when it mattered, was Bloomsbury—so much more frivolous, unorganized, and incoherent yet running deeper in spirit than Durkheim's sobriety. The only sober outcome appears in economic theory. The LSE too Labour to matter and, when it does matter, it takes a Fabian turn, and the Modern rides with the Salvation Army to later incarnate itself in the Attlee welfare state.

Bloomsbury in its affluent middle-class sensibility is at home in Cambridge. More aristocratic Oxford is still, at the time the Modern crosses the Channel, too preoccupied with the late Stuart agony of "church and loyalty" to feel the Modern head-on. Catholic or High Church is the agony the breakdown of the ancient ideas allows. Cardinal Manning is no Clarendon; spiritual awakening is the whiff of a shadow the Modern in its ideas casts at Oxford. T. S. Eliot sensibility is the reflection of the Modern at Oxford, as Eliot is the truest and the most profound radical anti-modern. He is a radical anti-modern, not because of his non-geometric language or his ridicule of the Modern's everyday "mundanity", but because of his mysticism. Apart from his mysticism, he best represented the British in the face of the Modern. He was a contemporary Druid. He was one who best deserved the OBE. He was buried most deservedly in Westminster Abbey with the kings and a handful of lords of the crown.

The ideas of the Modern without the paradigm are more destructive of pre-existing sensibilities as they corrode rather than challenge, seep into things rather than transform them. The ideas infiltrate without the solace of a paradigm. Theatre's response starts with Osborne's anger—some elements of Schiele's anguish here for the same reasons—but ends with Pinter's anguish. Pinter's *vide* is not the one Durkheim feared; Beckett comes much closer to that. In Pinter, the *vide* originates from ambiguity, anguish from unfulfilled interpersonal terror. The only optimistic face of the Modern appears in England not as part of the paradigm but as a type of new sociability, as evinced by Elmswood Studios and the B films and Alec Guinness, always hazy, black-and-whites of low pigment. In England, without the paradigm, the Modern, when paradigmatic, could only be about sociability. If the Modern disorganized Bloomsbury with its sitting in the aristocratic parlors of the affluent middle class, half a century later when the Modern is about to exit the world, the ideas of the Modern organized the urban lower class sensibility in their new-found status of relative affluence in finding new modes of sociability as they resituate themselves from the working-class semi-suburbs to the heart of aristocratic urbanity, selling others' wares at Boots and Marks and Spencer, and theirs at King's Road. Theirs is yet a rebellion against their working-class roots, a rebellion with a smile, with optimism and search. Much as Eiffel was the symbol of optimism and good spirit, a new sensibility in anticipation of a new sociability, the new Londoners keep a smile in their outfits and music; Mary Quant and the Beatles. As the Modern as a paradigm wanes, the ideas find their existence in the new paradigm of sociability in London's new urbanites. On the fringe of the elite, or in cohabitation with it, their new sensibility is not to transform the society-makers of England. The upper classes still rule the day. Whether the ideas of the Modern or the proximity of their alter-class in their merry ways is corrosive for the elites of England, they still remain most grounded in their aristocratic abodes. The Modern would wait until the Suez debacle or better the end of the Macmillan government. Wilson was no Ramsey MacDonald to sit with the Tories. If Osborne had already come about it was no different from Schiele, a double torment, the torment of the Modern and the torment of the having no modern abode. Things will only settle later in Pinter's theater and Mary Quant's apparel. King's Road and Carnaby Street will challenge Regents Street and Piccadily. Finally the working class has come in from the suburbs to shape the taste of London for which the women and the young were harbingers. What wonderful years! Yet the British Modern would never be like the Continent's, even after its century-late arrival.[18]

Essentialism has to be the privileged domain of a "paradigm study". *Only* in essentialist terms can we fix the uniqueness of the Paradigm of the Modern and in the dialectical method capture the vicissitudes of its history, its rise and its fall.

The Context Historicized:[*]
The "Double-Contextuality" of Versailles and the War

The end of the Modern was caused neither by the Devil nor by the Dragon but by a kidnap, due to the Modern's inner contradictions. For Durkheim, to battle the Dragon by nationalist practical reason was tricky. It had to be there, but its excesses destroyed the equilibrium and hence made it available for a kidnap.

Clemenceau's nationalist hubris was agitated by French self-doubt facing the Germans. His archaic vengeance, added to it the surprise victories of the Marne and Verdun, made him take the internationally nationalist road and emulate the British, whom the French always re-

---

[*]   This is diplomatic history of a special kind. When diplomatic history is written it is done through a study of documents and results tested in treaties. What I am doing here is examining that history through the voices behind the documents, the sensibilities that govern these documents, and intuiting the degree of the existing will behind the treaties, what these treaties represented in the minds of their architects and the conflict of views and the rivalries in their kitchen. In this manner, the study of diplomatic history becomes a wonderful tool for constructing the sensibilities, that is, for intuiting the world of meanings and the dense culture of aspirations that inhere in and, for us, shape what we have called the world of sensibilities. *Seminar, 27 June 2002, Budapest, Collegium Budapest.*

garded with concealed awe. The French, however Napoleonic, always felt at their heart inferior to the Germans for their modern might and armor, and for the size of their population, and to the British for their diplomacy. Clemenceau won the war, won at the Marne and Verdun, but lost the Republic and the Modern at the Paris peace talks.

The Paris Peace Talks: Double-Contextuality

Now I can turn to the narration of my dialectic: Much has been written on the Paris Peace Conference and Versailles and the treaties at the end of the First War, but none really has underlined how the Great Powers projected themselves into their own future from their immediate past and how in that manner they impacted the future of the globe.[19]

My contention has been that a good part of what would follow in the interwar period was cast at the Paris peace talks. That period was also the seedbed of the so-called Second War. I take the two wars as one constituting the two episodes of one Great War from 1914 to 1945.[20] This period is what I label the period of double-contextuality (Chapter Two), in which the Paris peace talks play a pivotal role.

During the peace talks several intertwined processes were taking place. One, the victors were allies on the one hand but rivals on the other when the territories to be parceled out brought their rivalry to the surface. The French extracted from the Germans what they had lost in 1871. For the British it was the Eastern war which punctuated their vast gain. More important for us in the understanding of the dynamics of the peace talks is the way each state projected itself into the future, which played an overall role in how they negotiated. With respect to this latter question there were also internal divisions. For the British the divide was between Balfour's low-key and resigned attitude of deep conservatism and Curzon's pretensions of grandeur of low Toryism. Lloyd George, on the other hand, does not seem to have his own projection. He is more imbued by the moment of the negotiation context with not much projection into the future. The French with the singular will of Clemenceau had given up the Third Republic in a betrayal of the French public. The French state had taken on the pretense of a great colonial power, perhaps in its hidden competition with the British but only in response to an exaggerated image of them. At Paris, the French with Clemenceau were trying to be a world power on the model of the British. Consequently, France forgot its Third Republic modernity, which could have been a much stronger projection with a global resonance. Instead the French opted for a British position, which had much less power for shaping the future in the moving century. This was the French irony. They lost both: firstly, world power status on a par with the British since the French lacked the resources and population to match the Germans, and secondly, their internal strength based on the Third Republic's project of modernity, which had enabled them as a power to sit at Paris. All this unique opportunity to influence the rest of the century with their Paradigm of the Modern was thus lost at Versailles for the sake of subduing the Germans as a great power in the Hall of Mirrors.

The Italians' project was none. They made noise and eventually had Mussolini come into that vacuum to fill what the Italian state could not formulate in Paris. Mussolini came to the post-Paris post-Versailles conferences on a special train as if to observe but not jumping in, perhaps just to avoid being snubbed. The winner in the global context of the then-retreating British and the retrogressing French was to be the Americans on the one side, strong and single-minded in their newness, yet restrained by Congress from enacting their projection. They needed the second war to project their mega narrative (see the section on American modernity) onto the universe; with Pearl Harbor the Congress turned around for the support of that project. And, on the other side, as the French retreated from their project of modernity with a volte face and the British scaled down operations for the politically most unsettling period of the interwar years—perhaps because they gave up the world project that their internal politics had turned into such un-clarity—the political vacuum was to be filled by Germany in radically decimating the project of modernity inherent in the Durkheimian Third Republic, which Clemenceau forsook in his imaginary competition with the British. In that sense, I argue that it was the French who betrayed their own project most at Versailles at the greatest cost to Europe and the West, because of their hubris in defeating the Germans and their insecurity vis-à-vis the British. It was their hubris that destroyed their project and left Europe barren for Hitler's anti-modern project to easily take over and overwhelm France as well as for the confusion of its intellectuals after the 1930s. The treason of the clerks was a consequence of this betrayal, and the reactionary intellectuals of shallow discourse were again to leave France most vulnerable to a Hitler kidnap.

Needless to emphasize, we are talking about a period in which a handful of elites decided these matters, which were presumed to cast the future of their own societies. Their concern about their populations would appear as afterthoughts or at best as future constraints on these projections. In Paris "the people" never entered into the consideration of the negotiating parties. Obviously, this factor greatly facilitates the writing of the projections and the researching of their content.

In that context Clemenceau gives up that sensibility, that particular modern of moral individualism, for a poor imitation of the British as an imperial power, not realizing how at that moment the British had become so archaic, as revealed in their colonialist choices at the peace talks. Clemenceau's hubris in defeating Germany, his revanchism, for a total destruction of Germany, became his and France's nemesis, only to lead, after several years, to the great surprise of Benda's *Trahison des Clercs* and the Modern's loss of faith, its "crise de foi".[21] Clemenceau, who translated radical individualist sensibility into the political process and transformed it as the Third Republic in its truest form, was also the one who betrayed it at Paris for his desire to destroy the Germans.[22] It was the nation-state struggle at the symbolic level that did Clemenceau in. His revanchism à la Scipio Africanus and his latent envy of the British led him to undermine Third Republican nationalism, the nationalism of civil society, and to revive the seventeenth-century notion of the aggrandizing state.

In retrospect, thus, I think it was the French who most betrayed the Modern at Versailles. The English had already reconciled themselves to a holding-operation: How to extend the historical life of an aristocratic middle-class elitism,[23] which Balfour, to my mind, best represented. Curzon's view was perhaps more ambitious but perhaps less feasible; it would have been most utopian to aspire to creating a nineteenth-century empire (perhaps most Wellingtonian) as Curzon had probably imagined. Balfour wanted a lease of life, hence the British were willing to play into American hands, partly because the latter appeared most powerful and partly because of British suspicion and dislike of France as a world power—a view perhaps implanted by the Napoleonic conflict. Hence, it was not the British who played the major historical role for the casting of the future in Europe. It was in the East that they cast their future.

In terms of their future history, the British had already withdrawn

SEVEN • A Stylized History of the Modern

to a backseat as the war dragged on to four demanding years, most contrary to what they had imagined. The Boer was the most of a war they had seen, and that was bad enough to repeat it in scale. The British entry into the war had been quite light-hearted. When Asquith received on the train the news of the German declaration in the morning papers on his way to the country, he pedalled to his afternoon siesta and waited until the next morning's cabinet meeting for a decision. He never anticipated the scale the war would develop into. The British had expected a three to four-week war, nothing on the scale of the earlier Boer conflict.

Although Lloyd George came in to replace Asquith when the war took a radical turn, the earlier mindset did not change much. This perhaps was the single most important factor why the British during the peace talks withdrew from assuming the role of being the player that would shape future history; they would rather, at a much lower cost, settle for a world status quo in which they would be able to extend their conservative order. Armistice Day, whether real or not, deserved the greatest celebration. When Lloyd George attempted to pick a further fight at a later date, he was shown the cabinet door. (The coal strike and the rest which followed the war might be a test of how correct Balfour's vision had been.) A new world had emerged, unstoppable with or without the British. An alternative view, say from Curzon's position, to recreating an imperial Britain as a world power would have involved the misfortune of the rise of a more radical "left" society; Curzon's reactionary position would not have been feasible.[24]

The war had destroyed the three different types of archaic empires: The Romanovs, the Habsburgs, and the Ottomans; it gave a chance for a modern empire, the German, to cleanse itself of its feudal elements.*

---

* Feudal is not archaic; it signifies a different order than archaic; the former is a fragmented polity, the latter a centralist despotism.

The British got an extension to their middle-class empire, but the future of the world was left to the powers of the Modern Age: the French and the Americans. At that juncture their differences and how they had related to their differentness become most crucial. I will conclude that the French gave up their own definitions most readily in order to assert themselves as a world power; their weakness as a power only enhanced this ambivalence, making them much less influential and making their definitions much less global contrary to the potential of universalism it ideologically contained.

The Americans, on the other hand, were more adherent to their world view without any doubt. Distance had a more coherent normative structure contrary to their more archaic and naïve definitions. I am referring here to the Americans' ideas of nationalism and citizenship, the idea of a nation derived from ethnic-tribalism and of citizenship from a generalized idea of a mixture of creed and race. But in spite of their anti-Enlightenment political vision, they had a unity of belief and action, which is what made them so powerful vis-à-vis the withdrawing British and French ambivalence because of their international pragmatism; that is, the French had the most appropriate blueprint but a weak base with a disproportionate global ambition. Italy had no power, and as a player had to sit in the trolley making too much noise in her discontent. Her conflict with Wilson had significance for the others in bringing things to a head in testing the three visions that the British, the French, and the Americans represented. That was the Italian role, a second-class seat, and lots of noise to force things in the front room.

Let me now turn to how the French compromised on the Third Republic after the War.

Elites in Search of a New Century:
The *Belle Époque* vs. The Third Republic[25]

Clemenceau, the epitome of the Third Republic statesmen, the creator of the radical socialist government, the man who made the Republic to mold the state and thus to create the Third Republic as a political institution, became, at the Paris peace talks, a Talleyrand with a vengeance. The opportunity to subdue the Germans, to humiliate them, took the Republic out of the French state and turned it into a power with imperial posturing, a *Guignol*. There was already so much Third Republic past and Third Republic institutionalization as to make this volte face into an empire, a non-possibility; and a half-empire is always a *Guignol*.

With the impact of the War, everywhere in Europe the new classes recreated their past *belle époque* with whatever was available in their political store. The War had packed away the *belle époque* for good, but now the petty bourgeoisie had to have their revenge. Their opposition to the *belle époque* took different forms in different political contexts. For example, in Turkey it was the Third Republic in its authoritarian form. In Hungary, it took a Marxist turn in Béla Kun and György Lukács. In Berlin, a distant Third Republican solution was attempted to be grafted on after the Marxian uprising was brutally quelled. A Durkheimian solution in Turkey was perhaps inevitable when a strong centralist state was available, whereas in Hungary without a state tradition the Marxian road was perhaps readier to be taken. Vienna lost its imperial equation with no chance for its revival and, with the ensuing turmoil, had to settle on an undecided course and sought a quasi-Durkheimian grafting of urban socialism. Britain, on the other hand, went on a binge with a view to downscale all operations. They gave up not on the geography but on the spirit of the empire. Worried about its cost, they could not once more imagine feeling the emotional cost of rising to its defense. Bloomsbury was the closest the British could come on their empire-island to Tristan Tzara, to Klimt and Hugo Ball.

The world would await another war for the United States eventually to move in as a Fortinbras unscathed by the past, new in armour, shining with hope but alien to the history of Elsinore. A new light which the old men of Elsinore had exhausted in their lateral movements: in witnessing the last upsurge of their deep, dark side, fearing the dangers of the Continent's underlying firmament would boil over, they would accept the new Fortinbras without consciously asking questions about its source. Fortinbras was there to sweep aside all that remained of the past, the king and Hamlet, the empire or the republic, and, in marching from Normandy to Berlin in 1945, to reverse the pre-existing norms of modernity. The French track was packed away for good at the global level. It took time for the rest to adjust. The French were thrown into total disarray until de Gaulle in 1958 pulled the rug out from under the Republic to forge a bourgeois alliance with Bonapartism by short-circuiting the petite bourgeoisie.

The Plan was not to recreate the Third Republic as society had thought, endorsed by France and professed by *Le Monde*, but to become a new arrangement. Now the State, with Big Capital, was harking back not to Bonaparte but perhaps more to Louis Phillipe, the bourgeois king. While French society was still immersed in the grammar of the Third Republic and the Revolution, the State of the Fifth was built on a new equation, an equation which kept the old middle classes at bay but created a new middle class on their coat-tails. State and capital "*pantoufled*". This system had one inner weakness; when the state and capital are so much confounded, how can we account for the necessary legitimation? How to maintain a facade of impartiality? This lack of division between the state and capital for the society of the Revolution and the Third Republic was momentous. For the Fifth Republic it was only a little confusion, a necessary cost of doing business, a little confusion but nothing to upset its logic (e.g. the Roland Dumas case). Yet for the society of the Third Republic this was momentous corruption. Here the two republics parted company and the true divisions once more emerged, emerged in the radical differentness of their modes of operation, in the economic logic of the two republics, which otherwise bore more or less the same face. Only in ideological darkness would they look almost alike. The rebellion of its 1968 was "reactionary". It failed to tear asunder the shroud that darkened their difference. It had its roots in the *fin-de-siècle* Modern.

Modernity's Two Tracks: French vs. American

For the earlier French version, modernity went ahead and capitalism followed, at times the tail wagging the dog. Hence capitalism was only accepted willy-nilly, with a lot of restraint and control, always with ambivalence, always with a devil in itself to fight, to restrain, to calm or to control. The Fifth Republic solved this problem by putting the state more squarely on the side of capital, and making the harmony issue secondary to accumulation, accumulation for national glory. Harmony was now to be elicited by national glory in accumulation on a global scale. Putting the cart before the horse was the credo of the Third Republic, but history vindicated the Fifth Republic over the Third, at least for the last quarter of the century—how much of it is due to the changes in the century, how much to the ingenuity of putting the cart before the horse, is of course impossible to tell.

In the American way, capitalism went ahead and modernity followed suit. Here, the problem is that when the institutions of the Modern are secondary, the nation-state and universalist citizenship follow only limping and are never fully forthcoming. Here, the question is how to steady the accumulation and rational action that the capitalist economy requires in the long run. In North America, it was self-discipline and Protestantism which secured it. In Latin America, constant *coups d'état* and dictatorships that trimmed the Modern for capitalist accumulation, but always for short-term capitalist accumulation with the hope that the long term would only be the aggregation of the short terms.

Clemenceau, the epitome of the Third Republic, the leader of the Republic which defined the Third Republic, gave up the Republic at Versailles by emulating Talleyrand, caught in the British game instead of expanding the boundaries of Republicanism, thus betraying the Revolution for the imperialism of the late nineteenth century.

In conclusion, my argument is that French hubris, not of the Modern but the *revanchism* for 1871, won at the Peace Conference. It was Pershing and his fresh troops and the British blockade aggravated by the Turnip Winter that prepared the final defeat of the Germans. Blocked on the Marne, Wilson's carrot was enough to tempt the Germans to demilitarize. Once demilitarized there was no way they could convince their troops to fight again although they had not vacated French territory. At the end, Wilson's carrot was not available to the vanquished. The intra-war period, the Modern weak of heart and Will, let the Modern's worst enemy, the Nazis, gather fuel. The war was eventually finalized only in 1945. Now the powers to arise at the two extremities of the Modern's geography, the Americans and the Russians coming in from the two sides of Europe in their own versions of the Modern which the Modern of the *fin de siècle* would be hard put to understand. The Soviets had kidnapped the Modern in the name of the Modern, the Americans had all its language and promise but none of the core. I suggest that it was the American context of modernity that allowed the new town to emerge with such power to offset the norms of modernity; i.e. the French transformed the countryside (metaphorically speaking) to leave primordialism altered but unaccounted for, while American modernity, when unchecked by any rivals and without the freeze of the Cold War, created the terrain for the new primordial to articulate itself as the "new town". Could that be its "vulnerability"? Was not that new town a niche for Jihadism and Al Qaeda, the new town rejecting the Modern only subterraneanly but charged with its ideas, yet only in the negative?[26]

Notwithstanding the rise of the Modern's deepest enemy, the Nazis, notwithstanding the loss of nerve in Paris, and notwithstanding the new course the French take after Versailles, the Modern in its original form still pervades as the model paradigm until the Great War is concluded with the ending of the second war in 1945. Its swan song still gets to be delayed by yet another forty years; the two supra-national powers that emerge after the war, in their competition still using the language of the Modern for their global hegemony; on the east, the Modern is in the "ends" that the regime chooses itself to present, on the west, the regime claims to represent the Modern in its everyday practices, in the "means" it identifies its hegemony with.[27]

Now it was the Ghost which had to be beckoned.

The East of Europe got derailed from its Parisian march to modernity (Czechoslovakia's Masaryk) by the Soviet unreality of skipping stages for a misunderstood modernity. It was as if part of Elsinore was forsaken to the Ghost. Germany was split between Fortinbras and the Ghost, its rival. Britain followed the American road with an elderly nonchalance and in resentment, some of its elite turned to the Ghost for opposing Fortinbras in the latter's late-comer naiveté taking over Elsinore for its seeming destruction. Kim Philby was a patriot and a loyal servant of his monarch for sure. He only too much resented the incursion of Fortinbras with such lack of couth, a quarterback in Elsinore Castle.

It was only in the final defeat of the East that the Modern could now be dropped for the hegemonic language of the supra-powers. In 1989, with the end of the Cold War, the Great War and the *fin de siècle* that had led to it—by accident—the "hundred years" concluded, from the rise of the Eiffel Tower to the dismantling of the Berlin Wall. It was only by purging the ghost that the Modern's language could be purged.*

• • • •

Finally, here Durkheim's crisis and the crisis of its particular modernity converge. I will suggest the end of modernity as writ in Durkheim's paradigm comes to a close as the twentieth century closes, primarily because of the success of Durkheim's paradigm as a political project in a particular global context. The French escaped their crisis when Clemenceau gave up the Third Republic at Paris for imitating the British, and de Gaulle, after a lapse of indecision and turmoil of four decades, could put the Fifth Republic in its stead with such ease. If Clemenceau had not diluted his republic, neither would the dark years of the thirties have occurred to that extent, nor could de Gaulle have so easily pushed aside the Republic in the name of the Republic and instituted a quasi-Napoleonic regime.[28]

---

* There are different days and different dates that a period ends. In retrospect it is we who choose one of the ways, a done date to mark the end of an epoch. I have taken the end of the Cold War and the Soviet hegemony over half of Europe for that signifier.

Double-Contextuality

Ascendance, contradiction, and conflict, and perhaps, subsequent demise have so far been dealt with here as parts of a totality, as one complete episode of the rise and demise of the Durkheimian paradigm of
modernity. Success as ascendance, and contradiction and conflict as
multiple crises, will however unfold in our model according to their
global context. They all come to a crescendo when the global environment feeds—elective affinity—or numbs the internal processes to simmer. In the former case we have either the success or the contradictions
and conflict coming to the fore, in the latter a simmering crisis moving
sideways, corroding its context but not transforming it. We will, in our
"story", see the examples of both motions.

The external international environment, the context, thus has in our
story determined the timing of change, that is, whether the crisis unfolds or whether it simmers, with the society thereby constantly drifting
to "lower-levels of equilibrium". For this second layer of analysis—an
analysis not of the structural sources of crisis but of the way and the
time that it is revealed—I have used Smelser's model of the "value-added" in a simplified, two-stage format.

Back to Paris at the end of the 1950s:
The Finality of the Modern

Edith Piaf was the torment of the waning of the Modern while Egon
Schiele had been the Modern's torment without an abode. Piaf is from
within, Schiele is from without. Schiele was in double jeopardy, living
the Modern's torment with no modern to belong to; he is in Vienna
living his Paris pain; his is the biggest agony. Piaf is crying within and

from the soul, as the soul deserts her as it wanes when it has no more Will; "je" has to inject a will personal and pitiful in its stead: "*je ne regrette rien*" is the personalization of that bygone will; the swan song of the Modern. Ultimately, what seals the end of it all is Pink Floyd and *The Wall*. Pink Floyd sings to the passing of the Modern, to the self-corruption, to the corrosion of the Modern when left without the paradigm, as the paradigm has moved on to its extinction. The Beatles a few years earlier had been the Modern's complete innocence. They represented the optimism of the Modern, its last songs in full earnest. They are the babies of a lost era, naïve and pure as could be. They are as delicate as a handful of lost orphans. Their fragility is their greatest power.

Paris on *pellicule* is always black-and-white, sepia only when it goes to Biarritz for summer or the weekend; the Côte d'Azur is Technicolor from day one and comes into the French consciousness only much later in time and as the reworking of the late Empire, i.e. ante-modern, and always a day too far from Paris. Paris is always in black-and-white as it was in Bogart's *Casablanca*; Paris is Paris during the Occupation, black-and-white; yet Paris is not Paris in the great joy of the Day of Liberation. That is when Technicolor starts to set in. Technicolor does Paris in; it brings Gene Kelly and singing in the rain—indeed most brilliant and most seductive.

Godard, Truffaut, Melville, Resnais, in the same vein as Old Wave Renoir and Carné, try once more to recover Paris, the Modern, in its black-and-white, injecting a good part of the film noir of the great American cinema—forever the greatest—of the pre-Korean war days. This last hurrah, epitomized in Delphine Seyrig[29] and Marienbad, one in speechlessness and the other in the void, lasts until Eric Rohmer's

Ma nuit chez Maud, cerebral as ever, and words start to take over, sentiment gets ossified, the *vide* is formulated and the surreal is expunged—Durkheim is back, back to revenge his mirror image, to stab his Dada in the back. Then Rohmer continues in color, pastel only for nostalgia. We are back to the end of the sixties.

By 1966 and Rohmer in color, the death-knell of the Modern is as clear as ever, making the search for the Modern so desperate in Berkeley and Paris! The student movement was reactionary; they wanted to institute the authentic Modern once and for all according to its bygone self-image, for its spirit far on the wane. They were all too earnest, as often happens when a period settles into its wasted end. The children were defending their fathers' dream.

Back to Paris before Rohmer's colors: the last sounds of Paris in black-and-white might have been Léo Ferré, and Juliette Gréco—for her chansons, for her life story, for her *mélancolie*, for her radical politics, for her romance with Miles Davis, for her turtlenecks, and for Aznavour playing the piano.

Yet for my story it is the voice of the itinerant Dalida that makes that Paris generic, universal, and definitional for all—Dalida from the edge of the Modern, just as it was for Schiele. The *vide* less defined but more defining, lurking from behind yet with no abode, the periphery of the Modern, Alexandria, in Europe and not in Europe at the same time. After the Suez invasion blackens the sunlit skies of the Levant and turns the entire Levant to sepia forever, Dalida's only remaining abode is Paris and absinthe. Suez ends all that the Modern pretends—pretends in both senses of the word—in the Levant.

Dalida comes into her own in that mourning of half-belonging: Paris is the true home of all illusionary migrants. Dalida eventually gives it all up, Paris, Rome, Alexandria and her disfigured life: to end the Modern, the Levant, forever, for herself, for Alexandria, for Egypt and for the million years of the Jews of the Levant, harbingers of the Modern on its Near-Eastern periphery.*

• • • •

The French intellectual current, the Existentialism of the 1950s, was to my mind a last effort to shore up the Modern, already on its last legs. Sartre, who, I find, has been exaggerated as a thinker, had the right title for his book: *L'être et le néant*.

Only in the last decade of the century, a little less than a hundred years from Dreyfus and the Rules of the Sociological Method, was the ghost purged forever (1989). Elsinore maintained now mostly as a stage set, Fortinbras still juvenile but not young any more, and the armor still shiny but no more with the same shine of novelty as before, the memory of the Third Republic's modernity could not any more be recalled with half the reality of *The Lord of the Rings*.** The virtual has become the real, and the real only a half-remembered virtuality, Durkheim dead and long buried, sociology had become media studies, and anthropology a collection of ethnographic studies of relativism—another name for Rashomon.

---

* Dalida was not Jewish. She came from the large Italian community of Alexandria, but I think her mix of joy and sorrow, festive and triste, was the real voice of the Jewish ethos of Alexandria as the end was peering around the corner. I find her voice more Jewish than any other Jewish voice of Alexandria. Alexandria was as modern as you could get on the shores of the Mediterranean. Class, far more than any ethnicity, defined identity in Alexandria.

** At the time this was written, it was *The Lord of the Rings* which preoccupied everyday discourse. When this essay gets published, I guess another "tale" will envelope public consciousness.

SEVEN • A Stylized History of the Modern

After the war, in the face of a serious Soviet challenge, the Americans were holding up the Modern by its own bootstraps. It was the necessary hegemonic language when the Soviets were trying the Modern but neither with its spirit nor with its essence. In 1989, with their victory over the Soviets, the Americans could now drop the shoe. This is where my story ends.

In Flanders fields the poppies blow
Between the crosses, row on row.

(John McCrae)

Notes

1.   This book is a product of many years of research, thinking and teaching. For research, it was a year's work at the Public Record Office, to be continued at the Yale library for some personal papers in the original of the junior staff at the Paris Peace Conference—the juniors are much more helpful if one wants to discover the sensibilities, as their frustrations reveal in their personal letters, a good guide to the borders of the prevailing sensibilities, and their success a guide to the core of the paradigm. In terms of thinking the obvious sediment starts at Cambridge in particular with Frank Hahn's tremendous sense of humour while being so strict and so logically rigorous when it comes to analytical investigation of theory—the best of the Viennese logical positivists. In fact, I take Hahn and Matthews's article "The Theory of Economic Growth: A Survey", *Economic Journal* (December 1964) as the example for a beginning of "analytical sociology".

As for the sections on the *fin de siècle* are no direct research but the poetry, in particular, Apollinaire and, as a precursor, Gérard de Nerval, which might also tell the bent, the bias endemic in that discussion, but which, I feel, best uncorks the depth of the *fin-de-siècle* sensibilities. For the practical, for this period, the best research, of course, was to walk the streets of Paris in the early 1960s when the *fin de siècle* still remained "alive and well".

The old buses with open platforms and the smell of the cheap coal of the metro, catching the "scent" of Paris before the "Drugstore and the Defense", that is, before Pompidou intervened. The matrix of that scenting Paris in its walks is the many reels of black-and-white cinema. In particular, the cinema of Renoir to me best reveals the rich texture of the *fin de siècle* in the 1920s. What always remains enigmatic to me is Marcel Carné's "resistance" to the Germans in his *Les Enfants du Paradis*, which goes very far back in history and insists on being very "non", if not "anti", *fin de siècle*. Is it that they (together with Jacques Prévert, who wrote the scripts, and Arletty and the other artists, J. L. Barrault (a junior) also blamed *fin-de-siècle insouciance* for the German victory? The Maginot line is nothing without a paradigmatic will. Durkheim's bravery, later enacted by Marc Bloch, would easily show that the Modernists were no less than heroes. It was the Tiger, Clemenceau, who betrayed that Will for a minor idea—minor juxtaposed with the Paradigm of the Modern—of an empire à l'anglais.

The literature on the Modern, modernity, modernization, each signifying different things, is immeasurably voluminous. It might be futile for some to see another rendition of the concept which has animated so much discussion. I claim that what I have done in this theoretical/analytical investigation is novel.

For a primary source I had the aid of volumes of the collection of *L'Illustration* (1919–1936) that I inherited from my father.

2.   It is said that whenever Adenauer crossed Elbe he would exclaim "Asia Asia".

3.   A few counter examples might help to underscore the particularity of my view in looking at the history of the practice of the Modern. Touraine looked at it, but it is hard to distinguish the innate ideas of the Modern in a systematic and analytical manner, as I claim to do, from just being a hegemonic paradigm: what is modern, what is hegemonic not clear. In other words, Touraine follows in Foucault's footsteps, but how much Foucault is about the Modern and how much about hegemony is never clear. At the other extreme, for Rabinow, the Modern is French but not sociological. He is too narrow while Touraine is too broad in covering the Modern. As we shall see, the Modern is sociological and hence Rabinow's French misses the analytical problems—Touraine is too broad hence unspecific, and Rabinow too narrow, and both miss the universal character of the Modern when they want to underline the pitfalls of the Modern paradigm. They lack the sociological, the paradigmatic nature of the question. I have taken the Parsonian track. The greatest hubris of all paradigms for their nemesis is their innate tendency to always "overextend" themselves as Parsons's paradigms showed their instability in their logical extensions. For us each paradigm overextends itself differently, hence it has a different history of nemesis; and its hubris is specific to it. In their essence, we discover the origins of the peculiarity of their own hubris. For the Modern, I am going to *fin-de-siècle* Paris to discover the roots of that essence (above Chapter Two).

4. In reference to Ivan Strenski, *Durkheim and the Jews of France* (Chicago: University of Chicago Press, 1997). Also, Yuri Slezkine, *The Jewish Century* (Princeton: Princeton University Press, 2004), who, in my view, never understood Western European Judaism and its emancipation. He often writes from a Russian experience and unduly elevates mysticism and alludes to an implicit *kabbalah*.

5. Faruk Birtek, "Recasting Contemporaneity – A Hypothesis in Rereading the New Politics of Localism: The New Assabiyah of the Town – Thomas Hardy Revisited", *The Post-Modern Abyss and the New Politics of Islam: Assabiyah Revisited*, ed. Faruk Birtek and Binnaz Toprak, (Istanbul: Bilgi University Press, 2011).

6. What about the question of multiple modernities that has recently surfaced as a point of contention? There are two types of phenomena which could be investigated under this. Neither would violate my claim that the Modern is a French phenomenon, its "coming into its own" was in Paris from 1898 to the 1920s, its hegemony lasting until 1989. The two types of the multiple modernity question are the two ways in which the paradigm of modernity gets reflected, extended, pursued. One is what I call the Paradigm of the Modern at its core and symbolizes itself with social practices donned externally by a particular set of habits, using the word in both of its senses. On the other hand, there are the social practices which have the Modern in their practice but not at their core. Below, they would appear in the historical examples of England and the Habsburgs. In these cases, there is not the paradigm of modernity at the core, but only its elements incorporated into its social practices; one has Parisian habits without Paris, the other is modernity without the politics of the Modern, as was the case with the Habsburgs. The Turks in their republic borrowed the institutions of the Modern but without its core and individualism, whereas the British the reverse, individualism without the Modern's institutions.

7. The real historical question is how that common sense comes about. Here I cannot offer, and parenthetically, no one has offered, a sufficiently analytically rigorous answer to the question of how a particular sensibility comes to rule, other than convincing yet conjunctural retrospective arguments for it.

Just saying that it arises from the French Revolution, a Phoenix and a Pegasus at the same time (Pegasus in reference to de Tocqueville's argument about the continuing centralisms) is no doubt correct but analytically very weak. It describes but fails to identify the causal links at the level where the result, the particular "common sense", is obtained. This particularity is central to the subject matter of this work. The French Revolution equation requires one more variable. Its "differential" is just that, a crude approximation but certainly not sufficient for claiming the origins at the level of concreteness for the sensibilities, which I am here mobilizing to explain the rise and the crisis of the Modern paradigm. This insufficiency is particularly strategic for explaining the two crises/failures of the paradigm of sensibilities on which I will focus. Here I am taking one instance, one sensibility, but identifying its "true" nature by first tracing it to its inception. I am explaining, analytically and causally, its rise due to its strengths and its demise on account of its internal limits, whether they be its internal hidden contradictions or its conceptual limitations.

8. Modris Eksteins, *Rites of Spring: The Great War and the Birth of the Modern Age* (New York: Doubleday, 1989). In historically constructing the Paradigm of the Modern I will broach my difficult subject with a critique of *Rites of Spring* by Eksteins, which has enjoyed a broad following, and show how we differ in reading the passage to modernity. Eksteins uses the metaphor of the "gare" to depict what he sees as the disarray of Modernity. Eksteins seems to view the world through spectacles borrowed from the *belle époque* and reads other parts of the work of Stravinsky and Nijinsky as not very different from the *belle époque*, which is often read as anti-aristocratic, populist, anti-conventional, and at times "street-mad". What he identifies, so erroneously, as the Modern has the language of the immediate past, the *belle époque*, to which the Modern was once a reaction; furthermore, he would read the same adjectives for a future in Berlin, again for us not the Modern but its antithesis. If Hitler had been the Modern, Eksteins's implicit choice, then how do we understand Dada's surrealist rebellions? The Modern is unsustainable for reasons much different from Eksteins's. It is the nation-state, the other leg of the Modern, which is much more to blame. The two legs don't rhyme, they

only undermine each other. Their imbalance is the most serious challenge for the politics of the Modern which has at the core the aspirations of the Millsian liberal project. For the Modern, Eksteins does not understand the strength and the first modern character of Paris in 1913. He takes a critique of art of the period, Samuel Rocheblave's exclamations of the lack of uniformity in Paris, as "barbarism", and his comment, "No school any longer, only a smattering of talent; no group any longer, only individuals" (Eksteins, p. 48), as the symbols of Paris's decline and weakness, totally missing the point that Paris came into its own in the Third Republic, at that time precisely through its most cerebral individualism.

9.   Faruk Birtek and Binnaz Toprak, "The Conflictual Agendas of Neo-Liberal Reconstruction and the Rise of Islamic Politics in Turkey: The Hazards of Rewriting Modernity", *The Post-Modern Abyss and the New Politics of Islam: Assabiyah Revisited*, ed. Faruk Birtek and Binnaz Toprak (Istanbul: Bilgi University Press, 2011).

10.   I must say that I feel privileged to remember Paris in the early 1950s and still maintain the impression of its glorious glitter. This was a decade before Pompidou intervened.

11.   Joseph Roth, *Report from a Parisian Paradise: Essays from France, 1925–1939* (New York: W.W. Norton, 2005).

12.   Roland Rosbottom, *When Paris Went Dark: The City of Light under German Occupation 1940–44* (New York: Little, Brown and Company, 2014).

13.   Èmile Durkheim in *Essays on Sociology and Philosophy, ed.* Kurt H. Wolff (Columbus: Ohio State University Press, 1960).

14.   Georg Stauth, "Critical Theory and Pre-Fascist Social Thought", *History of European Ideas*, vol. 18, no. 5 (1994): 711-728.

15.   Now, ENA is transported to Strasburg to be annexed to the European Union—most indicative of the transition from the Third Republic's scientific colonialism to the semi-Napoleonic Gaullist nation-state, and that only after going through many years of indecision, including the 1960s' UNESCO-type third-worldism, which prevailed when the building was at its nadir, manned by low-level clerks which went into bettering the post-colonial territories.

16. Nora Şeni, *Les inventeurs de la philanthropie juive* (Paris: La Martinière, 2005).

17. For a moment we will go to the edge of Europe and enter her competing sensibilities through the back door. The Ottoman elite of the end of the nineteenth century in their discontent with their pre-existing regime were split between the Habsburg and the Third Republican ways of salvaging their political society. The Habsburg version anticipates the War with a project of a Turco–Arab empire which would, after the war, evolve into an aspiration to a Turco–Kurdish polity. Yet, after the War with the victory of the nationalist elite, the French Fifth Republic sets the exact model for the creation of a republic with a deep hostility to earlier imperial formulations. The European periphery is a good refracting glass for seeing more radically the differences of orientation among the European polities (Faruk Birtek, *The Durkheimian Paradigm on Its Foreign Travel*, forthcoming). The gateway to these projects lies through their conceptualization of citizenship in the normative sense—though obviously the practice of citizenship is part of the cultural domain that the normative often fails to anticipate. How these two domains interact is yet another question. At the normative level, in regard to their concept of citizenship, we can pose the two paradigms.

Franz Joseph vs. Émile Durkheim: After the War, the dilemma for many of the post-War Ottoman intellectuals would be to sustain a Franz Joseph political paradigm in a world of Durkheimian sensibility. The answer to that had to be in the negative. The very logic of the Third Republic's Republicanism was assimilationist. Liberal *joie de vivre* was not for the Durkheimian élan to enjoy. The most republican regimes would be hard to keep within the aspired bounds of a limited mobilization of *selves*, diversity of founts of identity, and incongruous layers of loyalty. These would go very much against the basic grain of republican nationalism. Its logic, compelled by its grammar, led to a homogenizing process of recreating the "self" within the republican mold. A more clement international environment, a more affluent economy, a weaker need for industrial mobilization of labour, an economy of trade and commerce and services, might have allowed a hodge-podge of Durkheimian sensibilities with a Franz Joseph politics of citizenship, but that certainly was not available to the Turks at the time, nor was the world a place to allow a syncretism of multi-layered citizenship after Wilsonian doctrine put its stamp on the vanquished of the War. On the other hand, the very assimilationist logic of the republic would also erect barriers to any aspirations of multi-ethnicity.

I also loved the city. Budapest was much in the way I knew Europe in the early 1960s: a town of a struggling middle class who went shopping with their little bags and rode the tram or the subway. Budapest also woke me up to a thing in my past. I realized how much my grandparents' house resembled the shops and the houses of Budapest: the same kitsch, the same Thonet chairs, the same fake glass lampshades. It opened up a totally new vista in my thinking. For the first time, I realized that Turkish modernity was the history of a seesaw between the French republicanism of the end of the century and the Franz Joseph empire with its multi-ethnic politics and the operetta. Inspired by all this, I finished the first draft of a book in Budapest. I had some of the material ready in a draft form, but the Budapest observations gave it a very different turn. Instead of a linear story, it now contextualized the superior edge of the Durkheimian theory as a theory of the Modern over its alternatives, yet only to laden it with unforeseen hazards that would become its undoing. The study puts the Durkheimian theory to its historical test in the Ottoman-Turkish context and through its transformational processes in WWII. My discovery of Budapest was one of the turning points in my life. I realized that Durkeim's nineteenth century was more unique than I had initially thought. The Habsburg reality was different from Durkheim's yet so valid on its own. Please see the section on Budapest.

For my discovery of Budapest, I am most grateful to Claus Offe, who introduced me to the city. For that most educative experience, I am grateful to the wonderful institution of Collegium Budapest—now closed by the Orban government—and its general secretary, Mr Fred Girod. I have truly learned immeasurably from my discussions with him.

Thirdly, I met my co-author, Dr Laszlo P. Gatsby, in Budapest. This was an immeasurable blessing.

18.   The Modern's infiltration of England with a whiff of *fin-de-siècle* ideas lasts, like France, until Suez, or maybe with a few years delay until the end of

the Macmillan governments. Wilson was the new Ramsay MacDonald, but now to stay and stay forever. Hampstead had come to replace Bloomsbury. And now the Tories had taken refuge in the West End, in Chelsea and mostly in Belgravia, and put the Edgware Road in between them and Labour of Hampstead and its northern constituencies. Golders Green escaped this influence by breeding the intellectuals of the Left but itself almost secretly siding with the Conservatives. This withdrawal gradually from the last stronghold of the Tories in the north, in Bryanston Square, in Baker Street, to Eaton Square, or rather to Eccleston Square, or even to the more southwest, in the Pelhams, in Barons Court, had put them at a distance from the rest of London.

London under Wilson really split, a split that would last about twenty years in which the south of London would gravitate further to the countryside, uniting with Chiswick or even reaching out to Barnes, turning its back on St James Court and Regents Park.

How could the monarchy in this newly found solitude reproduce itself properly as they had never since 1688 been in the habit of self-regeneration; they were always put in the midst of the circle which regenerated the monarchy. The monarchy, once deserted in the 1960s by the gentry and their friends, escaping to the banks of the river and turning their backs on the royalty, had to have the flag flying although they had no means of recharging their self-identities. No wonder their young went astray. They went astray because the Tories had escaped them.* Thatcher was no royalty Tory, and, in any case, nobody from Chiswick or Eaton Square was going to return to join up with Regents Park and face the north once more. They had gone totally disinterested. It was into that crack that Margaret Thatcher could come and put a new seal on the Tories. The south of the river was now moving in, moving in from Battersea and around, jumping over the old Tories, shooting and hunting in Belgrave Square and Hans Crescent, the southern middling classes found the opportunity to displace the old guard; or rather they needed no displacement; they filled the seats the old guard had retired from and jumped to the rudder with Thatcher to sit down at the table with the Hampstead crowd to lay claim to a new conservative party, no more the Tories. The last ditch was Alexander

---

*   This was written in the early 1980s.

Soames, but he could only play the bonnie prince Charlie and go to France as an ambassador. It was Thatcher's world, akin to Wilson much more than to Jenkins, Benn, or the Gordon Brown of the earlier generation. Thatcher had no counterparts among the earlier Tories.

19. Many books from Keynes to Margaret MacMillan have been written on the peace talks but the most illuminating I find is Arthur Walworth, *Wilson and his Peacemakers: American Diplomacy at the Paris Peace Conference, 1919* (New York: W.W. Norton, 1986).

20. Churchill called it "The Second Thirty Years War".

21. In reference to the Julien Benda's *Trahison des Clercs* (Paris: Bernard Grasset, 1927).

22. See, for example, Keynes, *The Economic Consequences of the Peace* (London: Macmillan, 1971).

23. I have, in particular, H. H. Asquith in mind.

24. For a better historical context with regard to how, I believe, the more authentic praxis of the Durkheimian paradigm ought to be searched in the Turkey of 1923–50 and not in France after the WWI, as I have already intimated. It better illustrates how the current demise of that paradigm could be suspected in the overall history of the changes in the last century when seen from a very bird's-eye view.

When the French at Versailles opted for an "empire-nation" (Frederik Cooper, *Citizenship between Empire and Nation: Remaking France and French Africa, 1945–1960*, Princeton: Princeton University Press, 2014) to play at world politics, ridden with the hubris of a self-imagined great power, and prioritized that external posturing instead of rebuilding the Third Republic internally and converting the world to their own modernity, they paid more attention to colonial hegemony. Consequently, from a historical point of view the Third Republic in a less ambiguous format is left to be searched in the adventures of the Turkish Republic from its Young Turk inception to its Republican construction, epitomized in the rise of Ankara as the new Capital and in the total demise of Istanbul and its *belle époque* ways. In a larger context, it would take another half century for the American definition of modernity, nation and citizenship to prevail, to force the Turks by the end of the century into double-talk: the Third Republic vs. the global village.

25.   For a brilliant account of the same in a different historical context, see Şerif Mardin, *The Genesis of Young Ottoman Thought: A Study in the Modernization of Turkish Political Ideas* (Princeton: Princeton University Press, 1962). This work has set an example for my thinking.

26.   Birtek and Toprak, "The Conflictual Agendas of Neo-Liberal Reconstruction and the Rise of Islamic Politics in Turkey: The Hazards of Rewriting Modernity", *The Post-Modern Abyss and the New Politics of Islam: Assabiyah Revisited*, ed. Faruk Birtek and Binnaz Toprak (Istanbul: Bilgi University Press, 2011).

27.   Edward Shils's *Encounter* magazine was what we read before *The New York Review of Books* came along. Here, Ignazio Silone, Arthur Koestler, Milovan Djilas, and even Ionesco wrote. It was our bread and butter, modern, Left, and non-Soviet. We never knew it was a CIA project to bolster Europe against its eastern ghost; we should have perhaps deciphered it from its name, *Encounter*; we just thought it was a little odd for the name of a magazine. The name might have been the thing that perhaps secured Shils the CIA funding for a journal which, with regard to its contents, certainly did not sit well with the McCarthyist late 1950s and the early 1960s of Washington.

28.   This text was written between 1988 and 2005 in many wonderful places as I acknowledge in my introductory appendix. Unfortunately, I have no record to claim clairvoyance. Yet, today in 2007, while putting together this text in a form that could be published, Sarkozy got elected. Sarkozy is the revenge of Esterhazy, he is anti-Dreyfus as if dropped off the cover of *Punch*. This is the final hurrah in the ending of the Third Republic and the Modern as we knew it. Sarkozy had "escaped" the Lycée, the Left Bank, and the Grand Écoles. Science Po until the 1970s was a hotbed of latent monarchism and host to the right-wing student movement.

29.   In life Seyrig had the most mesmerizing voice—I was lucky to be in the audience once when Delphine Seyrig and some of her colleagues had a round table at the Théâtre d'Odéon on the "événements" of May 1968. I never heard a voice, a manner of speech, a mode of self-expression as seductive, as heavenly as hers—no Dietrich, no Monica Vitti could compare. She inhaled as she spoke. As she spoke she would totally envelope you.

We are grateful to Selma Ertegun Foundation for their support.